SUFFERING

OTHER TITLES IN THE SEANET SERIES

DATE DUE

P

S

Ch

WILLIAM CAREY
LIBRARY

Suffering: Christian Reflections on Buddhist Dukkha

All scripture quotations, unless otherwise indicated, are taken from the Holy Bible, New International Version®, NIV®. Copyright © 1973, 1978, 1984 by Biblica, Inc.™ Used by permission of Zondervan. All rights reserved worldwide. www.zondervan.com

Published by William Carey Library
1605 E. Elizabeth St.
Pasadena, CA 91104 | www.missionbooks.org

Laura Snider, copyeditor
Hugh Pindur, graphic design
Rose Lee-Norman, indexer

William Carey Library is a ministry of the
U.S. Center for World Mission
Pasadena, CA | www.uscwm.org

Printed in the United States of America

15 14 13 12 11 5 4 3 2 1 BP800

Library of Congress Cataloging-in-Publication Data

Suffering : Christian reflections on Buddhist dukkha / edited by Paul H. De Neui.

   p. cm. -- (SEANET series ; v. 8)

 Includes bibliographical references and index.

 ISBN 978-0-87808-024-3

1. Missions to Buddhists. 2. Suffering--Religious aspects--Christiantiy--Comparative studies.
3. Suffering--Religious aspects--Buddhism--Comparative studies. 4. Christianity and other
religions--Buddhism. 5. Buddhism--Relations--Christianity. I. De Neui, Paul H.

   BV2618.S84 2011

   261.2'43--dc22

                            2010048901

DEDICATION

This volume is dedicated to all who live and serve to make
Proverbs 3:27 a reality.

"Do not withhold good from those to whom it is due,
when it is in your power to act."

CONTENTS

PART II MINISTRY IN THE MIDST OF SUFFERING

INTRODUCTION

For many years a little round stone sat on the corner of the desk of Rev. Gyomay M. Kubose, the founder of Chicago's Buddhist Temple. In his later years, this Japanese American was once asked if he had ever suffered discrimination during his life. His immediate reply was negative. His son, listening to the conversation, immediately refuted him, saying, "Father! What about all the years you spent in the relocation camp? You lost everything." The priest looked at him and responded simply, "That was war." Rev. Kubose went on to describe the personal significance of that small stone found along the creek near the Heart Mountain Relocation Center, Wyoming in his book Everyday Suchness (Bambooks, 1985).

In this round stone, I feel a peaceful, harmonious and perfect character—a character acquired through many years of hardships. As I feel its smoothness and roundness, I know that it was not so in the beginning. It must have had many sharp corners when it was cracked off from the mother stone and began its long journey down the rivers and creeks enduring the heat, the rainstorms and the freezing Wyoming winter. For how long, it is hard to tell, perhaps for thousands of years; and as it was rolled and tossed with the other rocks and stones, it was polished and the sharp corners disappeared. And today as I admire its round and smooth beauty, I know that it took many thousands of year, not just one day to become round and smooth. Beneath its simple beauty, I perceive a wonderful character.

As I go on my way down the creek of life, this stone teaches me patience and endurance. It teaches me to make the best of situations as they come, to accept and ride my waves of karma, for many things that occur are beyond the limit of my power.

In this way, I find peace and contentment from the sufferings of life. As I see many sharp corners and roughness in me, I feel that I am much smaller and inferior to the stone. This little stone on my desk is, indeed, a great teacher to me (93-94).

Suffering is an undeniable theme in Christianity and Buddhism. Both religions attempt to cope with the vagaries inherent in human existence. Life and suffering are inseparable. But are both groups talking about the same concept of suffering or not? Christ suffered once for many; Buddha said suffering was the fact of life for all. Christ went the way of the cross embracing suffering; Buddha taught a way out of suffering. In many non-Western contexts, daily suffering is the unquestioned reality of existence that must be tolerated as karmic fate. In many Western contexts, much time, effort and money are spent in a daily pursuit of the conquest or denial of suffering. Are there insights from each perspective that can inform the other? We believe so.

This volume, *Suffering: Christian Reflections on Buddhist Dukkha*, is an edited collection of papers presented on the theme of suffering at the SEANET XII Forum held in Chiang Mai, Thailand, in 2010. It was readily apparent that this topic would quickly become personal and introspective for a group of Christians privileged to serve in the Buddhist world. It was certainly one of the most productive, albeit painful, topics we have touched upon in the history of SEANET.

In the table of contents, chapters are organized under two main categories with a summary thesis statement for each. The first category of Conceptual Foundations of Suffering contains insights imperative for a Christian understanding about various Buddhist perspectives on suffering. These chapters also offer a variety of Christian historical, theological, and cultural responses. The second category, Life Ministry in the Midst of Suffering, includes further insights into Buddhist worldviews as well as narrative descriptions of life as experienced therein. These stories illustrate individual and group responses to the Christian gospel in the context of suffering as experienced in a variety of places in the Buddhist world. We believe that the insights in these articles will correct and inform those who are challenged to face the reality of and responses to *dukkha* from any religious background.

Due to the highly technical nature of this topic, a glossary of Buddhist terms commonly used in discussion about *dukkha* is included in this volume. It is the intention of the SEANET steering committee that this volume be made available to as many readers as possible, since inevitably we will all experience suffering ourselves or we will be required to give a word of hope to those who have experienced or are experiencing suffering in their lives. It is precisely because this topic is painfully avoided or ignored by many Western missional practitioners, even those serving in the Buddhist world, that this book is presented. We believe that an understanding of the concept of suffering from within Buddhist worldviews is a key component to communication of the Christian gospel that can enrich all who are involved.

SEANET serves as a networking forum wherein groups and individuals can meet to reflect and strategize together on topics particular to their collective mission. SEANET does not promote one particular strategy or one particular theology but seeks to learn from models of hope that show what God is doing around the world. Over one hundred and thirty attendees from fourteen countries contributed in a wide variety of roles to this conference, for which we are grateful. Special gratitude is given to each of the contributors and their respondents. Your thoughtful insights and timely corrections have brought this volume to its final publication. We are grateful for all the delegates and leaders of SEANET XII for the encouraging interaction that challenged and developed our collective thinking for improved missional practice.

In the process of creating any book for publication, one must depend on the contributions of others. Many thanks to Jenna Brand, who corresponded with contributors and did much of the initial editing. Very special gratitude to Zachary Lovig, my right hand man throughout this project. He experienced his own degree of suffering through re-reading each chapter multiple times, creating thesis statements, chasing down references, and generally formatting the text for improved readability. SEANET is indebted to all the staff of William Carey Library including general manager Jeff Minard, editorial manager Naomi McSwain, copyeditor Laura Snider, and graphic designer Hugh Pindur. Thanks to all who hand-carry this volume to those living in places around the globe where books cannot be sent. Most of all, we thank the reading practitioners who through their daily examples promote this topic from merely a stimulating discussion to faithful and fruitful living that brings hope to a suffering world.

May this book bring meaning and hope to the lives of the suffering through the knowledge of Him who suffered once for all that all might truly live (Ezek. 16:4–6).

Paul H. De Neui
January 2011

CONTRIBUTORS

Jane Barlow (pen name) has served in an Asian Buddhist country for many years where she lives with her husband and two children.

Bantoon Boon-Itt Ph.D., M.A. /M.M., B.D. and **Mali Vongsuly Boon-Itt**, M.B.A., B.Sc. are a husband and wife team. Rev. Dr. Boon-Itt is Senior Pastor of Fourth Church Suebsampantawong, Bangkok, Thailand. His degrees are from the Open University and Nottingham University through St John's College, Nottingham, UK and Trinity Theological College, Singapore. Mrs. Boon-Itt has worked in banking and in marketing, but today assists her husband in the ministry to improve the communication of the Christian message, making it comprehensible and relevant to Thais. In the seminars they run throughout Thailand the Boon-Itt's strive to alert Thai Christians to the fact that evangelizing methods have been concentrated on, but the expression of the message itself has been overlooked. They have four children.

Satanun Boonyakiat is from Thailand. He received his Ph.D. degree in Theology (Theology and Culture) from Fuller Theological Seminary. His M.Div. is from Trinity Theological College in Singapore. He serves as a lecturer at McGilvary College of Divinity at Payap University, Chiang Mai, Thailand. Currently, he is the dean of the college. In addition, he is actively involved with the Christian education ministry of the First Church of Chiang Mai. He is married to Dr. Sirikanya Boonyakiat who is an associate pastor to youth and families of the First Church of Chiang Mai.

Russ Bowers earned his Ph.D. from Dallas Theological Seminary. His published dissertation considered the opus magnum of Keiji Nishitani, a major contributor to Buddhist-Christian dialogue. He engaged in Christian leadership development in Cambodia for more than six years, and taught courses on world religions (undergraduate) and Buddhism (graduate) in the U.S.A. for four. He and his wife Glenna live in Burleson, Texas.

Anton Francis (pen name) was born in an Asian Buddhist country where he presently lives with his family and ministers to youth and their families.

Alan R. Johnson and his wife Lynette, have lived primarily in Thailand for over two decades. They have worked in church planting and various forms of formal and informal training with the Thailand Assemblies of God. In recent years they have begun pioneer work among the urban poor, developing a house church network and ministries to children in a series of slum communities in Bangkok. Alan is a graduate of Northwest University (B.A. in Pastoral Ministry), AGTS (M.A. in Biblical Studies), Azusa Pacific University (M.A. in Social Sciences), the Oxford Centre for Mission Studies/University of Wales (Ph.D.). His dissertation is an ethnographic work on social influence processes in a slum community in Bangkok. Alan and Lynette have two grown daughters.

David S. Lim serves as the President of the Asian School for Development and Cross-cultural Studies (ASDECS), which offers graduate degree programs in Development Management, Business Administration and Transformational Leadership, presently in three Southeast Asian countries. He is also the President of China Ministries International-Philippines that recruits Filipino missionaries for China. He had previously served as Academic Dean at Asian Theological Seminary (Philippines) and Oxford Centre for Mission Studies (UK). His Ph.D. in Theology (New Testament) was earned from Fuller Theological Seminary in Pasadena, U.S.A.

Alex G. Smith is from Australia. He earned his D.Miss. and M.A. degrees at Fuller Theological Seminary and his M.Div. from Western Evangelical Seminary. Smith is a veteran missionary to Thailand, co-founder and coordinator/chairperson of SEANET (South, East, Southeast, and North Asia Network) and he was adjunct faculty at Multnomah University for eighteen years. Presently he serves as Minister-at-Large for OMF International. He is an author, trainer and lecturer. Smith resides with his American wife, Faith, three sons and four grandchildren in the United States. His church planting experience in Asia convinced him of the need to reach whole families, not just individuals.

G. P. V. Somaratna is from Sri Lanka. He has a Ph.D. in South Asian History from the University of London. He serves as senior research professor at Colombo Theological Seminary in Colombo, Sri Lanka. Somaratna has worked in the metro-political cities of Sri Lanka for the last forty-five years. He lives with his wife in Colombo, Sri Lanka.

PART I

CONCEPTUAL FOUNDATIONS
OF SUFFERING

CHAPTER 1

WHAT IS BEING COMMUNICATED TO BUDDHISTS

Mali and Bantoon Boon-Itt[1]

When looking around the Buddhist world, it is easy to see there are a great many Buddhists who do not understand Christianity despite its message being proclaimed in these areas for hundreds of years. Why is this so? Why is it so hard for Buddhists to accept Christ? Why do some Buddhists not have a very good impression of Christianity? What have we, as Christians, been communicating to Buddhists? Could it be that Buddhists have misunderstood what Christians intend to communicate? Why have Buddhists found John 3:16 to be "gobbledygook" (Davis 1993, 9–11)? Why is there confusion because of Buddhists' worldview? Is the Christian message being presented to Buddhists in a way they have found incomprehensible and irrelevant? To answer these questions, we need to take off Christian spectacles and put on Buddhist spectacles. This involves firstly coming to grips with the Buddhist worldview and understanding that *dukkha* (suffering) is its starting point, and secondly looking at how the Christian message has been presented to Buddhists—in essence, learning how Buddhists perceive Christianity. We have been doing this in the Thai context. However, our findings may also apply to other Buddhist contexts. Wearing Buddhist spectacles, one can better appreciate the challenge in communicating Christ to Buddhists. In this article, we shall try to alert you to the challenges facing Christians.

While there are vast differences between Buddhist and Christian worldviews, there are still some strands of similarity. The more we learned about Buddhism, the more it became evident we had a problem of miscommunication. Miscommunication has occurred largely because Thai

---

1   Most of the material in this chapter has been extracted from Bantoon Boon-Itt's PhD thesis, "A Study of the Dialogue between Christianity and Theravada Buddhism in Thailand As Represented by Buddhist and Christian Writings from Thailand in the Period 1950–2000" (2007. United Kingdom: St. John's College Nottingham validated by The Open University).

Christians have overlooked the fact that they are communicating with people who have a different worldview. We have not grasped the need to understand Theravada Buddhism and so without realizing it have been communicating using a Thai vocabulary that is incomprehensible to Buddhists. The more we learn how Buddhists perceive Christianity, the more we realize the complexity and the challenge Christians face in communicating Christ to Buddhists. In order to avoid miscommunication, we need to apply the Christian message to the Buddhist context to help Buddhists understand Christian beliefs. Buddhists may then realize that the Christian message is not entirely foreign to them and that they may even gain some new insights from this religion. They may come to understand that Christians have an alternative response to *dukkha*.

It has been said that the presence of suffering in the world is one of the strongest arguments against the existence of a loving, almighty God. If Christians are going to seriously communicate with Buddhists, they need to address the mystery of suffering. Some Buddhists perceive the creator God as responsible for suffering since they see it as part of his creation. The Thai monk Buddhadasa, in his lecture "Christianity and Buddhism," said:

> God the creator of the world is *avijja* (ignorance). It is one of the powers in nature that exists as the source and cause for the birth of all things and which results in the birth of suffering in the world. God, who realizes that the creation of the world is a mistake, is referred to as *vijja* (knowledge or truth). It is the knowledge in nature that is the opposite of *avijja*—that creation in its essence is creation of suffering. God, who controls the world, to punish or to reward beings, is referred to as the law of *karma* ... God the destroyer of the world is referred to as *vijja* to be the cause for all suffering to ultimately cease to be. God who exists everywhere so that no action can be overlooked is referred to as the law of *karma*. *Avijja*, *vijja*, and *karma* can be comprehended by the one word "*dharma*" (salvific truth or the Buddha's teaching/doctrine). (1999a, 87–88)

Buddhists see the world in essence as suffering and the creator as *avijja*. Having established the fundamental importance of the need for Christians to understand how the Christian message has been miscommunicated in the Buddhist world, let us now examine what is being communicated to Buddhists as well as some of the challenges involved.

UNDERSTANDING THE BUDDHIST WORLDVIEW

Dukkha is the starting point in the Buddhist world. In words attributed to Buddha, "As before, so also now, I preach only *dukkha* and the cessation thereof" (Chandrkaew 1982, 1). Grasping the truth of *dukkha* is the first step on the path to being saved from it. This view of life as *dukkha* has a parallel in the Christian understanding of sin and salvation; until the reality of sin is acknowledged there can be no salvation, and until the truth of *dukkha* is grasped, one cannot move towards nirvana. The Buddhist will describe *dukkha* like this:

> Birth is *dukkha*; decay is *dukkha*; illness is *dukkha*; death is *dukkha*. Presence of objects we hate is *dukkha*; separation from objects we love is *dukkha*; not to obtain what we desire is *dukkha*. In short, the fivefold attached aggregate of existence (*pancupadanakkhanda* or *benjakhanda*— an individual being) is *dukkha*. (Chandrkaew 1982, 8)

The Buddhist is living in the world of samsara, the endless cycle of cause and effect with no known beginning. The cycle is known as *paticcasamuppāda,* dependent origination or the wheel of existence (Harvey 2002, 32, 54). In the world of dependent origination, *atta* (the self) has no independent existence. *Atta* depends on factors which are constantly changing. The "I" is hungry or thirsty, angry or pleased, conscious or unconscious, hot or cold depending on various external factors. The personal apprehension of the fact of this samsaric world leads one to nirvana. Nirvana is release from the wheel of samsara.

> *Nirvana* is, therefore, neither the annihilation of anything real, nor is it the union of an individual self or soul with the Absolute, nor is it entirely indescribable. It is just the realization of things as they really are, resulting in a permanent cessation of all the wrong views about things, and thus a transcendence of the worldly experience. (Chandrkaew 1982, ix)

Buddha described the samsaric world which exists in space and time as *anicca* (impermanence), *dukkha*, and *anattā* (not a self), the three fundamental characteristics of all existence.

> Monks, whether the *Tathagatas* (the Buddhas) have arisen or not, this fundamental law, this rule of the law, this lawful necessity, prevails,

namely, all conditioned (or formed) factors of being are impermanent (*annica*) ... all conditioned (or formed) factors of being are subject to suffering (*dukkha*) ... all things (*dharma*) are without the soul or substance (*anattā*). (Chandrkaew 1982, 3)

The understanding of impermanence is a basic part of understanding the First Noble Truth, which is *dukkha*. Nothing in the universe is fixed, all is changing (*anicca*). The whole of existence is in constant motion, arising and passing and re-arising.

One state (*dharma*), on perishing, makes room for its succeeding state by transmitting the whole of its energy (*paccaya satti*). Therefore, every succeeding state possesses all the potentialities of the state just preceding it with something more. In this respect, no two successive states can be definitely said to be the same or entirely different, but being the same process of a constant flux. (Chandrkaew 1982, 4)

Today there is greater awareness that the whole of existence is in constant motion, arising and passing and re-arising. Thinking of the human body, one observes that it changes over the years; almost every cell will have been replaced since birth, but also remains the same. The *Milindapanha* further illustrates this argument as follows:

A man, whose lamp caused the destruction of the whole village by fire ... cannot be guiltless on the ground that the flame of his lamp is not the same flame that burnt the village. The flame is, no doubt, not the same flame, but definitely not a different one (*naca so naca anno*), for the process of the flame is in the same continuity. (Chandrkaew 1982, 4)

The reality of impermanence is revealed through, and based on, the mechanism of *paticcasamuppāda* (the wheel of life, dependent origination). Understanding that all is dependent on the arising and passing of a myriad of factors is progressing towards enlightenment, nirvana. The idea of *anicca* refers not only to the world, but also to the people in it. The Buddhist view of an individual being is this:

An individual being is composed of two parts, viz., name and form (*nama-rupa*). The Form consists of the four primary elements of earth (*pathavi*), water (*apo*), fire (*tejo*) and wind (*vayo*). While the Name is divided into four groups, viz., feeling (*vedana*), perception (*sanna*), mental formations (*sankhāra*) and consciousness (*vinnana*). Thus, the matter (*rupa*) and the four mental qualities are traditionally called "The Fivefold Attached Group." All these five groups, though being separate elements, are not a haphazard process (*adhiccasamupanna*), but subject to the definite law of Dependent Origination. ... They are a continuous, unbroken series of activity that leads to one unit of an integrated personality as the particular ego-consciousness of the moment, in which the 'I' only builds itself up *a posteriori* on the basis of continued experiences ... Personality is ... not an unchanged entity but a process or stream (*santana*) of physical and mental forces that are arising and passing away. (Chandrkaew 1982, 7, 13)

Buddhist teaching on impermanence is that one is doomed to disappointment if one thinks he or she can grasp at anything. The pain of disappointment will be avoided if one recognizes one's own impermanence. A Christian can affirm the noble truth that all things except God change continually. From birth to death, our self-awareness grows or atrophies as we use or refuse to use our power of thought. We see existential suffering, mental or physical pain, as part of the process of development. Rather than something to be avoided, this pain or suffering is a growth factor (Peck 1999, 68–70, 144–46). This view of continual change can be seen as akin to the Buddhist view that the being is always changing. In popular Thai understanding, impermanence is used to express the uncertainty of life. So, we live impermanently. If we do not recognize and accept this, we set ourselves up for *dukkha*. The idea behind the word *dukkha* embraces the whole range of experience. The common English translation "suffering" is normally applied by Westerners to pain or distress of body or mind and is opposed to health and well-being. In Buddhism, *dukkha* also means unsatisfactoriness, imperfection, and change. Thus, *dukkha* underlies our life attached to samsara and the wheel of *paticcasamuppāda*.

Three categories of *dukkha* may be distinguished. The first, *dukkha-dukkha*, is suffering due to birth, illness, decay, and death. The second, *viparinama-dukkha*, is the suffering caused by the fact that all things are temporary. It is the inevitable suffering that comes because moments of pleasure cannot be extended. The third form of suffering, conditioned-ness, *sankhāra-dukkha*, is linked to the second. It is suffering because of the nature of the world, samsara. The understanding of this is not intrinsically pessimistic. On the contrary, it can lead one to free oneself from the conditioned and find release in the unconditioned, nirvana. Christians can make a parallel observation when we distinguish two kinds of suffering: the undesirable, leading to personality damage, and the beneficial, leading to growth in understanding. Everything changes, but God does not. God, in this sense, can be equivalent to nirvana.

The arising of *dukkha* is described in the teaching of *paticcasamuppāda* as conditioned arising.

> When one perceives a sound, odor, taste and so on, if pleasant, he is attracted; and if unpleasant, he is repelled. Thus, whatever kind of feeling he experiences ... pleasant, unpleasant or indifferent, if he delights in the feeling, cherishes it and persists in cleaving to it, then in so doing, lust crops up; but lust for feeling brings about attachment (*upadana*); through attachment arises becoming (*bhava*); through becoming arises birth (*jati*) and through birth arises decay, death, sorrow, lamentation, pain, etc. This is the process by which the whole mass of *dukkha* springs up. (Chandrkaew 1982, 10)

From this we can see the essence of *dukkha* is in the reception one gives to the experiences of life. One's attitude is the key to the experience of *dukkha*. There is no suffering without a person to experience it. As Chandrkaew explains,

> According to the doctrine of *anicca* (impermanence), the desiring of impermanent things can only lead to the 'I' or desirer suffering the loss of those things. If an individual recognizes that he is also impermanent, i.e. *anattā* (not a self), he will not take everything to himself.

> The three aspects of *dukkha* operating in life will not do any harm if we do not regard objects or states of existence in terms of possession, attachment, or I-ness, and my-ness. It is, then, not the 'world' or its transitoriness which is the cause of suffering but our attitude towards it, our clinging to it, our thirst, our ignorance ... And this is the reason why the Buddha sums up the entire *dukkhas* under the designation of the fivefold attached aggregate of existence. (1982, 10)

Buddha perceived that the three roots or causes of *dukkha* are *avijja* (ignorance), *kilesa* (defilement), and *tanhā* (craving, desire), all of which are powerful factors holding humans in the cycle of *paticcasamuppāda*, keeping them in samsara (Payutto 1995, 906–8). The law of karma is the natural law which governs this *dukkha* existence.

How does this occur? Firstly, *dukkha* is caused by *avijja*. This is not ignorance in the sense of lacking information, but of failing to be aware of the true nature of things. It is a failing or shortcoming in thinking, in the mind, and a failure to understand reality (Harvey 2002, 56). For the Buddhist, understanding will come through meditation as a means of triumphing over ignorance. By reaching a true understanding of *anicca*, *dukkha*, and *anattā*, nirvana may be attained. The Buddha realized that while not many would understand him nevertheless, in his compassion, he remained in the world and taught 'The Way' for the dedicated few. One should also remember that in Jesus' teaching, we have the statement, "For the gate is narrow and the road is hard that leads to life, and there are few who find it" (Matt. 7:14). Some Buddhists perceive they may have to travel many existences to achieve nirvana.

The second cause of suffering is *kilesa* (defilements, mental impurities or impairments). There are ten sources of *kilesa*: greed; hatred/anger; delusion; conceit/spiritual pride; false views; skepticism/doubt; mental torpor, sloth/discouragement; mental restlessness; shamelessness; and lack of conscience and moral dread. They are negative characteristics in the mind, linked together with *tanhā* (craving, desire). When an individual lacks mindfulness (*sati*), these *kilesa* can take over the mind, resulting in great suffering. Until a Buddhist is no longer disturbed by *kilesa*, one cannot be free from conflict or find inner peace.

In Buddhism, one's existence depends on the state of one's mind (*citta*); Christian teaching would also assert this stress on the mind. The writer of Proverbs in the Bible was aware of the importance of "mental forces." For instance, he wrote, "The most important thing is for you to be careful in the things you think. Your thoughts control your life." (Prov. 4:23). In the New Testament, Jesus said, "For out of the heart come evil intentions, murder, adultery, fornication, theft, false witness, slander" (Matt. 15:19). Moreover, Paul stressed the use of the mind in his argument on spiritual gifts in 1 Corinthians 14:14–15: "For if I pray in a tongue, my spirit prays but my mind is unproductive. What should I do then? I will pray with the spirit, but I will pray with the mind also; I will sing praise with the spirit, but I will sing praise with the mind also." Luke tells us that, having established in their understanding that Jesus had risen from death, Jesus then "opened their minds to understand the scripture" (Luke 24:45). Buddhists seek a mind free of *kilesa*; Christians seek to have the mind of Christ (Phil. 2:5).

Tanhā, the third root of suffering, is craving, sensual craving, or desire. Three types of craving or desire are defined: *kama-tanhā*, craving for happiness and sensual pleasure in this present existence; *bhava-tanhā*, craving for existence or self-preservation, which is the cause of rebirth (seen in the plant and animal worlds as well as among humans); and *vibhava-tanhā*, craving for non-existence. This does not mean craving for nirvana but refers to the desire to be rid of unpleasant situations. *Tanhā* (craving) is always linked to *kilesa* (defilements).

Having recognized the all-pervasive nature of *dukkha* in the Thai Buddhist worldview, we need to try to understand how it is dealt with. We need to look at the law of karma. Karma literally means "action or deed," but not all actions should be seen as karmic. The Buddha taught it was intentional actions, whether conscious or subconscious, that held karmic value: black (bad), white (good), black and white (mixed bad and good), or neutral (neither bad nor good) (Payutto 1988, 21–22). This fourth karma, neutral karma, is the result of the realization of *anattā* (not a self) and *sunnatta* (emptiness, devoid of self) when the self is seen as not a self. While involuntary actions are not held to be karmic, actions may result from the subconscious as well as the conscious mind. There can be no facile "I didn't mean it" as an excuse. Suppose someone is driving home having had too much to drink and unfortunately runs a red light and kills a couple crossing the street. In Thailand this is not considered manslaughter; the killing was unintentional. In karmic terms, intent or motivation is more important than one's deeds. In both Christianity and Buddhism, intention is held as significant (see Mark 7, 20–23; John 8:3–8; and Matt. 5:28). In our example, the driver did not know the couple; there was no intention or reason to kill them. The fault was in not observing the fifth precept to avoid intoxicants. The legal penalty according to *Thai Criminal Code* (1932), Section 290 (no intention to kill), is for dangerous driving. If the couple who died had not been on the road at that time, they would not have been hit. Perhaps the persons who died were due to die according to their karma anyway.

The belief in good begetting good, and evil begetting evil is fairly universal. The principle of the law of karma is pointed to in the Bible in Proverbs 11:18, "The wicked earn no real gain, but those who sow righteousness get a true reward," and in Proverbs 22:8, "Whoever sows injustice will reap calamity." In Buddhist thought, one's karma is of one's own creating. Christ denied this idea when he commented on the people killed by the falling tower of Siloam in Luke 13:4–5. They were not worse offenders than other people. Karma is, moreover, an important concept used both by state authorities in Thailand and by the majority folk Buddhists (those practicing Buddhism mixed with animism), to explain suffering, especially the bad fortune that attends the apparently meritorious or the good fortune that attends the wicked. The pervasiveness of the belief is exemplified by official road signs in a campaign to reduce accidents reading, "Accidents do not result from one's karma (*ubutdihade michai wanegum*)."

Good actions are referred to as *kusala* (skillful or wholesome) as they produce uplifting mental states in the doer, hence, wholesome states of mind. Skillful actions are considered merit (*boon*), which is auspicious or fortunate as it purifies the mind leading to good fortune. Bad actions are *akusala* (unskillful or unwholesome). Unskillful actions are inauspicious, bringing ill fortune or demerit (*apunna* or *papa*, *bap*). Thai Christians use the Thai word *bap* for sin. In Buddhist thought, the individual is neither sinful nor guilty when acting demeritoriously. An "unskillful" action or black karma leads to bad consequences and hence should be avoided. The Buddhist has no concept of being answerable to a creator or god, so "sin" and "guilt" lose their significance. But the sense of "shame" or "loss of face" is very Thai, if not Buddhist. The gathering of good karma is in one sense a distraction. One does not reach nirvana because of a favorable balance of white karma; one can merely hope to have a better life. A being may be reborn in another sphere in the next life. There are four planes of existence: firstly, the realms of loss and woe—lower worlds, akin to hell, then the animal kingdom, the sphere of ghost-beings and demons; secondly, the seven sensuous blissful (sense-desire) planes—the realm of human beings, and the six lower heavens; thirdly, the sixteen heavenly form planes; and finally, the four formless realms where beings have no bodily form—the realms of gods and higher beings (Harvey 2002, 32–37). Harvey further explains,

> The law of karma ... is not operated by a God, and indeed the gods are themselves under its sway. Good and bad rebirths are not, therefore, seen as "rewards" and "punishments," but as simply the natural results of certain kinds of actions.

> It is, in fact, seen as particularly fortunate to be born as a human being. In the lower realms, there is much suffering and little freedom of action. In the heavenly realms, life is blissful in comparison with human life, but this tends to make the gods complacent, and they may also think they

are eternal, without need of liberation. The human realm is a middle realm, in which there is enough suffering to motivate humans to seek to transcend it by spiritual development, and enough freedom to be able to act on this aspiration. It is thus the most favourable realm for spiritual development.

> Buddhist heavens, then, are *this* side of salvation; for *Nirvana* is beyond the limitations of both earthly and heavenly existence. (2002, 38–39)

To reach nirvana, our actions should be based on the understanding of *anicca* (impermanence) and *anattā* (not a self) and therefore be neither black nor white. Not white with the desire for a good outcome nor black done under the influence of *kilesa* and *tanhā*. When we realize that we are *anattā* and act with equanimity producing karma which is neither black nor white—and so with no karmic result—then we have reached nirvana, the end of samsara. The cycle of samsara has no known beginning or end, but according to the Buddha, each person has had any number of past lives. How the cycle of samsara proceeds is explained by *paticcasamuppāda*, which is a fascinating topic but one we will look at later.

Attaining nirvana is release from *dukkha*, samsara, and the karmic burden that ties us down via the understanding of *anattā*, that there is no "real me," no "self." The concept of *anattā* is that of "not a self," having no permanent substratum or soul. If one grasps the teaching of *anicca* and applies it to oneself, one will see that one's life is as illusory as everything else. The doctrines of *anattā* and *anicca* are closely linked.

> Body, brethren, is impermanent. What is impermanent, that is suffering. What is suffering, that is without the self. What is without the self that is not mine, I am not that, not of me is this self. Thus should one view it by perfect insight as it really is. For the one who thus sees it as it really is by perfect insight, his heart turns away, is released from it by not grasping at the *asava* (mental intoxication). (Bodhi 2003, 45)

Buddha equated ownership with control. If one is in control of something, one "owns" it; if one is not in complete control, one does not own it. Following this, the doctrine of *anattā* states that individuals are not the owners of their bodies, for nobody can fully control his or her body.

Body, brethren, is not the Self. If body, brethren, were the Self, then body would not be involved in sickness, and one could say of body: "Thus let my body be. Thus let my body not be." But, brethren, in as much as body is not Self, that is why body is involved in sickness, and one cannot say of body:

"Thus let my body be; thus let my body not be." ...

"Now what think ye, brethren, is body permanent or impermanent?"

"Impermanent, Lord."

"And what is impermanent, is that weal or woe?"

"Woe, Lord."

"Then what is impermanent, woeful, unstable by nature, is it fitting to regard it thus: 'This is mine; I am this; this is the Self of me?'"

"Surely not, Lord."

"So also is it with feeling, perception, the activities and consciousness. Therefore, brethren, everybody whatever, be it past, future or present, be it inward or outward, gross or subtle, low or high, far or near, everybody should be thus regarded, as it really is, by right insight, 'this is not mine; this am not I; this is not the Self of me.'" (Bodhi 2003, 59)

From an understanding of *paticcasamuppāda* and the composition of an individual, *anattā*, soullessness, can be explained as follows:

Since the matter, feeling, perception, mental formations and consciousness are impermanent or perishable, and thus are *dukkha*, it is not possible to regard them as a self or as belonging to a self. The significance of this connection is that even the consciousness (*vinnana*) is included, which is the innermost mental faculty and always regarded as a self or soul, a permanent entity that "feels, that experiences now here, now there the result of good or bad deeds." ... the five-fold group of existence is called *Anatta* (not a self) because they are out of control, void, ownerless, unsusceptible to the wielding of power, and precluding a self. (Chandrkaew 1982, 11–12)

If the body and mind are really "self" we should be able to exercise ultimate control over them. However, *anattā* is not simply lack of control, which is only a factor in understanding "not a self." There is no room for a "first cause" or "Creator God" since existence is a process without a beginning but beginning always. And existence is the result of karma and *vipakakamma* (result of karma). No existing object is static and nothing can be considered in isolation, for everything, including an individual, only exists in a process. As Peter Harvey described it, "A 'person' is a collection of rapidly changing and interacting mental and physical processes with character-patterns recurring over time" (2002, 52). Insofar as there is action, reaction is inevitable, and so the life-process is extended to its inevitable destination determined by *sankhāra* (constructing activities, all formed things). However, what a person sets out to do either bodily, verbally, or mentally with intention will have its inevitable effect: favorable, unfavorable, or neither. This is the law of karma and *vipakakamma* and the related samsara (the cycle of rebirth) doctrine. The concept of *anattā* teaches that since one does not have definitive control over one's body, one should cultivate the conditions that conduce to nirvana. Buddhism teaches that each individual can work out his or her own way to reach nirvana through meditation, ethical behavior, and detachment. These Buddhist practices are simply a practical application of *paticcasamuppāda*.

Paticcasamuppāda is at the heart of Buddhism, underlying the Four Noble Truths. It describes the basic Buddhist worldview that everything is intricately interdependent. This is not the same as one thing causing another. Dependence is unavoidable; causes may be avoided. The doctrine states that being, this comes to be; from the arising of that, this arises; that being absent, this is not; from the cessation of that, this ceases. The wheel of life states the principle of conditionality, that all things arise and exist due to the presence of certain conditions, and cease once the conditions are removed. All are interdependent; nothing is independent except nirvana. The twelve linked factors (*nidana*) of *paticcasamuppāda* are in sequence as follows: *avijjā* (ignorance), *sankhāra* (mental formations, constructing activities), *vinnana* (consciousness; sixfold; of eye, ear, nose, tongue, body, and mind), *namarupa* (the five aggregates constituting individual existence), *salayatana* (the six bases of sense impressions—eye, ear, nose, tongue, body, and mind), *phassa* (sense contact), *vedana* (feelings resulting from sense impressions), *tanhā* (sensual craving), *upadana* (grasping; attachment or clinging to sensed objects, views, rules and practices, or the concept of self), *bhava* (becoming, conditions leading to birth), *jati* (birth, conditioned by becoming, the arising of the *khandas* and the sense bases), and *jaramana* (aging and death, the breaking up of the *khandas* and the sense bases). This traditional outline of *paticcasamuppāda* teaching is drawn from Payutto (1999, 26–32). There are also variations on these twelve linked factors that show the contributions of other conditions (Harvey 2002, 54–55).

Paticcasamuppāda can only be truly understood by the disciple who is prepared to meditate on its insights to make them his own. The difficulty of understanding *paticcasamuppāda* is confirmed by Buddha himself in the *Mahanidana Sutta*. When Ananda perceived *paticcasamuppāda* as easy to understand, Buddha corrected him:

> Do not say so, Ananda; do not speak like that. Deep indeed, Ananda, is this *Paticcasamuppāda*, and it appears deep too. It is through not understanding this doctrine, through not penetrating it, these beings have become entangled like a matted ball of thread, like a matted bird's nest, like *munja* grass and rushes, subject to the round of rebirth (*samsara*) in a state of suffering (*dukkha*). (Lertjitlekha 1998, 89)

Paticcasamuppāda unites and explains the Four Noble Truths—which, indeed, may be perceived as a simplified and practical form of *paticcasamuppāda*. It describes how *dukkha*, suffering, the First Noble Truth, arises; the Second Noble Truth, *samudaya*, conditioned arising, is the origin of suffering. By reversing the order, we get *nirodha*, the cessation of *dukkha*—that is, nirvana—which is the Third Noble Truth. And the Fourth Noble Truth, *magga*, the path to end suffering, is the way one must follow. It leads to the cessation of each linked factor. When we are aware of how we are conditioned, we can come to alter the flow of conditions by governing, suspending, or intensifying them. Thus we reduce *dukkha* and ultimately stop it entirely by transcending the conditions. Besides explaining the origin of *dukkha*, the formula also explains karma, rebirth, and the functioning of personality, all without the need to invoke a permanent self (Harvey 2002, 55–56). To escape this cycle, one has to embrace the truth of *anattā*.

> The argument of the Buddha is based on the observation that if anything could be called *atta* or one's self, one should have full control over it. So if we claim that there is an "individual," "I," or "*atta*" as a self entity, one should

have full control over it. This is the Buddhist definition of possession. In fact, since one does not have full control over our [*sic*] possessions, so one cannot claim them as his [*sic*]. (Lertjitlekha 1998, 88)

Buddhist practices are based on the understanding of *paticcasamuppāda* at ever deeper levels; hence, one aims to follow its cycle in reverse with the right view. As the teaching of *paticcasamuppāda* is key to the Buddhist understanding of *dukkha* and the release from *dukkha* (reaching nirvana), so is the cross of Christ key to the Christian understanding of sin and salvation (release from sin—entering the kingdom of God). We find it ironic that the word *vinyana* (act of consciousness), *vinyan* in Thai, has come to mean in the common mind "spirit, soul, or ghost." A Thai definition for *vinyan* is, "The thing that inhabits in the human body making it a person, when the body decays 'the thing' still remains to be reborn" (Official Thai Dictionary 1999, 1074).

HOW THAI BUDDHISTS PERCEIVE CHRISTIANITY

This may be learned from Buddhadasa, whose knowledge of Buddhist doctrine and expositions of Buddhism are seen as authoritative. For Buddhists, to end *dukkha* in the here-and-now is better than to believe in deity and heaven. Buddhadasa appears to think that the Christian teaching of the kingdom of God can be perceived as happiness associated with a self-entering the kingdom of God. The happiness or supreme bliss of a self is of a lower level than the enlightened person's release and bliss in the *lokuttara* (supramundane/ transcendental), nirvana. God is but our own creation.

> We first need to have the correct understanding of troubles. They come not because god is punishing us. The troubles we face are from and of our own creation, stemming from holding onto I/me-my/mine. When humans face more and more troubles, they find various ways of overcoming their troubles. They discover various principles, establish various rites, hypotheses, and even faith in a god so people can believe and hold onto him. It is only when true wisdom or the correct understanding is arrived at, that the true god will be manifested. Hence, everybody should see and realize for themselves that it is actually we ourselves who created god. (Buddhadasa 1999b, 19–21)

Those who hold onto a god have to surrender to that god. Believers are not to argue. It is rather oppressive, allowing neither freedom for actions nor thoughts. Everything has to be according to the will of the god. This is considered the lowest form of *atta* (self) belief suitable for the uneducated, those whose thoughts are still those of a child.

One learns to release oneself from the restrictions, reaching the stage of having *atta* for self. One does things for self, no longer needing to depend on a god, whereas a child needs to hold onto one. One learns to believe in one's own *karma*. One is not restricted by a god who allows us to do *karma* in only one life and all the *karma* one did will be written down for us to hear the verdict on the Day of Judgment. This second level of *atta* belief is slightly higher and gives more freedom. It also gives the hope that the *atta* that has performed the good, pure and right deeds will ultimately achieve the supreme unchangeable happiness. However, this level, of having *atta* for self and not *atta* that belongs to god, is still not the ultimate freedom. One is still imprisoned by and in oneself, in the prison of holding onto oneself, carrying oneself, and infatuated in oneself, without realizing that one is burning oneself in the fire of feeling of self: self satisfaction, love of self and like of self. For a Buddhist, this level is not the ultimate end of suffering. (Buddhadasa 1999c, 133–34)

Let us consider human selfishness. They even claim and use sacred things, or the deity, for their own selfish benefits. They worship, pray to the sacred beings, and act accordingly, in order to get what they want. If no benefits are granted, then they no longer see the object of worship as sacred ... The deity, the sacred objects, are to help me, to benefit me. Humans make merit so they can go to heaven. Is this not for a self, or is it really for the sake of *dharma*? (Buddhadasa 1999c, 157–59)

Those who do not know the truth will continue being infatuated with heaven. They aim to get to heaven, where they can get what they want, a city where there is supreme happiness, the eternal heaven of other religions. Heaven is used as bait for people to do good. People, therefore, become un-interested in ending *dukkha* in the here-and-now. Ending *dukkha* in the here-and-now is the real goal of Buddhism. Heaven is the first fundamental problem distracting people from achieving the ultimate goal of Buddhism.

They are concentrating on their *tanhā* (desire/craving) and *upadana* (attachment, grasping or clinging to sensed objects). We need to teach the people that the heaven they aspire to is merely a way of expressing a goal in terms of *puggaladhitthana* (exposition of the doctrine in terms of persons or by personification). It is suitable for those without the wisdom to grasp the real meaning. For some, even nirvana, which is the end of *dukkha*, becomes a city of deathlessness, or a city where there is supreme happiness that a human or even a *devada* (god/heavenly being) can experience. To express the goal in such a way is *puggaladhitthana*.

Buddhism solves the problem of how we are to live in this world without *dukkha*. We have to exist in *dukkha* without being *dukkha*, in other words, to be in the fire but yet remain cool. Buddhism gets rid of *dukkha* in the here-and-now. It does not aim to take one to heaven. Nobody knows where heaven is or whether it really exists. Buddhism's aim is not to get to heaven after death, or even after future lives. Whether heaven is real or not real, nobody can prove.

Buddhism eliminates *dukkha* which stems from holding onto I/me-my/mine. Buddhism provides practical steps for a person to follow without having to depend on external factors like god or any other powerful beings. There is no need to directly contradict anybody about god, hell, or heaven. Let them believe according to what they want to believe. Even if we need to relate to these topics, it is merely to help those without wisdom, those with such beliefs, so they can do good and abstain from the bad. They are unable to completely eliminate I/me-my/mine. Even if they are able to abstain from doing any bad and do only good, go to heaven and have happiness, they are still not free from the burden, and crushing oppression of what is called I/me-my/mine. Therefore, they need a better and higher principle which will be able to completely eliminate the power of what is known as *atta*,; a principle that can be used by not just humans in the here-and-now but among the *devada* (gods/heavenly beings) as well. (Buddhadasa 1999b, 19–21)

Buddhists will not rely on a god, as god will become something to hold onto, which is another kind of I/me-my/mine.

> We need not hope for mercy from god because the more one hopes in god, the more one is led astray from what can really eliminate *dukkha*. In fact, to be without I/me-my/mine, is the true Buddha, the true *dharma* (salvific truth/Buddha's doctrine) and the true *sangha* (the body of Buddhist monks) or the true god that truly can be depended upon. Otherwise it is just the outer covering of god, Buddha, *dharma* or *sangha* which itself can become the basis of something to hold onto in such a way that will eventually develop new, different and unique kinds of I/me-my/mine. ... When we can eliminate I/me-my/mine, we will reach nirvana which is the end of all *dukkha*. (Buddhadasa 1999b, 48–51)

Christians hope in the future kingdom. Hope to a Buddhist, however, is perceived negatively. In fact, it is a basis of *tanhā*, which causes the holding on to I/me-my/mine.

> *Tanhā* has its basis from the feelings from eye, ear, nose, tongue, body and mind. These feelings from the six sense impressions not only include the present immediate feelings. Feelings from the past can form the basis of *tanhā* in the present, by dwelling on the past. Feelings to be realised in the future, known as hope, also form a basis of *tanhā*. A more complicated problem because we can hope unfathomably and endlessly. (Buddhadasa 1999b, 66–71)

We can gauge the general perception of Christianity that was held by Buddhadasa and conclude that he perceived Christianity to be a less developed religion. Christians should not feel provoked but instead ask themselves why Buddhists have such a perception. What are the causes, and where does the misunderstanding lie? What have Christians been communicating or failing to communicate that leads Buddhists to have such a view? Phongphit is of the following opinion:

> One may argue that what Buddhadasa Bhikkhu considers as Christianity in his writings is a mere caricature of it. Yet it must be admitted that such a caricature has been made possible also because some Christians have

projected this kind of image. Another fact for many misunderstandings from the part of Buddhism is that there are few writings concerned with Christianity available in the language of the country. A Buddhist approach to Christianity is possible mainly through the reading of the Bible. Thus, the general view of the Buddhists towards the Christians is understandable. (1978, 45–46)

Thai Christians need to look again at how key Christian doctrines are being communicated. Christians can learn from Buddhadasa, who strove to make Buddhism understandable to his fellow Thais.

There is a great need to adapt words to express Buddhist ideas and doctrine so that they will be comprehensible to the general public. However, the key contents and messages have to be exactly the same as those found in the *Tripitaka* (the Theravada Buddhist Pali canon). Great care has to be taken that all key doctrines are complete and accurate and all Buddhist principles are harmoniously presented. Not only has the work to be acceptable to Buddhist scholars, but also easy to understand for those Buddhists who are not that well educated. Importantly, it should be practical and not requiring one to undergo extensive and complicated study. The elderly or those who are ill and dying, who do not have time, should be given the chance to hear it and comprehend the *dharma* (salvific truth / Buddha's doctrine) straight away and in time before it is too late. (Buddhadasa 1999b, 42–43)

Thai Christians should do for Christian teaching what Buddhadasa has done for Buddhist teaching. To make Christianity comprehensible to their Buddhist friends will require great acumen as the Christian ideas and concepts are so foreign and so very different to Thai Buddhist ideas. Key Christian words and doctrines are generally expressed by Christians in terms that are incomprehensible to Buddhists. For example,

Words such as God, sin, love, and salvation, produce different meanings in the minds of the Thai ... Buddhists are not interested in the concept of God, hell, heaven, resurrection, and forgiveness of sin. They do not have those concepts in their minds. If they have such a concept, it seems to be different from the Bible and too removed from their experience for them to understand. (Mejudhon 1997, 92, 348)

An in-depth understanding of Buddhism will help Christians appreciate why this is so. The following are examples of such words:

- God, to a Buddhist, can mean several things (Davis 1993, 10). The most common understanding is that "god" means one of many deities who occupy different heavenly realms.
- Self, to a Christian, is created in the image of God, intended to have a relationship with the creator God. But to a Buddhist, it is but the *benjakhanda* (the composition of an individual being, also known as the fivefold aggregate), a self that is *anattā*. Realizing that one is *anattā* gives freedom from *dukkha* via non-attachment, but Christians teach to love—love God and love others as we love self. To a Buddhist, this sounds like a *lokiya* (worldly/mundane) teaching of attachment.
- The goal for Buddhists is to reach nirvana; for Christians, it is to realize the kingdom of God in their lives. This can be perceived by Buddhists as a self doing things for the benefit of self—for self to reach heaven and be with God.
- Heaven and hell to most Buddhists (not for Buddhadasa, but for other Buddhists) are hierarchical heavenly and hellish realms where beings receive the results of their karma. But for Christians, heaven and hell mean the kingdom of God and eternal separation from God respectively. There are several views held among Christians about heaven and hell (Crockett 1996; Küng 1984; Wright 2006). N. T. Wright's view of heaven and hell, and new heavens and new earth, seems to have the best potential for use in the Buddhist context. This is an important topic but one we do not have time to go into here (Boon-Itt 2007).
- Freedom which the Buddhist seeks is *vimutti* (release) from *dukkha*, but a Christian seeks freedom from the bondage or power of sin.
- Sin, to a Christian means disobedience to God—to fall short of God's standards. But to a Buddhist, there is no such concept. There are bad deeds—that is black karma.

- For a Buddhist, the reality of existence in this world is *anicca*, *dukkha*, and *anattā*. For a Christian, the reality of worldly existence is that one lives in a creation sustained by God.

With these differences, it is not surprising that Buddhadasa held the view of Christianity that he did. Buddhadasa's perception of Christianity reveals that the Christian response today has to overcome an injudicious introduction of the Christian message to Thai Theravada Buddhists, an introduction lacking in-depth understanding of Theravada Buddhism. Christianity is now seen as a lesser, more primitive response to human existence, and Christian teaching is seen as the inferior teaching when compared to Buddhism. Without having first grasped the Buddhist worldview, one does not appreciate or understand the roots of Buddhadasa's perceptions of Christianity. If the Buddhist worldview had not been grasped before reading what Buddhadasa had said about Christianity, it would have been easy to deem him prejudiced. Trying to understand Buddhadasa's perspective brings the realization that it is Christianity that has failed to communicate. Only through efforts in trying to understand the other can Christians effectively communicate Christ to Buddhists.

There are several areas where words Christians use do not communicate to the Buddhist what Christians believe they are communicating. Only when we open our ears to the other side's response do we know what they think we have said. It is when Christians know the Buddhist worldview that we understand the incomprehensibility of much of what we are saying. Learning about Buddhadasa's perception of Christianity has exposed the gulf that has to be bridged. This gulf can only be bridged by first understanding the Thai Buddhist worldview. We need to enter each other's worldview to overcome the problem of miscommunication through incomprehension. In particular, Christians should study Buddhism, but also be aware of the various views held among Christians on some important aspects of Christian theology. Christian concepts can then be effectively communicated to Buddhists.

Of all religions, Judeo-Christian beliefs would seem to be rather materialistic. From creation to redemption, resurrection, and eternity, God is seen as concerned with the material, with creation. God became incarnate in Jesus Christ in order to redeem humankind. Christians believe in the resurrection of the dead and the eternal life (Apostles' Creed). Thai Theravada Buddhists see it the other way around. This life is everlasting and this life is unsatisfactory (*dukkha*). The world and life is all *anicca*. If the element of consciousness in a *benjakhanda* (the composition of an individual being) group can relinquish all attachments, then that group will be able to reach nirvana—remainderlessness, freedom, peace. If not, then the karma remaining will "give birth" to another *benjakhanda* group. One's attainment of nirvana depends on one's own efforts to follow the Buddha's teaching. Christianity is not individualistic, whereas Buddhism is rather individualistic—possibly one of its attractions accounting for its popularity in today's Western world. Christianity is based on relationships—of human to God, to nature, to self, and to neighbor. While the individual must accept or reject his or her own salvation, he or she cannot live in isolation but must be reconciled, be in contact with God, creation, and fellow humans. For someone with the Judeo-Christian worldview, a big leap forward in understanding Buddhism will be adjusting to the concept of life continuing without personal agents—that means, there is will but no "willer," an action but no "doer," suffering but no "sufferer," death but no "person" to die. Having grasped how Buddhists perceive Christianity, let us now look at the challenge Christians face in communicating Christ to Buddhists.

THE CHALLENGE IN COMMUNICATING CHRIST TO BUDDHISTS

Thai Christians should be able to explain their faith to fellow Thais in ways that are comprehensible for them. Paul also stresses this need for clarity in explaining the Christian message (Col. 4:3–4). In Mark 10:17–31, Jesus uses three terms at different points of the story to communicate his message: the kingdom of God, eternal life, and salvation. Paul, the apostle to the Gentiles, rarely uses the term "the kingdom of God." He uses other terms such as "citizenship" instead. If the kingdom of God is central to Jesus's teaching, why then does Paul seldom use the term? It is because he adapted his usage to his context, and with a Gentile audience, did not use the "Jewish kingdom" concept but "citizenship" in relation to the Roman Empire.

The New Testament explains the mystery of the cross to different people in different ways. For example, for his Jewish audience, the writer of Hebrews emphasizes the high priesthood of Christ and the sacrificial system. At the cross, God's son made purification for sins (Heb. 1:3). John, also Jewish, uses the image of "lamb of God." God sent his son to be "the atoning sacrifice for our sins" (1 John 4:10). Peter looks at the cross with the understanding of atoning sacrifice. Jesus was crucified like "a lamb without defect or blemish" (1 Pet. 1:18–19). Paul seems to realize that the sacrificial language which was relevant for the Jews was less relevant for the non-Jews. He introduces both the idea of redemption and that of adopted sons to make the mystery of the cross understandable and relevant to the people of the Roman Empire. This was effective as a large proportion of the population were slaves. Thai Christians need to make the mystery of the cross relevant to Thai people where the language of atonement, sacrifice, redemption, or adopted sons fails to communicate any relevant meaning. Some key Christian concepts needing clarification are God, love, sin, salvation, and self. Each topic is broad and complex, but all present vital possibilities for developing the Thai Christian response to Buddhism. After grasping the Buddhist worldview and realizing how Buddhists comprehend Christianity, a Christian response to Buddhism can be developed more effectively.

So, how are we as Christians going to address the mystery of suffering? The Christian God, suffering with his creation, transforming and redeeming suffering, lies beyond the Buddhist worldview. However, an attempt to explain "the Christian God is a suffering God" can perhaps be put in more understandable terms by using the ideal human relationship found between loving parents and children. Parents love their children, but children are not their puppets; children have their own will. Hence the suffering of the loving parents. Neither nirvana nor the kingdom of God have room for suffering, nirvana being the realm of non-self and the kingdom of God being where death, mourning, crying, and pain are no more, as we read in Revelation 21:4.

We need to communicate Christ to Buddhists in a way that is comprehensible and relevant to their lives. When we are witnessing, teaching, or preaching, we should make every effort to help the Buddhist listener understand what we intend to communicate to them. We, brothers and sisters, servants of the Lord urgently need to help each other find more effective ways of communicating Christ to our Buddhist friends so that what is communicated (the message) can really touch their hearts.

CHAPTER 2

DOING A THAI CHRISTIAN THEOLOGY OF SUFFERING

Satanun Boonyakiat

The problem of suffering is real and complex. People in different cultures understand and respond to this problem in different manners. In Thailand, the worldview of the Thai people concerning suffering is greatly shaped by the Buddhist concept of suffering as reflected in the Four Noble Truths. All Thai people can remember the content of this doctrine as it is taught in the Buddhism course that is compulsory in all Thai schools. The Buddhist concept of suffering governs the understanding of Thai Buddhists, and it influences the responses of Thai Christians to the reality of human suffering. Within this context, a Christian theology of suffering that is relevant to Thai people can no longer be developed exclusively on the basis of Christian scripture and tradition, but it must take into consideration the Buddhist concept of suffering, especially the Four Noble Truths. Moreover, it can no longer be limited to academia, but it must enable the Thai people to respond to different types of suffering more appropriately.

The purpose of this paper is to develop a Christian theology of suffering that is relevant to the Thai context (Boonyakiat 2009). This study will briefly discuss three aspects of such theology: the reality and complexity of suffering, the causes of suffering, and the ways to the extinction of suffering. It will begin by exploring each Noble Truth and the related Buddhist teachings. Then, the Buddhist understanding of suffering will be compared and contrasted with the corresponding biblical and theological concepts of suffering. While the Christian view of suffering will be maintained, it will be reflected and enhanced by the insights gained from the Buddhist tradition. It is hoped that this study will enable Thai people and others, both Buddhists and Christians, to better understand and experience the way to overcome the misery of life that we all share.

THE REALITY AND COMPLEXITY OF SUFFERING

In light of the First Noble Truth, I will propose that a Thai Christian theology of suffering must acknowledge the reality and complexity of suffering. This section will show that the First Noble Truth can help Christians better comprehend the reality and complexity of suffering, and respond to it in a more constructive manner. Different from the traditional Christian approach to suffering that often prioritizes the intellectual and minimizes the problem of evil—Buddhism emphasizes concrete human suffering experiences and seeks to respond to them on a practical level. While Christianity tends to generalize suffering and attribute it to sin, Buddhism observes the sophistication of the human predicament and points to various reasons behind it. Therefore, the First Noble Truth has much to teach Christians about the complex reality of suffering. The First Noble Truth is the truth of suffering (*dukkha*). Buddha declared,

> This, O Monks, is the Noble Truth of Suffering: Birth is suffering; decay is suffering; death is suffering. Sorrow, lamentation, pain, grief and despair are suffering. Presence of objects we hate is suffering; separation from objects we love is suffering; not to obtain what we desire is suffering. Briefly, the five groups of existence connected with clinging are suffering. (Bodhi 2003 LVI)

Here it is important to note that the Pali word *dukkha* has a much broader sense than its English equivalent, suffering. In ordinary usage, it can be translated as "suffering, pain, sorrow, or misery," but it also conveys wider concepts such as "imperfection, impermanence, emptiness, and insubstantiality" (Rahula 1996, 16–17). For Buddha, suffering had three basic meanings. First, *dukkha-dukkhatā* is the state of suffering in terms of feeling and sensation. This term is close to the English word "suffering." Second, *viparinama-dukkhatā* is the state of suffering that is inherent in change or the state of suffering which is concealed within the infidelity of happiness. This kind of suffering is caused by changes within and the cessation of happiness. Third, *sankhāra-dukkhatā* is the state of suffering due to formations. All things are under the conflictual state caused by birth and decay. They are not constant or perfect within themselves, but they exist as part of the cause and effect continuum. Thus, they will cause suffering (i.e., the feeling of suffering) whenever they become the objects of craving or clinging.

From this understanding, the First Noble Truth does not merely address physical and emotional pain, but it also includes the state of suffering that is inherent in the change and conflictual state resulting from impermanence. Buddha pointed out that human beings must encounter various kinds of suffering. Physical and emotional suffering associated with birth, old age, and death is unavoidable because it is the true basis of human nature. The feeling of suffering is the result of craving or clinging to someone or something. Human beings also suffer in the sense that they are under the stressful and conflictual nature caused by impermanence. Therefore, the essence of the first Truth is rightly accepting the reality of suffering as it is, and perceiving life and the world as they are (Dhammapitaka 2003, 906).

Similar to Buddhist teachings, Christian scripture testifies that human suffering is a complex reality. There are innumerable examples of suffering—for example, physical pain, toil, guilt, oppression, conflict, disaster, illness, punishment, death, and spiritual torment. The list could go on. These biblical examples are not abstract teachings about suffering, but they are actual experiences of men and women who tried to make sense of their predicament and sought to be freed from it. Therefore, suffering in the biblical perspective is not illusory but an undeniable fact.

The complexity of suffering is also revealed through its various biblical expressions. scripture uses many different words to convey this idea—for instance, affliction, agony, anguish, distress, hardship, oppression, pain, trouble, and tribulation. These expressions are derived from different Hebrew and Greek roots that portray the many faces of suffering. While some words primarily describe physical pain, others emphasize the psychological suffering of individuals and communities. Some terms, such as *'āmāl*, "distress, trouble, toil, effort, misfortune, misery, or adversity," can also mean "trouble associated with or caused by wickedness or to name that wickedness itself" (Thompson 1997, 435–36). Some words indicate the terrible suffering of individuals and the whole Israelite nation caused by enemies. In the New Testament, the term *paskō*, "suffer or endure," includes a wide range of human experiences. It is found forty-two times in the New Testament. Most of its occurrences refer to the sufferings of Christ and Christians for Christ's sake (Michaelis 1985, 904–23).

Therefore, it can be said that both Buddhism and Christianity agree that suffering is real and complex. The problem of suffering is not only an intellectual problem that requires a logical explanation, but also a tangible challenge that demands a proper response. Moreover, various expressions and manifestations of suffering in both religious traditions reveal that it is more appropriate to speak of many problems of suffering rather than a problem of suffering.

This understanding is clearly supported by the concrete situations of human misery. Suffering can be classified in various ways. It can be distinguished by its different targets—individuals, communities, nations, regions, or the whole human race. It can also be differentiated by the way in which it affects humanity—namely physically or nonphysically. Physical suffering primarily influences persons' or communities' bodily sensations, such as physical pain, physical disability, hunger, thirst, disease, and death. Nonphysical suffering mainly affects their inner beings intellectually, emotionally, psychologically, and spiritually. It is revealed in conflict, anxiety, depression, disappointment, abandonment, shame, guilt, and so on. Nevertheless, these types of suffering are closely connected since humanity consists of both physical and nonphysical dimensions. Pain unquestionably affects a person holistically. Finally, suffering can be classified by its degree of intensity. It ranges from minor personal pain to severe regional or global hardship caused by poverty, illiteracy, starvation, environmental pollution, natural disasters, oppression, war, terrorism, or AIDS. History shows that the Holocaust is not the only witness to the radical reality of human suffering. While we are uncertain about the exact number, we know that in this century alone millions suffered and died under brutal and inhumane political leaders around the globe. For this reason, suffering calls for a theological response that takes it seriously, a theology that is not just an academic exercise or merely addresses a particular kind of suffering without considering its diversity.

THE CAUSES OF SUFFERING

This section will study the Second Noble Truth, the Truth of the Cause of Suffering (*samudaya*), in comparison with some of the causes of suffering that Christian theology espouses. While there are many interpretations of the causes of suffering in Christianity, I will focus on two interpretations that relate to Buddhist teachings: suffering is the result of sin and suffering is a mystery. To illustrate these themes, I will use retribution theology and the book of Job respectively. I will argue that the Buddhist and Christian interpretations of the causes of suffering are similar in some aspects, but different in essential aspects. The law of karma is comparable with the principle of retribution, yet these concepts are not identical because the former is essentially the natural law of cause and effect whereas the latter advocates a sovereign God who is the supreme judge, the Trinitarian God who is higher than the rigid law of cause and effect. Moreover, the book of Job challenges both the law of karma and retribution theology by proclaiming that the cause of the individual's misery can remain a mystery.

After Buddha acknowledged the reality of suffering, he moved to the truth of the cause of suffering. While there were several possible causes of human suffering, Buddha taught that the basic cause was *tanhā*. He said:

> This, O Monks, is the Noble Truth of the Cause of Suffering: Craving, which leads to rebirth, accompanied by pleasure and lust, finding its delight here and there. It is the craving for pleasure, the craving for existence, the craving for non-existence or self-annihilation. (Bodhi LVI)

In order to accurately understand the truth of the cause of suffering, one must understand the meaning of the term *tanhā* and the law of karma. While *tanhā* is rendered "craving or desire," Buddha clearly stated that it referred to craving or desire in two specific manners: craving which leads to rebirth and craving which is accompanied by, and constantly finds its delight in, pleasure and lust (Humphreys 1990, 91). The truth of the cause of suffering is closely related to the law of karma. The term karma literally means "action or doing," but, in Buddhism, it generally refers to "action based on intention" or "deed willfully done." According to Buddha, good karma produced good effects, and bad karma produced bad effects. Therefore, the law of karma is the natural law of cause and effect, of action and reaction. It indicates that human beings receive the fruits of their actions according to the natural process (Dhammapitaka 2003, 156–57). This principle is summarized in the well-known Thai phrase *tum dee dai dee tum chua dai chua*, "good actions bring good results, bad actions bring bad results." Under the law of karma, craving brings about feelings of suffering in this life, and it enslaves human beings in the circle of birth and death.

It is significant to understand that the law of karma does not merely describe a direct and immediate connection between actions and results, because it also teaches that the results of one's karma can take place later in this life or in lives to come. However, Buddha affirmed that the law of karma is certain, and that individuals will surely reap the fruits of their karma in some subsequent existence (Bodhi 1995, 135–36). It is also crucial to mention that karma is not the spiritual or divine being that will provide reward or punishment but "the power of a voluntary thought, word, physical action, or dominant attitude to produce a fitting consequence in the life of its author or possessor" (King 1962, 113). This implies the rejection of the idea of a sovereign God who is the supreme judge. Moreover, the individual must be responsible for oneself. No one can help others from the law of karma. Therefore, the idea of a savior has no place in the Theravada Buddhist worldview. An individual must control and be responsible for his or her own destiny.

The first Christian interpretation of the causes of suffering which is comparable to the Buddhist understanding is retribution theology. Although the idea of God's retributive punishment of the sinner is often rejected by many people in the present day, it can be found throughout the Bible. In the Old Testament, there are numerous references to the retributive dimension of the divine punishment of sinners—in both narrative and didactic material. Examples are to be found in the narratives of the flood, destruction of Sodom and Gomorrah, death of Aaron's sons Nadab and Abihu, stoning of Achan and his family, and destruction of Samaria and Jerusalem, to mention a few. Didactic passages are frequently found in Deuteronomy, the prophetic books, and wisdom literature. In Deuteronomy, prosperity and long life are rewards for people's faithfulness to God. In the prophetic books, the prophets consistently warn the people, and their leaders in particular, to turn back from their sin because it will bring disaster for the whole nation. Nevertheless, the prophets also testify that the law of retribution is not absolute (Isa. 54:7–10; Jer. 23:5–6; Ezk. 36:22). A final restoration of Israel after the judgment of suffering and exile is not solely the result of the people's repentance and obedience, but it is primarily understood as "a unilateral manifestation of God's mercy over his judgment which transcends the scheme of reward and punishment" (Beker 1987, 43).

Biblical wisdom literature offers a more complex theological understanding of retribution. While the book of Proverbs advocates retribution theology, Ecclesiastes and Job put it into question. While several sayings in Proverbs emphasize God's retributive punishment and reward, many passages concentrate on a direct correlation between human deed and its consequence rather than divine intervention. Thus, the book of Proverbs witnesses both judicial and act-consequence aspects of retribution. God's role as judge is affirmed in the teaching that wrongdoers will not go unpunished (6:29, 11:21), but the wise and righteous will be granted what they desire and will be delivered from harm (10:2, 11:4). At the same time, a close connection between deed and consequence is revealed in many proverbs (10:4–5, 25:23).

In the New Testament, the principle of retribution can still be found, but the focus shifts from temporal retribution to a future and final judgment (Erickson 1998, 609). Several passages reveal that God's justice will be fully executed at Christ's second coming (Matt. 24–25; Rom. 2:1–16; Rev. 20:11–15, 21:1–8). In addition, the New Testament message of the final judgment is closely related to an invitation to be reconciled to God through Christ. People are called not only to repent from their sins, but also to have a right relationship with God (Mark 1:15; John 3:16–21; Acts 2:16–38).

A comparison between retribution theology and the law of karma reveals both similarities and differences. On a surface level, these teachings are similar in two aspects. First, they affirm that much suffering is the result of human wrongdoing, which is influenced by sin or *tanhā*. Second, the act-consequence aspect of retribution is very close to the law of karma in the sense that it advocates an intrinsic correlation between deed and consequence, whether good or bad. Therefore, it is fair to say that retribution theology shares certain characteristics with the law of karma, specifically the notions that every human act produces its effects or results, and suffering experiences come upon individuals from their wrongdoing itself, not from somewhere else. It is also appropriate to hold that the Buddhist understanding of action and result is a kind of wisdom tradition which parallels that of the Old Testament. Bad karma is comparable to the "foolish acts" mentioned in Proverbs that produce bad results. This understanding is very helpful for Thai Christians because it helps them realize that some of their suffering experiences may be the direct result of their wrongdoing, not God's punishment. Therefore, they should not view God as a heartless judge who purposely inflicts pain on them, but they should be more responsible for their actions, knowing that their immoral actions will surely bring about suffering.

Notwithstanding, I will argue that retribution theology and the law of karma are fundamentally different because of two main reasons. First, these doctrines perceive the relationship between wrongdoing and suffering in a different manner. According to Buddhism, the law of karma indicates that human beings receive the consequences of their actions according to the natural law of action and effect, not the judgment of God. The connection between action and consequence is also viewed as inexorable and mechanical. It is not under the control of any supreme being. Moreover, the process of karma fruition is enigmatic. The individuals may not receive the result of their action immediately, but will somehow reap its fruit later in their lives or in some subsequent existence.

Contrary to that, the principle of retribution teaches that God is the supreme judge who gives reward and punishment, and he is also the creator and sustainer of the relationship between act and result. Even though the act-consequence aspect of retribution is similar to the natural law of cause and effect, it does not deny the reality of God, and it does not divorce the correspondence between action and result from him (Koch 1983, 61). In any case, scripture leaves no room for a purely mechanical law of retribution. God is believed to be active in the association between human action and consequence (Murphy 2002, 117). The pattern that God has established is also viewed as a straightforward connection between deed and result (as reflected in several sayings in Proverbs), not a complex process that will somehow come to fruition at a later time. Moreover, retribution theology as a whole points to the supremacy of God that surpasses an unalterable connection between action and consequence. In the final analysis, it is God—not any system—that determines the destiny of humankind. Through his mercy and grace, God does not respond to humankind according to their deeds. His forgiveness and restoration is available for those who truly repent from their sins (Ps. 32:1–5, 103:1–13). More importantly, Christ's redemptive work on the cross obviously frees human beings from the results of their transgressions and reconciles them to God (Rom. 5:6–10). The Holy Spirit frees them from being slaves to sinful nature and fear, and testifies that they are God's children (Rom. 8:12–16).

The second difference between the law of karma and retribution theology is that they offer opposite solutions to suffering caused by human immoral deeds. According to the law of karma, suffering is basically caused by human *tanhā*. Therefore, one must not attach to anything or anyone, but must depend upon the self in dealing with one's desire and ignorance. In contrast, a theology of retribution teaches suffering is God's punishment for human sin. Consequently, one must repent from his or her sins in order to receive God's forgiveness, and, at the same time, enter into a genuine fellowship with him.

From this comparative study, a Christian theology of suffering in the Thai context affirms that one of the causes of suffering is sin. Some suffering experiences of the individual can be viewed as direct results of wrongdoing and manifestations of divine retributive punishment. However, this understanding should not be confused with the law of karma in Buddhism. Even though these doctrines concur that there is a connection between acts and consequences—whether good or bad—they understand this connection very differently, and they offer opposite solutions to suffering that is caused by human misconduct.

Consequently, I would argue that it is possible and appropriate for Thai Christians to use the term "the result of karma" (*pon kum*) in place of the term "the result of sin" (*pon kong bab*) in communicating the gospel to Thai people. However, they should not use these terms interchangeably as if they are identical when they describe the Christian faith. For instance, "the due penalty" mentioned in Romans 1:27 in the Thai Bible is translated *pon kum*. This translation is relevant to the Thai, but it is misleading because it signifies the people suffer under the law of karma rather than the judgment of God. On the contrary, Thai Christians should affirm the essence of retribution theology—that much of human suffering is the result of sin, and many individuals' painful experiences can be the result of their sins. Therefore, when an individual faces hardship, that person should humbly and carefully examine himself or herself to see if the suffering is the result of sin. Then the individual must repent. This response to suffering also applies to those who have not been reconciled with God through Christ. People may be far from physical suffering, yet they constantly undergo spiritual suffering. This kind of suffering will ultimately lead them to God, the only person who can free them from the suffering that greatly afflicts their soul.

The second Christian interpretation of the causes of suffering that relates to the Second Noble Truth is the notion that suffering can be a mystery. While the law of karma affirms that suffering is the result of *tanhā*, and retribution theology asserts that it is the result of sin, scripture also reveals that suffering can be a mystery that is beyond human comprehension. The book of Job is the clearest demonstration of this puzzling reality. It challenges both traditional Christian and Buddhist interpretations of the cause of suffering by proclaiming that the reason for suffering ultimately locates in divine wisdom, not in human knowledge. As a result, a proper response to suffering may not be repenting from one's sin, but rather sustaining one's faith in God. This understanding can be found in the book of Job's prologue, the three-circle dialogue, and Yahweh's speeches.

In the prologue, the author makes clear that Job was "blameless and upright; he feared God and shunned evil" (1:1) and the reason for his severe affliction was Satan's questions about his integrity (1:6–12, 2:1–6). The point the author wants to stress here is not the trial caused by Satan, but the fact that Job's suffering was not caused by his sin. He was truly an innocent sufferer. The author is proclaiming there is such a thing as innocent suffering. Therefore, at the beginning of his writing, he courageously challenges the common and long established notion that one suffers because of one's sins. More specifically, he argues that "the connection is not often obvious, and life is much more complex than this simple formula.

Human suffering is more than a system of rewards and punishments" (Anderson 1976, 67). In the Thai context, the book of Job indicates that not all sufferers are guilty of bad karma. It is possible that individuals suffer in spite of their innocence. The law of cause and effect may generally work, but it is too simplistic in the light of the complex reality of suffering.

The lengthy dialogue between Job and his friends indicates the significance the author attaches to it. David F. Ford interestingly points out that this dialogue and debate may represent the attempt of a tradition to face its limitations and move through a crisis. In other words, the author tries to tie together traditional belief with a new experience. The readers are immersed in a complex argumentative exchange and are given considerable responsibility to wrestle with these complex issues and make sense of them (Ford 2007, 122–23). The author does not simply mention the reality of innocent suffering and totally disregard traditional retribution theology. In contrast, he describes the conventional view with unsurpassed eloquence and fairness, notably in the speeches of Eliphaz, Bildad, and Zophar. The three friends, however, reverse the cause and effect and say, "If the person suffers, he or she must have sin." In doing this, they go beyond the general idea of retribution and assert that all suffering is caused by sin (Dillard and Longman 1994, 209). It must be admitted that there is truth in this principle and scripture affirms that both obedience and sin have consequences.

Job's arguments against his friends clearly rejects this overstated retribution doctrine. While the friends continually accuse him of his sin, Job asks them to point out this sin for him specifically. Of course his friends are unable to fulfill Job's request. They constantly return to the general principle of retribution or merely tell Job he had a secret sin (11:6). In addition, Job argues that, in numerous other cases, the wicked have not been punished, but have prospered (Job 21, 24). In the final analysis, Job's life experiences forcefully prove human suffering is much more complex than a simplistic system of rewards and punishments.

In Yahweh's speeches (Job 38–41), he neither blames Satan nor gives the reason for Job's suffering. In contrast, he proclaims the mystery and complexity of creation, which is beyond human comprehension, in order to remind Job that humankind has no right to accuse God as being unjust. God acclaims he structured the world according to his blueprints (38:4–8) in order to show that justice is also in the structure of the universe. He declares that the whole creation is under his control (38:16–39:30); as a result, he wisely and caringly watches over people just as he wisely manages the entire universe and caringly provides for creatures (Hartley 1988, 49). These speeches, therefore, affirm God's graciousness and kindness to all the works of his hands.

Through his encounter with God, Job finds a new power which sustains him in the midst of his predicament. He does not discover any explanation for his suffering, but he gains a new attitude towards life. Turning from his concern to a larger world and wider providence, Job eventually realizes that God is the true center of all things and nothing is beyond his concern. All things are created by him and are dependent on him. In all circumstances God is still fully present at the center, directing and sustaining all things, seen and unseen. Consequently, human destiny is in the hand of God (Wood 1966, 20). Human life is within the divine cosmic purpose. God's purpose, however, is far beyond what humans could ever comprehend. Therefore, the cause of suffering can remain a mystery and one can go through incomprehensible suffering by continuing in faith in God.

In conclusion, the Buddhist and Christian interpretations of the causes of suffering are similar in some aspects, but they are fundamentally different. These differences lead to very different and even opposite solutions to the problem of human suffering. While Buddhism teaches that human effort is the answer, Christianity believes that only God can ultimately deliver humankind from suffering. Hence, the next section will study the Third and Fourth Noble Truths—the truth of the extinction and the way to the extinction of suffering—in comparison with the Christian understanding of God's response to the problem of human suffering.

THE WAYS TO THE EXTINCTION OF SUFFERING

In this section, the Buddhist teachings of the extinction of suffering (the Third Noble Truth) and the way to the extinction of suffering (the Fourth Noble Truth) will be examined and compared with a theological understanding of the extinction of suffering. The focus will be given to the Christian understanding of God's response to human suffering as found in a theology of the cross. I will argue that Buddhism and Christianity share some responses to the problem of human suffering because several aspects of the Middle Way are very similar to the biblical teachings. Therefore, Buddhists and Christians can help and learn from one another in overcoming suffering. From a Christian standpoint, it can be said that the Noble Eightfold Path can also help Christians overcome suffering to a certain extent. Nevertheless, I will propose that Buddhism and Christianity ultimately offer opposite solutions to the problem of suffering. Buddhism teaches that it is human effort that leads humankind to nirvana. On the contrary, Christianity believes that only God, through Christ, can deliver humankind from suffering. While proper attitudes and actions can empower sufferers and prevent unnecessary suffering in a certain degree, only God's redemptive work can bring suffering to a complete extinction. For this reason, a responsibility of humankind is to turn from sin to God and actively participate in the suffering of Christ and suffering of others.

After Buddha pointed out the truth of suffering and its cause, he proclaimed the truth of the extinction of suffering (*nirodha*) and the path leading to the extinction of suffering (*magga*). He said:

> This, O Monks, is the Noble Truth of the extinction of suffering: it is the complete fading away and extinction of this craving, its forsaking and giving up, liberation and detachment from it.

> This, O Monks, is the Noble Truth of the Path which leads to the extinction of suffering: It is the Noble Eightfold Middle Path, that is to say, Right Belief, Right Aspiration, Right Speech, Right Conduct, Right Means of Livelihood, Right Endeavor, Right Mindfulness, Right Meditation. (Bodhi 2003 LVI)

While the term *nirodha* is used in the Third Noble Truth, the ultimate goal of Buddhism is generally referred to as nirvana, which is an "absolute extinction of that life-affirming will manifested as greed, hate and delusion, and convulsively clinging to existence; and therewith also the ultimate and absolute deliverance from all future rebirth, old age, disease and death, from all suffering and misery" (Nyanatiloka 1980, 201). In order to reach this goal, Buddha taught that one must overcome his or her craving by practicing the Noble Eightfold Path or the Middle Way, which consists of Right Understanding, Right Thought, Right Speech, Right Action, Right Livelihood, Right Effort, Right Mindfulness, and Right Meditation.

Right Understanding refers to the adoption of Buddha's teachings about the world and the human condition. More specifically, it indicates the understanding of the Four Noble Truths. Right Thought refers to the wholesome thoughts, which are the thought of renunciation, the thought free from hatred, and the thought free from violence. Right Speech means abstaining from unwholesome words. Right Action is abstaining from killing living beings, dishonesty, and sexual misconduct. Right Livelihood refers to abandoning dishonest livelihood and keeping one's life going with right livelihood. Right Effort includes an effort to prevent evils that have not yet arisen, endeavor to abandon evils that have arisen, attempt to create noble qualities that have not yet arisen, and effort to maintain and develop good qualities that have arisen. Right Mindfulness is the awareness of one's bodily actions, feelings, mind, and mental qualities. It is constant care and caution, not allowing oneself to fall into harmful ways or to miss any opportunity for improvement. It is recognizing things that need to be done and performing one's daily responsibilities with sincerity and effort towards improvement. Right Meditation means bringing one's consciousness to a single point in meditation. It is only through Right Meditation that one can enter the state of serene contemplation that enables one to fully realize the truth of the three characteristics of existence. This realization, in turn, frees one's mind from the attachment with the five groups of existence. Consequently, one can attain the goal of nirvana, freedom from the wheel of birth and death and, in turn, suffering as described in chapters nineteen to twenty-one of the Dhammapitaka (2003).

The Noble Eightfold Path certainly brings about realistic outcomes for those who practice it. Proper attitudes and actions can prevent individuals from unnecessary suffering; for example, Right Understanding of the impermanence of all earthly things helps individuals realize decay and death is unavoidable. Instead of resisting this reality, they should accept it and learn not to attach themselves to impermanent persons or things. Similarly, correct attitudes and actions enable sufferers to overcome painful feelings. For instance, Right Thought—free from hatred, anger, and revenge—can quench resentment and bitterness caused by an unforgiving heart. Therefore, each aspect of the Middle Way has an important role in helping individuals overcome different forms of suffering in this life.

A comparison between the eight aspects of the Middle Way and biblical teachings clearly reveals that Buddhism and Christianity share a great deal of ethical concerns. Both religions give similar preventatives and solutions to suffering. For instance, the second and third meaning of Right Thought—the thought free from hatred but filled with compassion, and the thought free from violence but full of mercy—is comparable to the Beatitudes, in which the meek, the merciful, the pure in heart, and the peacemakers are blessed (Matt. 5:5,7–9). Right Speech—abstaining from unwholesome speeches—is equivalent to Paul's teaching in Ephesians 5:4: "Nor should there be obscenity, foolish talk or coarse joking, which are out of place, but rather thanksgiving." Right Livelihood corresponds to various biblical passages concerning work ethics (e.g., Prov. 12:24, 21:25; Eph. 4:28; 2 Thess. 3:6–13). Consequently, Buddhists and Christians should learn from one another about these particular doctrines. Furthermore, they should work together in promoting and executing these beneficial concepts in Thai society. Christians should not reject aspects of the Middle Way that do not contradict Christian faith since some of them are identical with biblical teachings.

However, I will argue it is incorrect to take these Buddhist and Christian teachings out of their original context and claim both religions offer the same solution to the problem of suffering. Considering the Middle Way and corresponding biblical teachings in light of their guiding vision indicates they are similar on a practical level, but they are very different in their essence. Therefore they suggest different, and even opposite, solutions to the problem of suffering. While Buddhism suggests that human beings can eliminate suffering by relying on their own efforts, Christian theology of suffering teaches that only God can ultimately save human beings from suffering.

Since the cross of Christ is the clearest expression of God's response to human suffering, we shall discuss the theology of the cross more fully. A theological heritage of Martin Luther, Kazoh Kitamori, Jürgen Moltmann, and Kosuke Koyama helps Christians better understand the relationship between the cross of Christ and human suffering. For Luther, the theology of the cross consists of three major aspects: a theology of revelation, an understanding that God makes himself known through suffering, and a theology of faith. First, the theology of the cross is a theology of revelation. The true knowledge of God can be found only in God's self-revelation. This revelation, however, is indirect and hidden in the suffering and the cross of Christ. The concept of the hidden God is at the center of the theology of the cross. In Thesis Twenty of the Heidelberg Disputation, Luther's reference to the *posteriora Dei*, the rearward parts of God, serves as an emphasis that in the same way that Moses was allowed to see God only from the rear (Ex. 33:23), we can only see the indirect revelation of God in suffering and the cross (Luther 1955). Even though God is revealed in the passion and cross of Christ, he is not immediately recognizable as God. As a result, anyone who attempts to speculate on the created order through human reason is incapable of discerning God's revelation and does not deserve to be called a theologian. In contrast, the person who is able to discern God's revelation through the suffering and cross of Christ deserves to be called a theologian (McGrath 1994, 149).

Secondly, the theology of the cross maintains that God makes himself known through suffering. For Luther, God is active in this matter and suffering is seen as the means by which human beings are brought to God. Here, Luther introduces the dialectic between *opus alienum Dei*, God's alien work, and *opus proprium Dei*,

God's proper work. The alien works mean "putting down, killing, taking away hope, and leading to desperation" and the proper works mean "forgiving, giving mercy, taking up, saving, and encouraging." Luther sometimes calls the alien works "the works of the left hand" and the proper works "the works of the right hand" (Kärkkäinen 2002, 222). However, Luther maintains that these works result from the same love of God, and the proper works are veiled in the alien works and take place concurrently with them. Consequently, the passion of Christ and human suffering represent the alien works of God through which he works out his proper work (McGrath 1994, 151).

Finally, the theology of the cross is the theology of faith alone. For Luther, the theologian of the cross is the person who, through faith, discerns the presence of the hidden God in the suffering and cross of Christ. At the cross, Christ suffered on our behalf and took upon himself our sin in order that we might possess his righteousness. However, it is through faith alone that the true significance of the cross is understood and through faith alone that its power can be appropriated. While the unbeliever only sees the helplessness and hopelessness of a dying man upon the cross, the believer recognizes the presence and work of the crucified and hidden God who is present in human suffering and actively works through it (McGrath 1994, 174–75).

Another person whose work significantly shapes a theology of the cross is Kazoh Kitamori, who brought the concept of the suffering God to new prominence in the mid-twentieth century. Perhaps the most significant contribution of Kitamori is the argument against a traditional Christian theology that maintains divine immutability and impassibility. He points out that Western Christianity is overly dependent upon Greek philosophy, which perceived God as immutable and impassible, and argues that, at the cross, both the Father and the Son experienced pain because of their essential unity (1965, 85, 115). Though many theologians disagree with Kitamori's idea that the pain of God is caused by an internal conflict within God's own nature, his attack on the doctrine of divine immutability has created a profound impact in Christian theology. It has been echoed and elaborated by many contemporary theologians, especially by Jürgen Moltmann.

Grounded in Luther's foundation and Kitamori's contribution, Moltmann brings a theology of the cross to its fruition. He argues that God reveals himself to humankind through suffering and the cross, not through power and glory. On the cross, God has not just acted externally, but he has suffered himself (1993, 205). Thus, the crucified Christ reveals the crucified God, and the suffering of Christ manifests the suffering of God himself. According to Mark, Jesus died with a cry of Godforsakenness (Mk. 15:34). For Paul, the Father abandoned and delivered up the Son for godforsaken people (Rom. 8:32). From this understanding, Moltmann interestingly points out that the Son suffered dying in forsakenness, but the Father suffered the death of the Son, and if God considered himself as the father of Jesus Christ, then he also suffered the death of his fatherhood in the death of the Son (1993, 243). Moltmann concludes that the concrete history of God in the death of Jesus on the cross can be understood as history because it contains within itself all the depths of human history. Consequently, there is no suffering that is not God's suffering, no death that has not been God's death on the cross, and no life and joy which have not been integrated into the eternal life and eternal joy of God (1993, 246). Whoever suffers without reason always feels he or she is abandoned by God. However, whoever cries out to God in this suffering joins in the death-cry of Jesus. Moreover, the trinitarian history of God is open to the future. It moves towards eschatological consummation so that the Trinity may be all in all. God is in us. God suffers in us. We are participating in the trinitarian process of the history of God. In the same way that we participate in the suffering of God, we will participate in the joy of God when he brings his history to completion (1993, 255).

From this understanding, it is clear God is interested in human suffering to the point of participating in our suffering. The history of God in the death of Jesus on the cross is truly the "history of history" because it includes not only the sin of the world, but also all suffering, pain, and death for humankind. However, God does not simply suffer with human beings, but he suffers for us. Through Christ's death, God shares in human suffering in order to redeem humankind from sin and its consequences. It is at the cross that God walks alongside humankind in our suffering, and it is here that he works out his justification and salvation. This is indeed the new meaning of suffering. Christ's resurrection and glorification after he has suffered and died also affirms that God will eventually bring suffering to an end. "He will wipe every tear from their eyes. There will be no more death or mourning or crying or pain, for the old order of things has passed away" (Rev. 21:4).

Another theologian whose work greatly enriches a theology of the cross is Kosuke Koyama. His major contribution to a theology of the cross is his vision of the crucified mind. This concept enables Christians to move beyond passively acknowledging God's presence in the passion of Christ and the suffering of humankind to actively participating in the suffering of Christ and that of others. Based on the image of Jesus carrying a heavy cross with no handle, not a lunch box or business briefcase with nice handle, Koyama suggests that the cross without a handle signifies extreme inconvenience, ugliness, inefficiency, insecurity, pain, and self-denial. Hence, those who would follow Christ must deny themselves and receive the mind of the crucified Lord, a crucified mind; as Jesus said, "If anyone would come after me, he must deny himself and take up his cross and follow me" (Matt. 16:24) (Koyama 1977, 1–2). Reflecting on various New Testament passages, especially Paul's statements in 1 Corinthians 1:18–25, 2:2, and Philippians 2:5–11, Koyama indicates that a crucified mind is a mind characterized by self-denial, following the mind of Christ (Phil. 2:5), which compelled him to enter human history, deny himself, participate in human suffering, and be crucified on behalf of sinful humankind. Hence, Christians who have this state of mind will be willing to deny themselves and participate in the suffering of Christ and of others (1977, 8, 12).

In summary, several aspects of the Middle Way are very close to Christian teachings, but Buddhism and Christianity ultimately offer opposite solutions to suffering. Buddhism teaches that it is humans' own effort that leads to nirvana, but Christianity believes that Jesus Christ is the only Way to salvation. The Middle Way and the Way obviously lead to different goals. The theology of the cross helps Christians better understand that the crucified Christ reveals the hidden God who was also crucified on the cross. It is here that all the suffering of humankind throughout history is embraced by God himself. Moreover, it is at the cross that Christ redeems humankind from sin and its consequences, especially suffering. Therefore, human beings should respond to God's saving act by repenting from their sin and trusting in him. Furthermore, they should learn to participate in the suffering of Christ and suffering of other people.

CONCLUSION

In conclusion, a Christian theology of suffering that is relevant to the Thai people must take into consideration the Buddhist concept of suffering, especially the Four Noble Truths, and it must help the Thai people respond to the complex reality of suffering on a practical level. I have briefly proposed three aspects of such theology. First, a Thai Christian theology of suffering acknowledges the reality and complexity of suffering. The First Noble Truth reminds Christians that suffering is a complex reality that demands not only a rational explanation, but also a proper response. A Thai Christian theology of suffering can no longer follow the traditional approach that generalizes suffering and discusses it under the problem of evil and theodicy. On the contrary, it must specifically address different kinds of suffering and attempt to respond to them appropriately.

Secondly, reflecting on the Second Noble Truth, a Thai Christian theology of suffering resists any attempt to generalize suffering and declares that this complex reality can be attributed to several causes. Among many Christian interpretations of the causes of suffering, two positions have been presented in this study because they are more relevant to the Thai context: suffering is the result of sin and it is a mystery. I have argued that the law of karma and the principle of retribution share some similarities on a surface level, yet they are different in their essence. While the former is the natural law of cause and effect, the latter advocates a sovereign God who is higher than the rigid law of cause and effect. The book of Job indicates that the cause of suffering can remain a mystery, and one can go through incomprehensible suffering by faith in God.

Finally, responding to the Third and Fourth Noble Truths, a Thai Christian theology of suffering agrees that proper attitudes and actions can certainly empower sufferers and avert preventable suffering to a certain degree, yet it sincerely and humbly declares that only the redemptive work of the Triune God can bring suffering to a complete extinction. This message is truly good news for Thai people and others. It is a great comfort to know that humankind does not face suffering alone, but there is a compassionate God who is present in the suffering of humankind. It is a great hope to hear that beyond humans' limited ability to complete the Noble Eightfold Path leading to the end of suffering there is a Savior who is the Way to the end of suffering. It is also a great encouragement to hear that human effort is not useless because though it cannot free the individual from suffering, it becomes an act of participating in the suffering of the one who has already freed them from suffering. More importantly, it is a great joy to know that those who believe do not have to be afraid of suffering, but they can embrace it, knowing that in so doing, they are participating in God's redemptive work for all humankind.

This brief discussion simply highlights some aspects of a Christian theology of suffering in the Thai context. While some of the questions about the subject matter of suffering have been answered, many questions still await Thai theologians who want to fulfill their calling in the Kingdom of Thailand. More careful studies need to be done and more Buddhist-Christian dialogue is needed. Nevertheless, I hope that this study will achieve its goal, even as a small step, of helping Thai people and others, both Buddhists and Christians, better understand and experience the way to overcome the misery of life that we all share.

WHAT YOU DON'T KNOW CAN HURT YOU: IGNORANCE AS A CAUSE OF SUFFERING IN BUDDHISM AND CHRISTIANITY[2]

Russell H. Bowers, Jr.

"Man is born to trouble as surely as sparks fly upward" (Job 5:7). For this reason, all religions ponder the nature of and cure for suffering. Western Christianity's knottiest apologetic problem for the past hundred years has been justifying belief in God in the face of human pain. If God is great and God is good, why the groaning of humanity and creation?

But Buddhism is par excellence in its ideology of suffering. Metaphysical questions do not address this problem; hence, consideration of them was often dismissed by the Buddha (e.g., Sutta 63 of the *Majjhima Nikaya*) (Burtt 1982, 35–36). What he did reiterate were the Four Noble Truths: the pervasiveness, origin, cessation, and path that leads to the cessation of suffering. These were the subject of Siddhārtha Gautama's first sermon after his enlightenment, and remain basic to all the various forms of Buddhism practiced today.

Buddhism's first Truth, then, posits the pervasiveness of suffering. The Pali word is *dukkha* (in Sanskrit, *duhkha*), "sorrow," "suffering," "imperfection," or "unsatisfactoriness." Together with impermanence (*anitya*) and "no-self" (*anātman*), suffering comprises one element of the *tilakkhana*, the three characteristics of all existence. That life is characterized by *dukkha* does not mean, however, that all sentient beings writhe in constant agony. Rather, its implication is that nothing in this phenomenal world ultimately satisfies; that things and people and experiences are bound to disappoint if we look for lasting pleasure in them; that life is somehow out of joint and unsatisfactory, like an axle attached off-center to its wheel (Larson 1984, 351). No one English word captures

---

2   This article printed by permission of the author who holds the copyright.

its nuances. It is "illfare" as opposed to *sukha*, welfare (Smart 1984, 371; Larson 1984, 351). There are three types of *dukkha*—torment (such as old age, sickness, and death), absence of pleasure, and the necessity of giving up that which one loves and to which one has become attached.

Upon first hearing this Truth, outsiders often prematurely conclude that Buddhism is essentially pessimistic. But the Buddhist rather sees recognition of suffering as realistic—facing life as it is and then dealing with it. In fact, understanding *dukkha* as unsatisfactoriness is no more pessimistic than Qoheleth's assessment that all is meaningless; that there is nothing new under the sun; and that neither wisdom, pleasures, toil, achievements, advancement, nor riches in themselves truly satisfy. It is no more pessimistic than asserting that all have sinned and fall short of the glory of God. Buddhism considers this first Truth to be a reasonable assessment of the human condition, a refusal to play either ostrich or Pollyanna, and an attempt then to deal with what is (Lacombe 1980, 113–17). Viewed this way, it may provide a better introduction to the Christian gospel than "God loves you and has a wonderful plan for your life"—a statement that strikes many thinking Buddhists as either meaningless or juvenile.

With no loving, omnipotent God to defend, Buddhism need not concern itself with a theodicy, but may immediately proceed to examining the cause and cure of suffering. The cause turns out to be *trsnā* (Pāli *tanhā*)—thirst, craving, clinging, selfish or blind demandingness. People crave pleasures, possessions, experiences, and continued existence. If we fail to get them, we suffer. If we gain but later lose them, we suffer. We may gain them only to find that they cannot ultimately satisfy, and so once again we suffer. We may crave for nonexistence or nirvana, but wanting even that causes us to suffer. The First Noble Truth declared the pervasiveness of suffering. The Second reveals the cause—we suffer because we thirst. Thirst is divided into at least three broad categories—thirst for sensual pleasure (*kāmatrsnā*), for embodiment (*bhavatrsnā*), and for deliverance through annihilation (*vibhavatrsnā*). As our thirst grows it produces *upādāna*—"grasping" at things to try to seize and claim them.

Certainly, the Bible affirms that evils grow out of inordinate desire. Jesus warns that "desires for other things [can] come in and choke the word, making it unfruitful" (Mark 4:19). Peter cautions against "the corruption in the world caused by evil desires," urging Christians to abstain from them because they "war against your soul" (2 Pet. 1:4; 1 Pet. 2:11). John advises that "the cravings of sinful man, the lust of his eyes and the boasting of what he has and does—[come] not from the Father but from the world. The world and its desires pass away" (1

John 2:16–17). Paul implies that those who gratify "the cravings of [their] sinful nature and [follow] its desires and thoughts" are "by nature objects of wrath" (Eph. 2:3). James teaches that evil desire leads, in turn, to enticement, sin, and death (James 1:14–15). Even outside the scripture, Thomas à Kempis laments, "What, indeed, gives more trouble and affliction than uncontrolled desires of the heart?" (1955, ch. 3). Christians, then, agree with the Buddha that craving often begets suffering.

However, for the Christian not all desire is wrong. The biblical words for desire are used for a variety of longings: good, bad, and indifferent. Key Old Testament Hebrew words that can be used in these three senses are *awah* and *hāmad*. Words like *awah* and cognates often imply a desire springing from the depths of one's being; *hāmad* and cognates are most often used of desire for something or someone visible to the eye. New Testament Greek words used for good, bad, and indifferent desire include *epithymeō* and *oregomai*. In addition to these two, *hēdonē* is used in a bad sense in all of its five occurrences in the New Testament; *epithymeō* and its cognates almost entirely or entirely in a good sense in their thirteen occurrences. By contrast, in Buddhism even the craving for nirvana must be abandoned. Desire itself is not our enemy; evil desire is. God himself desires (Ps. 51:6, 132:13–14; Isa. 55:11; Hosea 6:6); Jesus desires (Luke 22:15); the Spirit desires (Gal. 5:16), and at times grants what people want (Ps. 21:2, 37:4, 103:15, 145:16,19; Prov. 10:24, 13:4). Christians are commanded to desire certain things (1 Cor. 12:31, 14:1; 1 Pet. 2:2). So desire *in se* is not bad. The question for the Christian is, "What is the source of and cure for the *evil* that prompts evil cravings and their lamentable consequences?" rather than, "How can we eliminate *all* desire?"

As profitable as such an inquiry might be, thirst (*tanhā*) and its production of unsatisfactoriness or suffering (*dukkha*) is not the subject of this paper. The causal link that Buddhism observes between craving and suffering is obvious. This paper rather seeks to explore *why we thirst in the first place*. If we can discover what initiates and drives our *tanhā*, then we may have isolated what is even more fundamental to our suffering than the craving itself.

Why then do we thirst for things? Buddhism proposes three hindrances (sometimes called "poisons" or "unwholesome roots") as the culprits. Because of them we crave and cling, and hence perform those intentional deeds (karma) that lead to rebirth and suffering. They are greed, anger, and delusion. These *kleśas* (or kilesa) are depicted in the hub of the Tibetan wheel of life as a cock, a snake, and a pig, constantly chasing each other round and round, and thus driving the whole process of samsara. The most basic of these three is delusion. Because we are deluded or ignorant of the true nature of reality, we imagine ourselves and the things around us to be enduring entities. Hence, we grow greedy to gain and retain things and pleasures, hoping in them to find meaningful, lasting enjoyment. When they do not (since they cannot) provide this, we grow angry. Then the process repeats over and over.

Our most basic enemy, then—that which causes us to crave—is *avidyā*, "lack of light," the "darkness of ignorance," the state of mind that does not correspond to the way things truly are because it mistakes passing phenomena for reality. The word is related to *moha*, confusion. Such misperception encourages craving and hence suffering. As Bodhi says, "All the defilements ultimately stem from ignorance, which thus lies at the bottom of all suffering and bondage" (Bodhi 2005, 308). *Avidyā*, it should be noted, is not as much a lack of information as it is a positive misconstrual of reality (Matilal 1980, 154–64).

That *avidyā* is our fundamental problem is underscored by Zen master Ju-Ching (1163–1228):

> Descendants of the Buddhas and the patriarchs first rid themselves of the five hindrances, and then rid themselves of the six hindrances. The six hindrances consist of the five hindrances plus the hindrance of the darkness of ignorance. If we only eliminate the hindrance of the darkness of ignorance, we thereby eliminate the five hindrances as well. Although we get free of the five hindrances, if we do not get free of the hindrance of the darkness of ignorance, we cannot attain to the practice and realization of the Buddhas and the patriarchs. (Nishitani 1982, 185)

If, then, we could but know ourselves and the nature of this world, we might stop clinging and thereby cease suffering. Here is how ignorance leads to craving and hence suffering:

> We view the world through a mind that is often fundamentally unclear, unsettled, and confused. Not surprisingly we fail to see things as they truly are. At this point it begins to become quite apparent just how and why craving leads to suffering. There is a discrepancy between our craving and the world we live in, between our expectations and the way things are. We want the world to be other than it is. Our craving is based

on a fundamental misjudgment of the situation; a judgment that assumes that when our craving gets what it wants we will be happy, that when our craving possesses the objects of its desire we will be satisfied. But such a judgment in turn assumes a world in which things are permanent, unchanging, stable, and reliable. But the world is simply not like that. In short, in craving we fail to see how things truly are, and in failing to see how things truly are we crave. In other words craving goes hand in hand with a fundamental ignorance and misapprehension of the nature of the world. (Gethin 1998, 73–74)

The mind and truth are crucial in Buddhism. The defining moment in Siddhārtha Gautama's career was his enlightenment. In that experience, "ignorance was banished and true knowledge arose, darkness was banished and light arose" (Bodhi 2005, 66). Enlightenment is what made him the Buddha, and a similar awakening to reality is what every practicing Buddhist seeks. The importance of the mind is stressed throughout the Buddhist scriptures. For example:

3. I do not perceive even one other thing, O monks, that leads to such great harm as an undeveloped mind. An undeveloped mind leads to great harm.

4. I do not perceive even one other thing, O monks, that leads to such great benefit as a developed mind. A developed mind leads to great benefit....

9. I do not perceive even one other thing, O monks, that when undeveloped and uncultivated entails such great suffering as the mind. The mind when undeveloped and uncultivated entails great suffering.

10. I do not perceive even one other thing, O monks, that when developed and cultivated entails such great happiness as the mind. The mind when developed and cultivated entails great happiness. (Bodhi 2005, 267)

Or, in the opening lines of the *Dhammapada*:

We are what we think.
All that we are arises with our thoughts.
With our thoughts we make the world.
Speak or act with an impure mind
And trouble will follow you
As the wheel follows the ox that draws the cart.
We are what we think.
All that we are arises with our thoughts.
With our thoughts we make the world.
Speak or act with a pure mind
And happiness will follow you
As your shadow, unshakable. (Byron)

The *vipassana* ("insight") meditation taught and practiced throughout the world has as its goal the practitioner's intuitive recognition of the three characteristics of existence (*ti-lakkhana*) discussed above and consequent grasp of the true nature of the world—namely, emptiness. Such insight stops new passions (and suffering) from arising and, along with calming the mind, is necessary to attain enlightenment (Bercholz and Kohn 2003, 327). The first link in the chain of dependent arising (*pratītya-samutpāda*)—that which causes rebirth to suffering—is ignorance. Hence, if we can overcome ignorance (the root of the craving that is often blamed), we free ourselves from suffering (Bodhi 2005, 353). Understanding is "the key to salvation" (Jayatilleke 1974, 32–33).

We must not, however, misconstrue the Buddha as prescribing abstract, theoretical ideology as the cure. While the Noble Eightfold Path leading from thirst and suffering to nirvana does include insight (the antithesis of and cure to ignorance), it also urges morality and meditation. (The first two elements of the Path are Right Understanding and Resolve—representing insight [*prajñā*]. The next three—Right Speech, Action, and Livelihood—are matters of morality [*śīla*], and the last three—Right Effort, Mindfulness, and Concentration—deal with concentration [*samādhi*] or meditation [*dhyāna*].) Thus, the cure to craving begins with banishing ignorance from the mind. Truth, however, must not remain merely cerebral and theoretical, but must be lived once it is known. The Buddha's cure is holistic.

Clearly, however, Buddhism perceives ignorance behind human suffering. There may be an intermediate step—craving—but our *avidyā* or misapprehension of reality causes that craving and hence our suffering. In fact, although the Buddha assigned "thirst" as the cause of suffering in his first sermon, it may be that later he considered *avidyā* to be primary and *tanhā* secondary (Frauwallner 1973, 150–71; Jones 1991, 138; Jayatilleke 1974, 201, 228). We experience angst and pain, and then are reborn to slog through yet more, because our ignorance of reality and the craving it engenders causes us to thirst for and cling to passing things, experiences, and people. If we only knew better! After all, insight-wisdom, the polar opposite of ignorance, is "the ultimate liberating factor in Buddhism" (Thera 2003, 83; Pye 2003, 14,n. 6). "The work of Buddhist practice then is quite simply to cultivate those conditions that set in motion and bring about the process of the ceasing of ignorance leading to the ceasing of suffering" (Gethin 1998, 157). "At root the cure for suffering lies in freely diverting our dispositions toward a life of insight" (Smart 1984, 376).

At this point, we shall turn from the nexus in Buddhism between ignorance and suffering, to Christianity's connection between the two. We find, *mutatis mutandis*, a similar link.

Jesus defines eternal life as knowing God (John 17:3); not knowing him consequently leads to ruin (2 Thess. 1:8). Eternal life in Christianity is a good thing, quite different from the endless round of birth-suffering-death-rebirth (samsara) from which Hindus seek deliverance in *moksha* and Buddhists in nirvana (for a discussion of the Christian view of eternal life, see Thompson 1989, 35–55). Further discussion of such future suffering would be fruitful, but this paper will instead focus on how ignorance of God contributes to suffering in this life.

In Hosea's day, Israelite society was unraveling; Assyria threatened on the borders and would soon take his nation into captivity. The prophet lamented that God's people were being destroyed from lack of knowledge (Hosea 4:6). Isaiah was astounded by how thoughtlessness led idolaters to feed on ashes. They were deluded, unthinking, bowing to blocks of wood that could not save. In Isaiah 44:18–20 ignorance is described not as a lack of data but as a deluded view of reality. Jesus grieved that if only Jerusalem had known what it should have, the city would have survived. But because she did not know, "your enemies will build an embankment against you and encircle you and hem you in on every side. They will dash you to the ground, you and the children within your walls" (Luke 19:41–44). The above three passages forebode calamity and destruction, but less disastrous forms of suffering also follow ignorance. In a postresurrection appearance, Jesus instructs two disciples on matters which, had they known and believed, would have prevented sadness and disillusionment during his time in the tomb (Luke 24:13–35). The Apostle Paul instructs the Thessalonians about future events so that they will not be uninformed and grieve unnecessarily (1 Thess. 4:13–18). Denigration of thought can easily lead to despair and loss of faith among Christians today as well (Rice 2004, 23–25). By contrast, knowledge of Christ and Christian doctrine leads to stability and loving growth (Eph. 4:11–16).

Hence, in the Christian faith, ignorance of God and his ways leads to suffering—emotional and physical, in this life and in eternity. In Buddhism, ignorance of the impermanence, selflessness, and unsatisfactoriness of all dharmas leads to suffering—emotional and physical—in this life and in the continuing cycle of samsara. What both faiths warn against is ignorance of the true nature of reality, since "one thing on which Buddhists and Christians agree is that understanding how things really are is essential to our salvation" (Williams 2002, xvii). But each understands differently what that nature is. In Christianity, what is most real and foundational for all else is the infinite-personal God (Ps. 102:12,24–27; Heb. 1:10–12). In Buddhism, what is most real is the void that eternally empties itself of its emptiness and expresses itself as form. Despite attempts to equate these two, they are in fact quite different—one might even say, utterly disparate. Both cannot be true. Which (if either) is?

This paper shall not attempt to establish the answer but simply suggest one avenue of inquiry. Buddhism is based on the insights of Siddhārtha Gautama. These were gained under the bodhi tree and are said to be derived from not only his logical ratiocination but also his extrasensory perception and unlimited clairvoyance. He knew more than Brahma, enjoyed "a total vision of reality" (Jayatilleke 1974, 33, 48–49, 53, 63, 67, 100), and was more than a mere human being (1974, 19, 26–27, 59). Even so, he subsequently (and wisely) urged his followers to not blindly accept his word, but examine for themselves the validity of his ideas (the goldsmith verse, quoted in Thurman 1978, 25). Nevertheless, and despite the fact that there have been (and will be) other enlightened ones, Buddhism is essentially a system built upon Siddhārtha Gautama's thought.

The Christian vision of ultimate reality, by contrast, purports to be based not upon the cogitations of any one person, no matter how perceptive or systematic, but rather upon the self-revelation of God. God chooses to reveal himself to individuals who are not portrayed as inherently better or wiser than others, but who are by contrast at times reluctant and even miscomprehending recipients of this truth. Significantly, God's self-revelation is not conveyed simply by words, but often by *deeds* that are inexplicable apart from his existence and intervention. In particular, Israel's exodus from slavery in Egypt, return from captivity in Babylon, and continued national existence, and Jesus' physical resurrection from the dead, are amazing deeds of God done in part "so that you might know that I am God" (Ex. 14:4, Jn. 20:31).

First, Israel: Pharaoh's objection to Moses's request that Israel be let go to hold a festival to Yahweh in the desert is, "Who is Yahweh, that I should obey him and let Israel go? I do not know Yahweh and I will not let Israel go." So the plagues and deliverance that follow are designed so that Pharaoh (Ex. 7:17, 8:10, 22, 9:14, 29, 11:7), the Egyptians (Ex. 7:5, 14:4, 18), Israel's present and future generations (Ex. 10:2, 4:5, 8–9), and ultimately the whole earth (Ex. 9:16; Jude 5) will know that Yahweh is and that Yahweh is God. Second, the resurrection of Jesus has a similar didactic and apologetic purpose. It is what powerfully declares that he is the Son of God (Rom. 1:4), just as his crucifixion demonstrates God's love (Rom. 5:8; 1 John 3:16). These are but two examples. At least seventy-five times in the book of Ezekiel, God predicts or performs deeds (usually of judgment) so that Israel, Moab, Philistia, Egypt, the nations—even the trees—might know that Yahweh is God. God delivers Goliath to young David so that "the whole world will know that there is a God in Israel" (1 Sam. 17:14). The apologetic impact of the deeds of God on behalf of and in answer to the prayers of his people continues that motif throughout scripture and today.

Because of these predicted and accomplished deeds (as well as other evidences), an impartial observer could reasonably infer the existence of the God who announces and performs them. The Buddha, by contrast, rules out *a priori* any possibility of a transcendent reality (other than nirvana). A Western critique might be that the Buddha's method at this point is faulty; he has committed *petitio principii*. There seems no logical reason why a transcendent creator could not exist; Buddhism simply assumes he doesn't and eliminates him. Of course, Buddhism proposes thoughtful and articulate arguments against theism as well—particularly the problem of evil, and the question of whether human freedom or responsibility can be said to meaningfully exist in a universe ruled by a sovereign, omnipotent God. The present point, however, is that even before it proposes these objections, Buddhism appears to eliminate the possibility of God out of hand without allowing theists to present evidence or counterarguments for consideration.

Despite the Buddha's insistence that his word be tested and not simply accepted, both Buddhism and Christianity are grounded at least in part on faith, containing elements that appear fantastic and mythological to outsiders. After a discussion of Buddhist cosmology, with its multiple world systems populated by thirty-one classes of beings over eons of time, Gethin writes, "What can be said with certainty is that we have no evidence, either in the ancient texts or in the different contemporary traditions, for a 'pure' Buddhism that does not recognize, accommodate, and interact with various classes of 'supernatural' beings. Such a pure Buddhism is something of a theoretical and scholarly abstraction" (Gethin 1998, 130). The Christian worldview also embodies beings and descriptions that many people consider mythological—angels, demons, a three-tiered world with a solid sky, fantastic future visions, and so on. The Buddhist universe is astoundingly older than the twelve to fourteen billion years suggested by Western science; for those Christians who hold to a young earth model, the universe is many orders of magnitude younger. But biblical descriptions of the sky as solid need not be taken literally any more than such phenomenological phrases as "the sun rose." Neither is the young earth model necessary to evangelical Christian faith. It must be acknowledged, however, that this faith does entail acceptance of the existence of unseen, nonempirical beings, forces, and realities.

The question, then, is, are the thoughts of Siddhārtha, as cogent and penetrating as in places they are, a sufficient and reliable guide to the true and deepest nature of reality (Jones 1991, 138–47)? Or are the events surrounding Israel and Jesus (to say nothing of such issues as the chemical complexity of life) suggestive of the mind and work of God? Is the deepest nature of reality such that all that exists is impermanent, selfless, and unsatisfactory, without beginning? Or is there a self-existing, unchanging being outside the time-space universe, who brought that universe into existence, interacts with and so demonstrates his existence through it, and who will someday end that universe and create a new? Is it wise to eliminate *a priori* the possibility of a transcendent God before any proposed evidence for him is presented and weighed?

Both faiths propose causes for suffering other than ignorance. Chief among these in Buddhism is karma—the natural consequences of past intentional thoughts and deeds. Even the Buddha is said to have suffered physical distresses because of karmic influences from previous lifetimes. Though not necessarily so, belief in karma may lead to a sense of resignation. Low status or sudden tragedies may stem from deeds unremembered, done by a person unknown in time long past. Clearly such a state of affairs could lead to a sense of fatalism, disenfranchisement, or vague guilt.

Christians are also said to suffer for reasons other than their ignorance of God and his ways. Among these are the effects of living in a fallen world (Rom. 8:20–21; Gen. 3:17–19), spiritual conflict beyond the individual's ken (e.g., Job 1–2; John 9:1–3), and discipline designed to encourage development (Heb. 12:1–13; James 1:2–4). When suffering comes, particularly as a result of opposition to one's Christian faith, believers may commit themselves to their faithful creator and continue to do good (1 Pet. 4:19).

Christianity assigns the chief cause of human suffering not to ignorance but to sin—to a defect not of thought but of will. The story of the fall, which introduced suffering and death to human experience, illustrates this. The first human couple had received God's directive—"you must not eat from the tree of the knowledge of good and evil"—but chose to disobey it. This is not ignorance but rebellion, not a deficiency of the mind but defiance of the will. Later discussion acknowledges that the woman, though not the man, was deceived in the process of temptation (Gen. 3:13; 1 Tim. 2:14), but even so, what happened was a clear choice to contravene a known directive.

The New Testament concurs that decisions of defiance—not deficiency of data—stand behind the downfall and suffering of humanity. God's eternal power and divine nature are understood from creation, so that people are without excuse. Knowing God, then, people choose not to glorify him, but become futile in their thinking and descend into a downward spiral of delusion and debauchery (Rom. 1:18–32). Human choice not to honor the God who is known, then, is more basic to human woe than is ignorance. Not only do those who sin suffer, but also others around them and future generations may suffer consequences from their actions. Hitler brought trouble not only on himself but most of Europe as well. Ignorance may be considered secondary to sin, since one source of it is the hardening of the human heart (Eph. 4:18; Rom. 1:18–32, which argues that futility of thinking, foolishness of heart, and depravity of mind follow upon the sinful human decision to ignore God).

Similarly, not only suffering but the craving that leads to it is occasioned as much as by sin as by ignorance—perhaps even more so. Christians crave because they choose to love the present more than the age to come, or prefer praise from men to praise from God. This *avidyā* in the sense not of no worldview but of wrong worldview, does not stem from lack of data regarding the existence and superiority of the coming age or praise and eternal reward that may be obtained in it (e.g., Matt. 25:23). Rather, the problem is a lack of faith in these promised realities—or a disastrous decision of the will to devalue them. The king sends his servants to invite guests to his banquet—they have the invitation—but they refuse to come because of preoccupation with smaller matters (Matt. 22:1 6). Many hear the word (dispelling their ignorance), but allow the worries of this life and the deceitfulness of wealth (i.e., desires) to choke it, rendering it unfruitful (Matt. 13:21). Some people live as enemies of the cross of Christ not because they have not heard of that cross, but because by their own choice, disobedience, or lack of faith their god is their stomach and their mind is on earthly things (Phil. 3:17–20). Christians are called upon to conduct their lives by faith (in the unseen, unending reality and superiority of the future world), not by sight (2 Cor. 5:7). Abram's nephew Lot, who based his life decisions on sight rather than faith, suffered the disdain of his fellow Sodomites, and the loss of his possessions, sons-in-law, and personal integrity (Gen. 13:10–11, 19:9, 25–26, 30–38). The problem, as in Buddhism, is not lack of worldview, but wrong worldview. It is a faulty value system knowingly and willfully chosen.

Ignorance, then, is not the only—or even the chief—source in Christianity of the craving that leads to suffering. Sin, unbelief, a disinclination of the will, a short-sighted preference of the present and temporary over the future and eternal, induce this thirst even in many professing and practicing Christians. Christian theology assigns this corruption of the will to a consequence of the fall of Adam and Eve, and does not see it as an original component of the human heart at creation.

Perhaps something similar happens in Buddhism, although it is not as frequently discussed and certainly not in the character of sin against a god. A Buddhist begins by taking refuge *by faith* in the Buddha, the dharma, and the *sangha*. Doubtless, there have been those who have heard of these and have begun walking the Path, but who later choose to turn aside for present pleasures. The problem for such Buddhists then would not be primarily ignorance, but willful choice to abandon that Path.

It is all too easy in either tradition to falter in this way. Good intentions of heart and mind do not always or easily translate into actions of hands and feet. The Apostle Peter and his companions discovered that fact when, having been explicitly warned by Jesus about his impending arrest and crucifixion, they fled and denied Jesus when the soldiers arrived. Because our wills are weak, help is often needed—"Watch and pray so that you will not fall into temptation. The spirit is willing, but the flesh is weak" (Matt. 26:41). Similarly, the *Tathāgata* knows how the minds of living beings "delight in petty doctrines and how deeply they are attached to the five desires" (Watson 1993, 135). A Buddhist who veers away can change course and return to the path. In Mahayana an errant Buddhist might find help: the Buddha himself as well as numerous bodhisattvas employ *upāya-kauśalya*, skillful stratagems or liberative techniques adapted to each individual, to help aspirants find and persist in following the Path (Bowers 2005). Even in Theravada, the example of the Buddha and subsequent *arahants* can encourage the wavering. But in an even deeper sense a Christian can find forgiveness and "grace to help in time of need" (Heb. 4:16). The indwelling presence of God disallows a life ultimately dominated by sin (e.g., 1 John 3:9). And he or she is surrounded by "a great cloud of witnesses" whose examples can spur on the fainthearted (Heb. 12:1).

Interestingly, both faiths anticipate a decline in serious practice of them. Buddhism foresees a degenerate age (*mappō* in Japanese) that will require the fifth Buddha, Maitreya (presently a bodhisattva), to descend to earth and renew preaching of the dharma when Buddha Gautama's teachings have completely decayed. The Christian New Testament anticipates that "there will be terrible times in the last days" in which "evil men and impostors will go from bad to worse" (2 Tim. 3:1,13).

What Buddhism promises those who, through enlightenment, overcome ignorance and craving is nirvana—the extinction of ideas, concepts, and desires, and of the suffering that grows out of these; the exchange of individual consciousness for a transcendent state of freedom and bliss. The Buddha could not describe in detail what this means (Bodhi 2005, 367–69). What Christianity promises those who, through faith in Christ, come to know God is eternal life—unending personal existence with a body superior to the present one in an environment of beauty and bliss. If the Buddhist version of true reality is wrong, a Buddhist deprives himself or herself of many innocent pleasures in this life, gains no future benefit from doing so, and risks forfeiture of eternal life. If the Christian version is wrong, he or she is "of all men most to be pitied" (1 Cor. 15:19) and will be reborn to again endure the cycle of suffering and death (if Buddhism is correct), albeit probably with good karma if the Christian ethic has been consistently followed.

In Buddhism, suffering only ends when an individual breaks from his or her ignorance through enlightenment; abandons perceiving himself as an individual, and the selfish craving that grows out of that perception; and achieves nirvana. Those Buddhists who embrace the bodhisattva ideal delay ultimate individual entrance into nirvana until all other sentient beings are enlightened. Cessation of suffering may thus take a long time. By contrast, in Christianity, suffering ends for the child of God when he or she dies (which occurs for each individual only once). The book of Revelation suggests the completeness of that end and the paradigm shift that allows for it.

"Now the dwelling of God is with men, and he will live with them. They will be his people, and God himself will be with them and be their God. He will wipe every tear from their eyes. There will be no more death or mourning or crying or pain, for the old order of things has passed away." He who was seated on the throne said, "I am making everything new!" Then he said, "Write this down, for these words are trustworthy and true." (Rev. 21:3–5)

Of course, a bodhisattva can experience nirvana even in the midst of samsara. Likewise, a Christian can experience peace (John 16:1–4,33), joy (Matt. 5:11–12), and perspective (Rom. 5:3–5) in this life in the midst of suffering. But ultimate release is much nearer for the Christian than for the Buddhist.

Abandonment of *avidyā* through regarding reality as insubstantial, changing, and unsatisfactory should not lead a Buddhist to ascetic self-denial, but to a Middle Way between asceticism and indulgence. Similarly, a Christian's recognition of the passing nature of this world in contrast with the ultimate, lasting nature of that to come should lead to a Middle Way of thankful enjoyment of everything God richly gives for his or her enjoyment without falling into the trap of placing ultimate value on these (1 Tim. 6:17; Col. 2:20–23; 1 Tim. 4:1–5; Phil. 4:11–13; Eccles. 5:18–20; Luke 12:15; Matt. 6:24–34; 1 Tim. 6:6–11).

As mentioned above, the path to and practice of Buddhist enlightenment entails more than merely adopting a new theoretical mental construct that accepts the self and the world as impermanent, insubstantial, and unsatisfactory. Rather, both moral behavior and the practice of meditation are essential. These three components—the insight (*prajñā*) that accepts the Buddha's analysis of reality, morality (*śīla*), and Buddhist meditation (*samādhi* or *dhyāna*)—are the three categories of steps in the Eightfold Noble Path, which itself comprises the Fourth Noble Truth.

Similarly, biblical Christianity entails far more than mouthing theological ideas—such as that God exists, that Jesus is God's son and humanity's savior, that the individual has accepted Jesus as "his savior"—no matter how true or necessary they may be. Those who profess to believe the "wisdom" of those theological ideas are expected to live lives of "morality" that reflect and commend those ideas. Furthermore, it is assumed that people who profess to believe the ideas of Christianity will practice Christian "meditation" upon the scriptures (both private and public) so that they may be grounded and grow in their faith.

SUMMARY

This article does not attempt to be exhaustive but merely suggestive for further study of elements of the ignorance-suffering link in Buddhism and Christianity. The following items are among those that emerge:

1. Buddhism and Christianity agree that ignorance or misconception of true reality, together with the behaviors such ignorance encourages, results in human suffering—both in this life and beyond.

2. Buddhism and Christianity differ on the nature of true reality— Buddhism proposing the three characteristics of emptiness, selflessness, and suffering; Christianity urging recognition of one transcendent, infinite-personal God who creates all else.

3. Buddhism and Christianity differ on the means for coming to understand the nature of true reality. Buddhism grounds itself in the thought of Siddhārtha Gautama, as then tested by each individual's own thought and practice. Christianity proposes the revelation of the transcendent, creator God both in word and (particularly) in deed. Such revelation, while going beyond what human reason can discover, does not contradict the basic laws of reason.

4. Buddhism and Christianity differ on the relative importance of ignorance in producing suffering—Buddhism viewing it as the primary reason why people thirst and cling, Christianity proposing that sin is more fundamentally the cause. People throughout history often do what they know is wrong.

5. Buddhism and Christianity agree that the possessions and pleasures of life do not ultimately satisfy. Both urge a "middle way" between extravagant indulgence and ascetic denial.

6. Both holistically embrace thought and practice, urging that all who abandon ignorance for truth should practice moral behavior. Not all the professed adherents of either faith, however, have consistently done so.

CHAPTER 4

SUFFERING AND COMPASSION IN BUDDHISM AND CHRISTIANITY

Alex G. Smith

Suffering is a universal experience of all humanity and common to adherents of all religious persuasions. The philosophical sources and causes of suffering may vary. The human responses to suffering are variegated. The multiple processes for living with suffering and for overcoming it differ, depending on human perspectives and various religious beliefs held by community groups, families, and individuals.

Buddhism and Christianity are two of the great world religions, each with millions of followers across the planet. From their earliest times, both have been missionary religions, gaining new followers usually through outreach and peaceful proclamation of their beliefs. This was the pattern from their beginnings, often in the face of considerable personal pain and suffering.

Both religions have also suffered intense persecution from emperors, kings, warriors, and political leaders. Both have survived with great resilience and vitality. Over the centuries, while maintaining a solid core of unified fundamental beliefs unique to each, both have developed variegated forms and multiplied different denominations. Both faiths have coexisted for millennia, yet many Christians are largely ignorant of basic Buddhist concepts and many Buddhists know little about Christian beliefs. Many concepts, though at first seemingly similar, are often defined differently, including the meaning of suffering. The main discussion here will focus only on the concepts of suffering. Unless comprehension of each of these different perspectives is mutually understood, it is not likely that dialogue and communication will occur.

HISTORICAL BACKGROUND OF SIDDHĀRTHA GAUTAMA

Siddhārtha, meaning "every wish fulfilled," was born into a Hindu ruling family of the Kshatriya caste, in the Shakya warrior clan, located in the Himalayan foothills of today's southern Nepal. He was a welcome son to a childless royal family of the Gautama clan (Maguire 2001, 3). Legends of miraculous events accompanied his conception, birth, and entry into the world. A seer had announced that if Siddhārtha stayed in the palace, he would become a great secular ruler and be emperor of the world. If, however, he left the palace, seeking the spiritual path, he would endure hardship but eventually become a buddha and teacher of all.

As a future warrior-lord, Siddhārtha's background potentially opened the possibility for him to be exposed to receiving suffering and even to being involved in causing massive suffering. Both of these aspects would normally have given Siddhārtha pain but somehow he was mostly kept from that exposure. It appears that four events of guarded awareness in his life likely educated him contrariwise.

First, he was highly sheltered and protected within the palace enclaves. His father wanted to preserve him from experiencing suffering. The high, fortified palace walls kept him from viewing the real world outside. His father deliberately shielded him from seeing the ugly side of life—from pain, suffering, poverty, disease, death, and decrepitating human conditions.

Second, Siddhārtha may have gained a sense of the potential of suffering if he had been exposed to his wife's pain during childbirth, which is among the most excruciating experiences of humankind. However, this likely did not happen in palaces as such events usually excluded the presence of the males, particularly the rulers. We do not know whether or not Yasodharā, his wife and cousin, later described her situation of pain and aloneness to him or how it affected Siddhārtha. Nevertheless, not long before his Great Renunciation, when he abandoned the palace and his family, Yasodharā had already given birth to Rāhula, their first infant and only child, whose name meant "chain."

Third, was the shock that Siddhārtha experienced during the occasion of his secretive escape outside the walled palace. Through that unique opportunity, he was exposed to four desperate sights of humanity in travail—sickness, aging, death, and the naked poverty of an ascetic holy man. These sights of suffering profoundly shocked and affected him, and straightaway Siddhārtha set his sights on beginning a sincere search for the solution to suffering.

Fourth, was his instantaneous renunciation of position, palace, and privilege. That night, after he had returned to the palace, he immediately left his wife and tiny infant son without waking them. This set in motion an unusual stage for learning about suffering on a personal level. He joined up with five ascetic gurus (holy men) and for the next six years experienced deprivation, hunger, extreme discipline, and the self-denying rigor of personal pain in an ascetic lifestyle. At the end of those six years, while suffering from extenuated fasting, he became so weak that he almost drowned. This brought him to his senses, and he consequently turned from both extremes of affluence, on one hand, and asceticism, on the other, propelling Siddhārtha towards a quest of finding the solution to suffering through a more balanced Middle Way.

INDIAN RELIGIOUS MILIEU: HINDU WORLDVIEW

Another factor contributing to Gautama's understanding of suffering came from his Hindu mindset or worldview, the way he looked at the cosmos and viewed life related thereto. This conceptualization formed the mental map by which he interpreted the world around him, as it did all good Hindus and later Buddhists.

First, he espoused a monistic worldview of cosmology and the universe in which there was no external Creator God. All forms of life were believed to be part of one whole, similar to one all-encompassing "Mother Earth," though Buddhists rarely, if ever, use that term.

Second, this state of a constantly changing or evolving universe was its own continuous cycle of life, ever evolving and ever changing. Within this world, humans and all life-forms experienced repeated reincarnations through the transmigration of the soul via multiple rebirths. Each and every reincarnation was conditioned and caused by the accumulated karma from former lives.

Third, this circular form of causation affected each and every life, which was caught up in a continuous cycle of life from birth through disease, aging, and decrepitating conditions, eventually ending in death, only to be reborn into another incarnation.

Fourth, Hindus believed that because of past karma, suffering was therefore justified and a just recompense for the errors, evil deeds, breaches of morality, and sins in former reincarnations.

Fifth, in this process individuals were merely insignificant parts of the whole. They were unimportant elements working for the good of the whole. The whole was all-important, not the individual beings that comprised it.

Sixth, the whole was to find eventual completion or perfect fulfillment by the collective deliverance of all individual parts or living things.

Thus, Siddhārtha's sheltered background and this fundamental Hindu worldview became a platform which shaped his concept of suffering as he began to observe and experience it in his deliberate quest for answers.

THE BUDDHA'S VIEW OF SUFFERING

Through his search to understand suffering and to find a solution for it, Siddhārtha Gautama embarked on this third journey—one of inquiry, aspiration, and meditation. Having left the comfortable palace life and then having abandoned the ascetic way of life, he launched out to find an answer to life's problems using a moderate Middle Way.

BUDDHA'S ENLIGHTENMENT

This path brought him to Bodh Gaya (located in today's Bihar province of India) where, for forty-nine days, he meditated around seven separate stations. At the end of this time, he became the Buddha, the Enlightened One, or the Awakened One. He claimed to have perfect insight by which he recognized the basic cause of the world's problems—namely, suffering, along with its origin and cure. He summarized these into a basic code for Buddhism called the Four Noble Truths, which are as follows:

1. *Dukkha*—generally interpreted as suffering,
2. *Samudaya*—the arising or origin of *dukkha,*
3. *Nirodha*—the cessation of *dukkha*, and
4. *Magga*—the way leading to the cessation of *dukkha.*
   (Rahula 1974, 16)

SUFFERING AND THE FOUR NOBLE TRUTHS

According to the Buddha's insights received during his enlightenment:

Dukkha is suffering. The Buddha received this awareness from self-disclosed knowing that the whole world is in suffering. Suffering is the universal experience of all beings. It is existence itself. Humphreys speaks of "the omnipresence of suffering" (1951, 75).

The origin of suffering is *tanhā*, meaning desire, craving, passion and, in the Mahayana schools, attachment to emptiness (*sunnatta*). The Buddha believed that this *tanhā* was the root cause of all suffering.

Nirvana (blowing out, extinction) is attained when all *tanhā* (desire, craving, passion, attachment) is eliminated. This eradication causes all suffering to cease, a kind of "salvation from suffering," though Buddhists do not use the term "salvation."

Magga is the way to gain this deliverance through following the Noble Eightfold Path. By having the right wisdom (insight), the right ethical conduct (morality), and the right mental discipline (concentrated effort), one hopes to attain or achieve nirvana.

SUFFERING AND NO-SELF

Since, as part of his understanding of *dukkha*, the Buddha declared that humans have no real entity of spirit, soul, or ego, suffering is more a universal condition than an effect on individual personality. If Buddhists were to use the word "salvation," it would refer to the clearing or purifying of the mind, not the saving of the soul or spirit.

D. T. Niles, a world-renowned ecumenical leader from Sri Lanka, brilliantly clarifies the basic Buddhist doctrines of *anicca* (impermanence), *anattā* (no-self), and *dukkha* (suffering) in relation to Buddhist and Christian teachings when he says, "If we do not start with God we shall not end with him, and when we start with him we do not end with the doctrines of *anicca, anattā and dukkha*" (1967, 27). Niles continues to expound the contrast from a biblical and Christian perspective, saying, "The existence of God means the existence of an order of life which is eternal—*nicca* (permanence). It means that there is for the soul an identity which is guarded by God's sovereignty and remains through eternity—*atta*. Within this context, sorrow—*dukkha*—is seen to consist, not so much in the impermanence of things, as in the perverseness of our wills which seek these things instead of the things which are eternal" (1967, 27).

This view differs considerably from the Buddha's perceptions.

DEFINING SUFFERING ACCORDING TO BUDDHA

Suffering is the starting point for developing Buddhism. It is the fundamental primary insight of Buddha's enlightenment. Suffering became the focused presupposition and premise on which conceptual Buddhism arose. Suffering is seen as the basic nature of existence. In *What the Buddha Taught*, the eminent Buddhist scholar Walpola Sri Rahula explains this:

> At "the heart of the Buddha's teaching," was *dukkha*, which essentially means suffering, pain, sorrow and misery. *Dukkha* also portrays a deeper meaning including imperfection, emptiness, impermanence and insubstantiality. Existence is full of this suffering, as no state is stable, but is always changing, which is the nature of life. (1974, 16–17)

Dukkha has three aspects: (1) as ordinary suffering—*dukkha-dukkha*, (2) as suffering produced by change—*viparinama-dukkha*, and (3) as conditioned states—*samkhāra-dukkha* (Rahula 1974, 19–20). The first category includes suffering from the various succeeding stages of the cycle of life. This is therefore associated with unpleasantness and also separations, along with most physical and mental suffering. The second category refers to those conditions that are impermanent, changing, or fleeting and not everlasting. The changes of happiness or of joyful dispositions cause feelings to fade, elicit pain, and result in suffering. The third category of *dukkha* relates to what non-Buddhists see as the individual being, ego, "I" identity, or soul/spirit being. The Buddha held that a human is only a combination of ever-changing physical and mental forces or energies which may be divided into five groups or aggregates (*pancakkhandha*). These five *khandas* are matter, sensations, perceptions, mental formations, and consciousness. "The Buddha says, 'In short these five aggregates of attachment are *dukkha*'" (Rahula 1974, 19–23).

In his book *Christ and Human Suffering* first published in 1933, E. Stanley Jones (1884–1973) identifies the crux of the Buddha's attitude towards suffering. Jones was an American Methodist missionary and theologian who served in India, where he worked among many groups, including the Dalits. The following excerpts interpret this view:

> The gentle Buddha summed it all up in the startling conclusion, "Existence and suffering are one." He went further than saying that there is suffering in existence. The Buddha said that suffering and existence are fundamentally and inextricably one. (1933, 47)

SUFFERING AND KARMA

Buddhists generally believe that suffering results from the effects of karma generated from past lives. One suffers in the current life because of bad karma from former rebirths. Suffering is inescapable as long as karma (both good and bad) continues to plague humankind and all sentient beings, constantly driving them through the cycle of life. Suffering in Buddhist contexts and conceptions requires that one gives the highest priority and immediate attention to use one's energies in overcoming one's karma and consequent suffering in this present life. The first of "Twelve Principles of Buddhism" promulgated by Christmas Humphreys and reiterated by Beatrice Suzuki states, "Self-salvation is for any man the immediate task" (Humphreys 1951, 74–76; Suzuki 1959, 155–58). This is the major reason for Buddhists to be concerned about making massive merit.

Interpreting bad luck or other sad experiences in life often has serious consequences for families. It is not uncommon for parents or extended families to feel the shame of past karma, such as when a child is born with a deformity or contracts a debilitating disease. It is not unusual for family members to leave the baby or child on the steps of a temple or local hospital. The reason is that such conditions indicate bad karma from past incarnations, so the child with its current condition carries forward heavy karma.

My wife and I used to visit one particular hospital on Silom Road in Bangkok, near the Chao Phraya River, where, on the top floor, the medical staff cared for such abandoned children. Among them was a bright, young girl with an ugly elephantitis leg; another was the son of a careless policeman, a small boy who picked up his father's unprotected loaded revolver which discharged, shooting off part of the boy's leg; a third was a girl with advanced rheumatoid arthritis. A score or more suffering children were deemed to have such bad karma from former rebirths that they were abandoned there. Even adults such as elderly folk with advanced leprosy or HIV patients often consider their acute conditions of suffering to be the effects of karma from former lives rather than the effects of infectious diseases or their own personal unwise practices exposing them to potential affliction.

At times, the karma of Buddhists has overplayed itself. They feel fed up, frustrated, hopeless, and discouraged. For example, during the era of the Killing Fields in Cambodia, many became disenchanted with the religion and its images because their fervent prayers to the Buddha for help went unanswered. Many saw their loved ones slaughtered. They were left helpless, angry, and devastated at such senseless suffering. Hearing the gospel of hope and seeing Christ's love expressed through the practical compassion of His servants in refugee camps across the border helped some turn to Jesus. Some may also have done so out of ulterior motives. One example of this occurred among the 150,000 Southeast Asian refugees who, between 1975 and 1980, arrived in Thailand from nearby Buddhist lands. At the point of their exasperation and frustration, when civil war was raging and life was so uncertain, they sought for someone to depend on who would truly help them. During the concerted, caring ministry of many groups, the Thai Southern Baptists baptized 2,100 Cambodian and Vietnamese refugees during the three years following 1975. Many of the refugees were repatriated to third countries and started new lives and also new ethnic churches in the West. Some opened Buddhist temples there.

In recent decades, abject suffering has arisen in some Buddhist countries from national crises as well as from several shocking, unusual natural disasters. These heartrending events reminded Christian workers that theology divorced from the real needs of people is futile, as is social service without the clear proclamation of the good news which gives hope and confidence. Remember that Peter provided the crippled beggar in the book of Acts with both the saving name and the helping hand. Through this dual approach, the beggar was healed and his life transformed (Acts 3:6–8).

SUFFERING AND COMPASSION IN BUDDHISM

I have often been shocked at the attitudes and actions of Buddhists towards their own suffering countrymen and friends in Asia. On many occasions, arriving at scenes of car or bus accidents where Asians are lying scattered around—often injured or dying—I have observed so many of their countrymen standing by idly watching. At first I did not understand their concept of suffering. Two things were important in the thinking of those standing idly on those occasions. First was the belief that those injured or killed must have accumulated a significant amount of bad karma from their previous lives. Because of this, it was considered best to let them remain in whatever state karma had dealt them and not interfere lest calamity also fall upon the helpers. Second, many expressed fear, which came from their animistic folk Buddhist beliefs. They felt that if they got involved and someone happened to die, then the ghost or spirit of that person would attack them and cause all sorts of trouble for them and their families. Therefore, this fear called for taking a measure of protection, requiring noninvolvement with the consequences of karma. These vivid experiences, both observing and interacting with the standers-by, helped this young missionary understand Buddhist attitudes towards suffering and compassion.

On one occasion about forty years ago, my family was traveling down an old interior road from central Thailand to Ayuthaya, one of the ancient capitals of Siam. As I was driving, I noticed a military jeep coming towards us at a fast rate. Suddenly, the jeep swerved across the road, turned over several times, flew up into the air just ahead of us, and crashed down the embankment, coming to rest upside down on the other side of a waterway. It seemed like a scene from the movies. We immediately stopped to help and saw that a family was in the jeep and that the children had been thrown out, while the mother was lying injured and unconscious nearby. The distraught husband rushed over to her, picked her up, and started to struggle up the embankment with her in his arms. Several other passing drivers stopped, gawked and then drove on. Others pulled over but refused to help. My wife and I gathered the children and helped the man get his wife into the back of our Land Rover where our two young sons were sitting and drove them to the nearest hospital. While the doctors attended the mother, we tried with our limited language ability, to comfort the weeping children and shocked husband. That incident is still indelibly imprinted in our minds.

A key aspect of Buddhist compassion (*karuna*) is defined as eternal harmony. Christmas Humphreys's fifth principle of Buddhism declares:

> Life is one and indivisible, though its ever-changing forms are innumerable and perishable ... From an understanding of life's unity arises compassion, a sense of identity with the life in other forms. Compassion is described as "the Law of laws—eternal harmony," and he who breaks this harmony of life will suffer accordingly and delay his own Enlightenment. (1951, 74–75)

Thus, this kind of compassion differs from God's grace, love, and mercy. It is bound up with the concept of a worldview that centers on the unity of the whole in which each individual life is not significant in itself but exists only for the whole and its eventual completion, fulfillment, or even "redemption," though Buddhists would not use that term.

Furthermore, Maguire emphasizes that compassion in Buddhism says:

Karuna flows freely and spontaneously from the individual who realizes that there is no such entity as a separate self and, therefore, no such duality as self and other. Unlike the Christian concept of *agape*, it is not an act of loving someone as oneself, or expressing the love that is in one's soul, or being an agent of God's love ... There is no self, soul, or God—nothing to relate to, or to give up, in the expression of compassion. Instead, it's perceived as simply and absolutely the natural thing to do. (2001, 147)

Primarily, compassion was, as it seemed to the Buddha, the perception and recognition that the whole world lies in suffering. This is emphasized in the First Noble Truth. Thus, compassion here is more an intellectual awareness of that state than of any explicit emotional feeling or attendant action to alleviate the suffering state. In fact, the Buddha himself emphasized and taught that humans must depend on themselves alone to overcome karma and *tanhā*. Buddha declared that he could not help anyone. They must help themselves. They must be a lamp unto themselves. Significantly, Buddhist compassion seems to be knowledge-oriented or an intellectual ascent to the fact that all life equates with suffering. Buddhist compassion is not essentially the direct result of emotional feeling or of the call to respond with merciful action. However, as normal human beings usually do, many folk Buddhists often exhibit deep concern for their own loved ones.

It is commendable that in recent years some Buddhist groups or individuals such as in Taiwan and elsewhere have started to develop compassionate aid agencies, somewhat after the pattern of World Vision or Compassion. It is often common for Buddhist women to organize and run these Buddhist compassion services. On the outskirts of Lopburi in Thailand, a temple-monastery has set up hospital-like facilities to care for patients with advanced HIV. However, the presence of Buddhist agencies in times of natural disaster is still generally quite minimal compared with that of Christian aid agencies. Sadly, this HIV temple has become a place of exploitation, particularly of visiting foreigners. It is also against government policy, which encourages families to look after their own relatives who are HIV positive or suffering with AIDS. Some family members literally abandon their infective relatives at hospital steps or at temples or even just on the street. The gruesome models of naked, dead, mummified HIV bodies on display have also become an educational means to warn and shock the young who are brought by busloads to look at the patients and the ugly displays. One must ask, "Where is true compassion in this?"

The Mahayana Buddhists recognize Avalokiteshvara as the bodhisattva of compassion (*Kwan Yin* in Chinese, *Chenrezig* in Tibetan, and *Kannon* in Japanese). Like the thirteen former heads of the Geluk lineage before him, the Dalai Lama is also "a reincarnation of *Avalokiteshvara*" (Maguire 2001, 103). The laypeople and folk Buddhists usually consider this bodhisattva to be a female Buddha of compassion. However, this bodhisattva, like all others, is male, originally coming from India. Another enlightened bodhisattva of wisdom is Manjushri, who is also sometimes called upon for medical counsel and help.

Most Buddhist talk on alleviating suffering seems more like an intellectual recognition of the results of karma rather than an expression of loving compassion and service akin to that which Christ and his church demonstrate. The more Christians practice genuine care, merciful concern, and true loving compassion, the more our Buddhist friends will want to find out why we do so. Hopefully, as they frequently do, they will also adopt the Christian example and practice of compassion to reduce the suffering of humanity in the world.

THE BIBLICAL VIEW OF SUFFERING

The Christian teaching of suffering does differ considerably from that of Buddhism. By way of contrast, biblical presuppositions, sources, and solutions to suffering are unique. Here only a brief dealing with this aspect will be attempted, as many other books on suffering from a Christian perspective are readily available.

While the Buddha uses a single category—*dukkha*—to lump all suffering together, the Bible employs many different terms for various kinds of human suffering. Some of them are abandonment, abuse, accusation, affliction, afraid, agony, anguish, anxiety, betrayed, birth pangs, bitterness, brokenhearted, burdened, calamity, captivity, crucify, cruelty, death, denial, deride, desert, despair, detest, disease, exclude, fear, forsake, grief, groan, guilt, harm, harass, insult, killed, misery, mistreat, mourn, murder, oppose, oppress, pain, perish, persecute, punish, purge, ravage, regret, reproach, revenge, revile, scoff, scourge, shame, sickness, slander, slay, sorrow, spurn, starve, scoff, terror, thrash, toil, torment, tribulation, trouble, turmoil, violence, wail, weep, woe, worry, and wound. These multiple descriptive parts of speech for suffering indicate that rather than having one simple term for this state of life, God's word exposes the many different aspects of suffering in human experience—physical, emotional, mental, psychological, societal, and spiritual.

PERFECT ORDER OF ORIGINAL CREATION

However, these kinds of suffering were not part of human experience in the beginning. Nor were they part of God's purpose and plan. Nor did evil forces or karmic causes effectively plague these variegated kinds of suffering in the pristine age of creation. God created the world and all that is within it—including animals and humans—in a perfect, pure, and innocent condition (Gen. 1:1–2:25). When God reviewed his handiwork, he saw that everything was good—very good (Gen. 1:4, 10, 12, 18, 21, 25, 31).

He created man in his own image and, consequently, with desires and emotions which are not bad in themselves, just a part of personality. Creator God intended humankind to desire what is holy and good and to enjoy God's creation, his blessings, his provision, and God himself (1 Tim. 6:17). The preacher of Ecclesiastes declares, "This is what I have observed to be good: that it is appropriate for a person to eat, to drink and to find satisfaction in their toilsome labor under the sun during the few days of life God has given them—for this is their lot" (5:18). That was the Lord's intent before the fall and also after it.

THE SOURCE OF ORIGINAL SIN AND SUFFERING

After a time of perfect peace and purity on earth, as well as unclouded communion between God and humans, and the total absence of any sort of pain, misery, or even death, an event occurred, known as the fall of humanity. According to the Bible, by this event sin, suffering, pain, and death entered the human experience and the created order. This came about through the temptation by Satan of the first human pair and the response of their human willful disobedience against God's word and will. Thus sin entered the world as rebellion against a holy God (Gen. 3). Tissa Weerasingha affirms that

> The basis of Christian happiness is not things but in a relationship with the eternal—*nicca*. The misery, pain and dukkha of all human existence can be rooted in the fall of humanity due to disobedience and the primary ignorance (*avijja*). (1989, 16)

The process of the entry of sin in this Fall came through the lust of the eyes, the lust of the flesh, and the pride of life (Gen. 3:5–6; Luke 4:1–13). This rebellious choice resulted in the corrupted minds, corrupted hearts, and corrupted wills of the first human created beings (James 1:13–15, 4:1–3). Thus, sin as a thankless affront to Creator God became present on earth for the first time. Suffering and misery consequently followed.

RESULTS OF SIN AND SUBSEQUENT SUFFERING

God responded to the human rebellion of the first couple with holy love to save the race and with judgment in order to discipline. The serpent (Satan) was cursed. Eve, the mother of all, was to have pain in giving birth to her offspring. Adam, the first created human, was to toil in hard labor to provide sustenance, as the ground was cursed from that day forth (Gen. 3:14–20). Thus gainful livelihood and food production from then on normally required painful hard work. Furthermore, death entered for the first time and passed on to all humankind through Adam (Rom. 5:17; 1 Cor. 15:21). The curse also universally affected the condition of all creation, which "groans" for God's redemption (Rom. 3:10–17, 3:23, 8:18–23).

THE FACT OF SUFFERING IN EXPERIENCE

Scripture declares that since the fall, "Man is born to trouble, as the sparks fly upward" (Job 5:7). Job's life experience certainly exposited that reality. Jeremiah, a faithful prophet of the Most High God also had his fair share of pain, suffering, and sorrow. Another example is Peter's writing to suffering saints in his first epistle. King Solomon in Ecclesiastes points out the folly, frailty, meaninglessness, and vanity of life. He is not far from expressing certain aspects of the later view of Buddha's emptiness except that his conclusion is different from the Buddha. "The conclusion, when all has been heard, is: fear God and keep His commandments, because this applies to every person. For God will bring every act to judgment, everything which is hidden, whether it is good or evil" (Eccles. 11:13–14). On the other hand, the Buddha rejected the creator of the universe.

THE PAIN OF GOD AND SUFFERINGS OF CHRIST

Japanese theologian Kazoh Kitamori (1916–1998) contributed a landmark work on suffering in 1946 titled *Theology of the Pain of God*. He critically examined the notion that was then prevalent concerning "the problem of divine impassibility" (Chua 2005, 17). "He enlarged and enriched understanding of the character of God" beyond classical atonement theories (Chua 2006, 1–20). He suggested that "divine pain is constitutive of divine grace. The pain of God in Kitamori's writings refers not only to the suffering of the Son of God on the cross, as we commonly understand it, but also to the deep anguish of the Father who has lost His only Son" (Chua 2006, 2).

Among many scriptures he studied, three key texts ignited Kitamori's intuitive conceptualization: God's anguish over wayward Ephraim (Jer. 31:20), Herod's slaughter of innocent male infants (Matt. 2:16–18), and Simeon's prophecy of a sword piercing Mary's heart (Luke 2:28–35) (1965, 151–57). The human anguish of Bethlehem's mothers and of Mary too was indicative of the conflict within God, between love and wrath, giving rise to deep pain within. God identified with both, seeing them as expressions of his pain at the loss of his dear son. An insightful Kitamori affirmed Christ was born to die. Jesus's birth at Bethlehem and his cross at Calvary are intimately and integrally welded together. Similarly, the same sword that pierced Mary's heart also simultaneously pierced God's heart, for Jesus was both the son of Mary and the son of God (Chua 2006, 3).

Kitamori discovered that scripture suggests that God's anguish and love are in conflict: "God who must sentence sinners to death fought with God who wishes to love them. The fact that this fighting God is not two different gods but the same God causes his pain. Here heart is opposed to heart within God" (1965, 21). A similar call for this conflict is the injunction to love one's enemies (Rom. 5:10) (1965, 91). Kitamori declares that only when we recognize the birth and death of Christ as "the pain of God" and his resurrection as "the love rooted in the pain of God" do the facts of the historical Jesus become "the fact of the gospel" (1965, 33).

He points out that since a righteous God demands that sin must be punished, sin therefore should never be forgiven. But the "scandal of the gospel" is that God acted in an "ungodlike" and "improper" way, for God desired to forgive sin and embrace the sinner (1965, 119). "It is only within the pain of God that we are sheltered and protected from the wrath of God" (1965, 123–24). "Suffering is not uniquely a human experience; it is also a divine experience." One implication "of the Incarnation is that in the person of the God-man Jesus we see the unity of divine pain and human pain." Thus, "God knows our pain and suffering. For not only is the Son the object of God's pain, but through the Son all human beings have become objects of God's pain as well" (1965, 56–57; Chua 2006, 4). Therefore, the believers' union "in Christ" expresses our union with Christ in his suffering, death, and resurrection (Rom. 6:3–11; Phil. 3:10–11; 1 Pet. 4:12–14) (Kitamori 1965, 71).

GOD'S GRACE OVERCOMES SIN AND SUFFERING

God has made a way for freedom from suffering and deliverance from its root cause: sin. He provided that means through Christ Jesus, the only one who could eradicate sin and suffering. "The Father has sent the Son to be the Savior of the world" (1 John 4:14). Christ, who was without sin, became sin for humankind. He suffered and voluntarily died on the cross to free all from the power of sin and its attendant suffering. That suffering was taken up by the divine Suffering Servant (Isa. 52:13, 53:12). Christ emptied himself to become incarnated into suffering humanity (Phil. 2:5–8). He put aside his own will to do the will of Father God in the saving, efficacious work of the Suffering Servant (Luke 22:42). Rising again from the dead three days later, Jesus Christ conquered the power of death, suffering, and sin on behalf of all humankind once and for all (1 Cor. 15:57). Victory over suffering was thereby procured for eternity. So, for believers, suffering is not eternal but temporary. The future hope of salvation through grace by faith in Christ and of their final gathering into heaven for eternity assures true believers of total victory over suffering. In heaven, where God and Christ (the Lamb of God) dwell together, are also healing, beauty, service, but no more curse, pain, suffering, sin, evil, night, or death (Rev. 21:22–22:6). In Buddhism, karma is the unbending, inescapable iron law, engendering somewhat hopeless, fatalistic attitudes. "In contrast Christ's gospel offers hope, salvation and optimism for both present and future, even in the midst of suffering" (Smith 2001, 24–25).

BLESSINGS THROUGH SUFFERING

Many believers, even when under dire pain and suffering, have been a blessing to multitudes not so afflicted. The testimonies of suffering bedridden saints or those with debilitating conditions are powerful legacies to the valiant human spirit and the amazing grace of God. Who has not been encouraged and challenged by folk like Joni Eareckson Tada? Many others, young and old, are blessing too. In the midst of suffering, Christians can be vibrant witnesses to the sustaining power of the Holy Spirit. Many a Christian funeral on a thousand mission fields have given hope and strength to those outside of the gospel when they see the joy and faith exhibited in believers, rejoicing in victory over death. Another reason for this is that suffering and death are not fatalistic for believers. Since God understands our pain and suffers with us, Christians receive comfort and strength from God and so, even in the midst of dire affliction, are able to comfort others (2 Cor. 1:3–10).

God not only allows us to grieve in the right way, but also teaches us how to lament with hope and confidence of the eternal future. King David is an example of this over the death of Bathsheba's infant son and when he lost his rebellious son, Absalom (2 Sam. 12, 18–19). The Psalms are also full of human suffering, lamentations of the soul, and the comfort of God's acceptance and sharing in our pain. Christians do not grieve as those who have no hope.

CONCLUSION

The Buddha's idea of suffering is a primary, fundamental, and deeply basic first tenet of Buddhism. All life forms are seen to be in suffering. Life and suffering are inextricably one and the same. Life and existence are suffering. Suffering is life. Suffering relates to the unity and harmony of all life, with a concentration on the whole rather than the parts. Buddha sees that suffering also equates with the five integral components (*khandas*) of humankind. This belief of non-being (*anattā*) denies the soul-spirit concept of humans. The cause of this suffering is the endless cycle of life (rebirth), perpetuated by constant inescapable karma. The goal of Buddhism is to escape this suffering by eliminating desire and all attachment, thus gaining release from the cycle of life through attaining nirvana.

The concept of suffering in Christianity is very different from that in Buddhism, particularly with regards to cause and effect. The contrast with Christ and his vicarious suffering for the world is unique and difficult for Buddhists to comprehend. The reasons for suffering in Christian contexts are based on different presuppositions. Christians need to understand the conceptualization of Buddhist suffering as well as clearly studying their own theology behind suffering from the biblical viewpoint. One of the keys to the effective growth of the church among Buddhists may revolve around this vital issue of clearly understanding suffering. A second key may be in comprehending nirvana in conceptual terms of eternal life, but again from different premises as defined in Buddhism and Christianity.

Buddhism suggests that humans are naturally good and not flawed by sin. Yet the explanation of karma as the cause of all the suffering and chaos of society in this world does not fully satisfy their claim. E. Stanley Jones said,

> There is something lofty and grand about Buddha even when ... we must differ with him in this. Is not the corrupt nature of humans and their sin a major problem to be addressed? Jesus said that there is evil in existence, but get the evil out and you will find that existence is fundamentally

good. Jesus purposed, "I am come that they might have life and that they might have it more abundantly" (John 10:10). (1933, 49)

Hopefully, this topic has exposed significant theological contrasts, emotional and psychological insights, and valuable practical applications around this issue of suffering. May this be a means of empathetically, intellectually, and spiritually bridging into the Buddhist worldview with new strength and peace of mind in the midst of mutual human trials and tribulations. Both Christians and Buddhists experience suffering, pain, and tribulations, though they may view them differently. What are the common denominators for contact, compassion, and action? These need to be researched and concerted efforts made to alleviate suffering. Consider areas where church and *sangha* can work together in reducing societal and moral problems, especially family conflicts and violence, youth gang activity, drug rehabilitation, poverty, prostitution, and exploitation. Buddhist-oriented peoples know that suffering is a most vital topic and issue. To Christians, it also has possible eternal consequences.

The shame aspect of suffering needs to be addressed also. It is often important, though difficult, to communicate in Asian shame-based cultures, because with shame comes a form of deep suffering. Losing face, feeling embarrassment, keeping up appearances, not expressing true thoughts and feelings, sensing inadequacy because of karma—all are elements of that shame dimension and are integral parts of experiencing suffering. This needs careful study and loving application. The so-called honor killing of family members who break the norm of Asian community tradition is an expression of the deep conflict, shame, and searing suffering that require wise and concerted study, counsel, and change.

Biblical theologians with insights to deal with this central concept of suffering are needed. In communication this may be crucial for the advance of God's kingdom among 1.5 billion folk Buddhists on the globe. It is a painstakingly difficult task to struggle with the issues of this conceptual suffering. Much more reflection, meditation, and study are required on the theology of suffering. Christian scholars and writers should seriously analyze suffering, write about its causes, and define its solutions from biblical sources and Christian perspectives. At the same time, it is necessary to apply this with an understanding of the Buddhist connotations and with sensitivity to their situations.

Experimentation is needed to produce valuable results as lessons for future use. Are there better ways to engage the *sangha* in sympathetic dialogue on common points regarding *dukkha*, both intellectually and practically for the good of the community? What missiological insights can be discovered and applied from Kitamori's writings and studies on the relationship of suffering to the community and within the church?

Chuang How Chua of Singapore has suggested four key missiological applications from his extensive study of the writings of Kitamori (2008, 20–21). First, since suffering is an inescapable part of human experience, Christians should work to alleviate pain and suffering locally and globally. While total eradication of misery, pain, and suffering is not possible this side of heaven, much more can be done through the resources and personnel of the church worldwide (Chua 2008, 20). As God feels our pain, so believers should be more empathetic with the hurting world around them. As I was preparing this summary, I was reminded of God's voice saying to Saul, who was threatening and ravaging the Christians of his day, "Saul, Saul, why are you persecuting me?" (Acts 9:1–4). Here God identified his own feelings with those who were being persecuted. Similarly, we may argue, God feels the pain of the suffering world even more, particularly when the church neglects to give every effort to relieve the suffering around them. Remember the prophet Jonah's lack of compassion for Nineveh. It was opposed to the compassionate concern of God for the world's greatest city of that day (Jon. 4:10–11). At the same time, God was not just concerned for their physical suffering, but primarily for the root cause of sin and their need to repent so his mercy could be unleashed.

Of course, historically, missionaries have done much in attempting to help a hurting world. From the earliest days they established schools to educate the ignorant, provided opportunities for women to advance, built hospitals to help the sick, set up leprosaria to care for the afflicted, started orphanages for the abandoned, initiated efforts to deal with poverty and prostitution, and organized local training institutes for teaching better agricultural and industrial skills to assist in bettering their communities. In all of these, the gospel was also lived and preached. These were initiated in line with the passion, purpose, and pain of God. Yet today, there is still much more territory to be occupied in caring for the downtrodden and hurting.

Second, suffering "is a necessary component in missionary service. We learn from Kitamori the missiological purpose of pain that God experienced in embracing the world, the enemy of God, in love" (Chua 2008, 20). Romans 5:6–10 affirms that conflict. Likewise, when cross-cultural servants of the cross "live incarnationally among a people who have no knowledge of God, or worse, who are overtly antagonistic to the gospel, they should not be surprised when they encounter pain and suffering as if something strange were happening." Chua suggests that we should embrace suffering rather than suppress or deny it. "How missionaries understand suffering theologically and respond spiritually, in identification with the sufferings of their fellow human beings, becomes an essential part of the gospel witness. ... The people whom we preach the gospel to will model us in our attitude to pain and suffering" (Chua 2008, 20). This is the outworking of our position "in Christ" through real identification with Christ in his sufferings, death, and resurrection.

The Hebrews 11 hall of suffering has been replicated on a thousand mission fields through those who were martyred or died while serving suffering multitudes. Their remains are scattered in overseas cemeteries across the globe. Their commitment and dedication still challenge the enterprising youth of each generation. Yet today's attitude of numerous missionaries, both from first and third world, is often one of seeking comfort; escaping pain, suffering, and hurt; and acquiring material things. Not that we should be stoic about seeking suffering. But are we living Spartan-like lives, as aliens in a world hostile to Christ, with a better identification with those we serve?

Third, Kitamori suggests that in dealing with our pain we should let our suffering testify to the pain of God. The first way of doing this is, "to let our *loved ones* suffer and die" (emphasis in the original), thereby witnessing to the pain of God, through experiencing "the pain of God the Father who let His beloved Son suffer and die." Because God knows precisely the pain involved, "we need to trust Him when our loved ones suffer and die, and not demand healing as if it were our intrinsic right" (2008, 20). Chua observes, "This is a powerful theological counterpoint to the health and healing industry so rampant in the modern church today" (20). It may also say something about extensive preaching-healing campaigns on mission fields. Seldom are the negative results of failed healings, premature "conversions," or inoculation against the gospel publicized. Sometimes the problem here results from simplistic answers to enormous suffering without the preacher-healer accepting responsibility for the outcomes. This is not to say we should eliminate healing ministries, for Jesus sent out the twelve and the seventy "to proclaim the kingdom of God and to perform healing," usually in that order (Luke 9:1–2, 10:9; Matt. 10:7–8). Nor should we not expect God's spirit to work miracles or wonders. But have not many healers become flashy showmen using theatrics, often greedy for money, contrary to Jesus's command in the verses following the above texts? So certainly Jesus calls on all preacher-healers to remain humble and dependent only on God, to test their theology more accurately, to consider their methodology more seriously, to craft their message more carefully, to make their altar calls more specifically, and to accept responsibility more deeply.

A second way for us "to render service to the pain of God is 'for *us* to suffer and die'" (emphasis in the original). A biblical way to witness to the pain of God and the pain of Christ is to deny ourselves, take up our cross, and follow Jesus (Matt. 16:24). Suffering must be understood as part of the pilgrimage of those who follow Christ. "The central message of the gospel is not salvation from suffering. That would be Buddhism. Rather, the gospel is about salvation from sin, and that involves suffering" (Chua 2008, 21). It also involves clearly proclaiming Christ's redemptive gospel of salvation provided through his suffering. All missionaries and church workers need to follow more fully the example of the Apostle Paul in "serving the Lord with all humility and with tears and with trials … declaring … the whole counsel of God" (Acts 20:19–27). That calls for our service of suffering, of sacrificing, and of absolute submission to the Lord.

Fourth, a final missiological application on the study of suffering relates to the ministry of the church. According to Kitamori, "it is in the person of Jesus that we see the unity of divine pain and human pain." He sees the church as being the extension of the life and ministry of Christ. Jesus passed the baton of responsibility to every member of his church to bear the pain of God in the world. His people around Planet Earth are to relate human reality to divine pain. Chua interprets Kitamori's thought on this as follows, "A theology of pain must service an ecclesiological appropriation of pain and suffering, so vital in the mission of the church. In practical terms, it means that in order to relieve the suffering of the world, the church must be involved in suffering. The task of preaching the gospel must therefore include an active engagement with the existential human realities of pain and suffering, violence and death" (2008, 21) . To me, this reinforces and brings us back to getting involved with the first three applications above.

But let's keep balanced. Church and missions' strategic ministries to the multitudes comprise two basic simultaneous elements. This requires both empathetic practical service to the pain of God for suffering humanity, and the presentation of Christ "in word and deed" through his redemptive sacrifice, because that was the reason God identified with our pain. True transformation of societies, families, and individuals will only occur when both are effectively and mutually employed.

CHAPTER 5

CONTINUITIES WITH SUFFERING AS A BRIDGE TO EVANGELIZING BUDDHISTS

David S. Lim

How can we effectively evangelize our Buddhist friends? This paper proposes that for fruitful evangelism, we should use Buddhist terms, concepts, and teachings inclusive of suffering (*dukkha*) in order to lead people to a personal relationship with Jesus Christ and following him in a community that adopts this understanding of faith. Any diversion from this theological contextualization approach has been one of the main reasons for the failure to see Christward movements among Buddhists.

By "theological contextualization," we mean we can start with any term or concept from any worldview or religion including Buddhism which does not even believe in the existence of God. We can use each particular Buddhist's worldview to share the Christian gospel and invite them to accept the person and work of Jesus Christ. We can approach Buddhists in a common search for truth by using their understanding and interpretation of reality. We are hereby showing them that in humility we are sharing their journey to search for truth and enlightenment.

Leading people (including Buddhists) to Christ should be a simple matter. It is akin to gossiping: telling a friend (almost always excitedly) of a piece of good news; hence, new believers are usually the best evangelists. The harvest is ready (John 4:35) and plentiful (Matt. 9:37); we just need to pray for more harvesters (Matt. 9:38). The Holy Spirit has been "poured out upon all flesh" (Acts 2:17–18) "to convict the world of sin, righteousness and judgment" (John 16:8–11) and to guide people into all truth (16:13), for God desires that all will be saved and come to the knowledge of truth (1 Tim. 2:3–4; 2 Pet. 3:9).

We must expect spiritual hunger in the world. Our role is to be good witnesses, to choose the best way possible to win people to God's embodied truth (John

1:1–18); Jesus Christ is likeable good news if only we can package him correctly for our friends to accept. We have to share the gospel at their point of interest or need, perhaps most effectively at their point of suffering. Jesus may be introduced as their healer, provider, sustainer, friend, reconciler, comforter, life-changer, and even as Redeemer-God for Mahayana Buddhists (cf. Smith 2009).

EXPERIENCE OF SUFFERING

It has been suggested that suffering (*dukkha* and its various equivalent terms) be used as the starting point in evangelizing Buddhists (Johnson 2005, 197). We can use their common understanding and experiences of frustration, suffering, and the difficulties of life to introduce them to the biblical worldview and Christian faith. This may be most natural and most effective since suffering is the starting point of Buddhism's Four Noble Truths and may be most predominant in the worldview of Buddhists.

Approaching Buddhist suffering as an experience rather than a concept is not only more basic but more fruitful. To use the reality and experience of suffering may be the most natural starting point in ordinary conversations and in theological dialogues with Buddhists. This is called the incarnational or "scratch where it itches" approach (Smith 2001, 55–59). Like all human beings, Buddhists respond more positively at their existential point of need or weakness as statistically proven. People undergoing traumas and with felt needs are most responsive to the gospel. At this level, there is really no need to know, much less master, Buddhism's concept of *dukkha*. Just being a friend and being around at the time of their need is good enough. One just has to share Jesus as the answer to their suffering, and those friends will be ready to follow him without having to go into deep intellectual discussions on *dukkha*.

Experiences of suffering abound. They can range from the physical needs of sickness and hunger, to the emotional needs of heartbreak, identity crises (especially in teenagers), failed aspirations, and feelings of professional inadequacy, to the financial needs of poverty and bankruptcy, and to the spiritual needs of demonic oppression and involvement in the occult and witchcraft. Sufferings caused by social phenomena like ethnic discrimination, urban and cross-national migration, natural disasters, and violent conflicts are common to humanity. All these can lead to individual conversions and, if properly nurtured, to communal or mass conversions. Addressing people at their existential point of suffering may just be the main secret of church growth among Buddhists by Christians of all traditions, especially the recent Pentecostal/charismatic brands with the help of signs and wonders. God usually speaks in silence, but he shouts through suffering; how fruitful the harvest would be if only more Christians were around as friends to help alleviate each particular suffering—and more with deeds than with words.

What has been less tried is to do this kind of evangelism with Buddhist leaders and monks, and thus the lack of reports of success with educated Buddhists. Friendship, being there to address their personal experiences of suffering, would lead to much more effective evangelism and even people movements. They are human beings too, not just with "religious experiences" for us to dialogue with them about (Küng 1986, 312–13), but also with painful experiences (including intellectual doubts) for us to discuss, people we can counsel and minister to. Like ordinary Buddhists, they suffer not just from the daily needs to eat and rest but also from their call to total detachment from this life, particularly because living on earth does have its attractions (Davis 1997, 74). The key issue then is how to make friends with them so as to share Christ when they experience personal suffering.

WORLDVIEW ABOUT SUFFERING

How about intellectually addressing Buddhists' interpretation of *dukkha*? How can their concept of suffering also be used in effective evangelism? There are actually many congruencies and overlaps in the Buddhist and Christian worldviews, especially regarding suffering in temporal reality or earthly existence. We can see these continuities in the teachings of Buddha and Jesus themselves, in their scriptures, and in the teaching of their contemporary followers.

CONTINUITIES IN TEACHINGS OF THE FOUNDERS

In relation to their teachings on suffering, there are similarities in the teachings of Buddha and Jesus. Like Buddha, Jesus had urgent and good tidings (dharma/gospel) to deliver, which demanded of people a change of mind (*metanoia*, stepping down into the stream) and trust (*shraddha*, faith), not so much orthodoxy but orthopraxy. Like Buddha, Jesus worked from the assumptions that the world is transient and temporary, that all things are inconstant, and that humanity is marred. This is shown by humanity's blindness, foolishness, entanglement in this world, and lack of love towards fellow human beings. Buddha and Jesus both saw the root of this fallen state centered in human desires, cravings, egotism, and self-centeredness (Küng 1986, 322).

To solve this problem, both Buddha and Jesus pointed out a way of redemption from self-seeking, fallenness and spiritual blindness. This liberation is achieved not through theoretical speculation and philosophical reasoning, but through religious experience and inner transformation: a thoroughly practical way to salvation. Both of them did not require any special intellectual, attitudinal, or moral prerequisites for following this way of salvation; the individual had merely to listen, understand, and draw conclusions. No one was asked to explain their true faith or memorize an orthodox creed. This way is a *via media* (middle way) between the extremes of sensuality and self-torture, between hedonism and asceticism, a way that makes possible a new selfless concern with one's fellow humans. Not only do the general moral rules of Buddha and Jesus coincide; they also coincide in their ethical demands of kindness and sharing in another's joy, of loving compassion (the Buddha) and compassionate love (Jesus) (Küng 1986, 322–323).

Though these two founders lived in different contexts, they lived according to what they taught. In their ministry they were poor, wandering teachers, homeless and unpretentious, who lived simple lifestyles in solidarity with those who suffered. They believed that greed, power, and ignorance constituted the temptations which stood in the way of their mission and of people's well-being. And they uttered prophetic critique against the religious traditions and the formalistic and ritualistic caste of religious leaders who were insensitive to the sufferings of ordinary people.

CONTINUITIES IN TEACHINGS OF THEIR SCRIPTURES

The Teaching of Buddha (now placed in hotels like Gideon Bibles) states, "Do not vainly lament, but realize that nothing is permanent and learn from it the emptiness of human life. Do not cherish the unworthy desire that the changeable might become unchanging" (Dendo 1966, 24). Though the main Buddhist view is that of the impermanence of things, the virtue called for is not different from Jesus's teaching on contentment and freedom from anxiety (Matt. 6:19–34; Luke 12:13–34; cf. 1 Tim. 6:6–10; Ps. 49:16–17), especially, "Watch out! Be on your guard against all kinds of greed; a man's life does not consist in the abundance of his possessions" (Luke 12:15).

The same Buddhist book teaches the Second Noble Truth, which is that the cause of *dukkha* is desire:

Where is the source of human grief, lamentation, pain, and agony? Is it not to be found in the fact that people generally desire? They cling obstinately to lives of wealth and honor, comfort and pleasure, excitement and self-indulgence, ignorant of the fact that the desire for these very things is the source of human suffering ... From its beginning, the world has been filled with a succession of calamities, over and above the unavoidable facts of illness, old age and death. But if one carefully considers all the facts, one must be convinced that at the basis of all suffering lies the principle of craving desire ... If avarice can be removed, human suffering will come to an end. (Dendo 1966, 82, 228, 236)

This is congruent with the biblical teachings of Ecclesiastes 2:2–3 and James 1:14–15 where the lack of self-discipline in greed, lust, gluttony, and drunkenness is viewed to be the source of human suffering. The Buddhist view coincides with the biblical critique of materialism, hedonism, and consumerism, which would be a very important corrective to the prosperity gospel teachings in some Christian circles today.

There are similarities in the main ethical precepts found in the popular moral code of Buddhism: (1) Kill not; (2) Steal not; (3) Indulge in no forbidden sexual pleasure; (4) Lie not; (5) Take no intoxicating or stupefying drug or liquor. Interestingly, the last prohibition is not found in the Ten Commandments of Christian scriptures, nor is it taught in most Christian traditions.

Moreover, if any Buddhist is willing to study the Christian scriptures in their spiritual quest, especially in light of their experience of *dukkha*, Ecclesiastes may be particularly useful. The worldview that Qoheleth addresses is almost entirely congruent to that which Buddhists hold. "All is vanity" in this earthly existence, indeed (2:17–26). It is most helpful to show similarities in methodology, findings, and understandings of reality as well as the cause of and solution to suffering (Vasanthakumar 2005) even if one does not posit the existence of God.

Above all, both the Buddhist and Christian traditions believe in the same ultimate end: the hope of a future without suffering. Whether it is a nihilistic nirvana or a paradise-like one, as is the biblical heaven, both agree that suffering can and will be finally overcome. Most traditions in both camps also believe that this freedom from suffering can already be experienced in this life amid suffering too.

CONTINUITIES IN TEACHINGS OF CONTEMPORARY FOLLOWERS

Most Buddhist teachers today, especially the Nobel laureate Dalai Lama and Tzu Chi of cable television station Da Ai, emphasize the concept of love and compassion in response to the sufferings in the world. The Dalai Lama calls compassion the most precious thing:

> It is very important that we have a right attitude. There are many different philosophies, but what is of basic importance is compassion, love for others, concern for others' suffering, and reduction of selfishness. I feel that compassionate thought is the most precious thing there is. It is something that only we human beings can develop. And if we have a good heart, a warm heart, feelings, we will be happy and satisfied ourselves, and our friends will experience a friendly and peaceful atmosphere as well. This can be experienced nation to nation, country to country, continent to continent.

> The basic principle is compassion, love for others. Underlying all is the valid feeling of "I," and on a conventional level, there is an I—"I want this," "I do not want that." We experience this feeling naturally, and naturally we want happiness—"I want happiness," "I do not want suffering." Not only is it natural, it is right. It needs no further justification; it is a natural feeling validated simply by the fact that we naturally and correctly want happiness and do not want suffering.

> Based on that feeling, we have the right to obtain happiness and the right to get rid of suffering. Further, just as I myself have this feeling and this right, so others equally have the same feeling and the same right. The difference is that when you say "I," you are speaking of just one single person. Others are limitless. Thus, one should visualize the following: On one side imagine your own I which so far has just concentrated on selfish aims. On the other side imagine others—limitless, infinite beings ... The unbiased third person naturally can see that the many are more

important than the one. Through this, we can experience, can feel, that the majority—the other limitless beings—are more important than the single person "I." (2001, 1–2)

He applies this love to all relationships, including interreligious relations:

The development of love and compassion is basic, and I usually say that this is a main message of religion. When we speak of religion, we need not refer to deeper philosophical issues. Compassion is the real essence of religion. If you try to implement, to practice, compassion, then as a Buddhist, even if you do not place much emphasis on the Buddha, it is all right. For a Christian, if you try to practice this love, there is no need for much emphasis on other philosophical matters. I say this in a friendly way. The important thing is that in your daily life you practice the essential things, and on that level there is hardly any difference between Buddhism, Christianity, or any other religion. All religions emphasize betterment, improving human beings, a sense of brotherhood and sisterhood, love—these things are common. Thus, if you consider the essence of religion, there is not much difference.

I myself feel and also tell other Buddhists that the question of nirvana will come later. There is not much hurry. But if in day to day life you lead a good life, honestly, with love, with compassion, with less selfishness, then automatically it will lead to nirvana. Opposite to this, if we talk about nirvana, talk about philosophy, but do not bother much about day to day practice, then you may reach a strange nirvana but will not reach the correct nirvana because your daily practice is nothing.

We must implement these good teachings in daily life. Whether you believe in God or not does not matter so much, whether you believe in Buddha or not does not matter so much, as a Buddhist whether you believe in reincarnation or not does not matter so much. You must lead a good life. And a good life does not mean just good food, good clothes, good shelter. These are not sufficient. A good motivation is what is needed: compassion, without dogmatism, without complicated philosophy; just understanding that others are human brothers and sisters and respecting their rights and human dignity. That we humans can help each other is one of our unique human capacities. We must share in other people's suffering; even if you cannot help with money, to show concern, to give moral support, and express sympathy are themselves valuable. This is what should be the basis of activities; whether one calls it religion or not does not matter. (2001, 4)

His teaching that all religions prompt people to lead a life of righteousness and love can be affirmed to be generally true, though there are some extremist exceptions. Though his devaluation of dogma may be unacceptable to most Christians, his emphasis on moral virtue can also be affirmed.

We can even learn from the best of his teachings on compassion, which includes love of enemies:

Compassion ... can be extended even to one's enemies. Our ordinary sense of love and compassion is actually very much involved with attachment. For your own wife and husband, your parents, your children, you have a feeling of compassion and love. But because it is in fact related with attachment, it cannot include your enemies. Again it is centered on a selfish motivation—because these are *my* mother, *my* father, *my* children, I love them. In contrast to this is a clear recognition of the importance and rights of others. If compassion is developed from that viewpoint, it will reach even to enemies.

In order to develop such a motivation of compassion, we must have tolerance, patience. In the practice of tolerance, one's enemy is the best teacher. Your enemy can teach you tolerance whereas your teacher or parents cannot. Thus from this viewpoint, an enemy is actually very helpful—the best of friends, the best of teachers. (2001, 2–3)

For Christians this can provide good insight into understanding the teachings of Jesus and Paul "to love your enemy" (Matt. 6:43–48; Rom. 12:19–21).

Above all, there are large segments of Buddhism (in folk Theravada and most Mahayana and Tibetan) that believe suffering can be redemptive, especially through the vicarious suffering of the righteous to save the unrighteous, particularly in the concept of the bodhisattva. The true bodhisattva does not suffer for himself, but suffers with humankind, as explained by a spokesman for Buddhism in the West:

Our own pain we just suffer, learning to remove the constant cause of it, the desire of self for self. But others' suffering is more and more our personal concern, and it is a fact to be faced that as we climb the ladder of self-expansion and self-elimination we suffer not less but more. For as we increasingly become aware of the One Life breathing in each brother form of life we learn the meaning of compassion which literally means "to suffer with." Henceforth the suffering of all mankind is daily ours, and as the sense of oneness grows so does the awareness of "that mighty sea of sorrow formed of the tears of men." Here is the glory of the Bodhisattva ideal, to turn aside at the entrance of Nirvana, and to postpone that ultimate guardian of a thousand lives of effort "until each blade of grass has entered into Enlightenment." (Humphries 1951, 53)

Most popular among Chinese Buddhists is Amida Buddha, the bodhisattva of compassion. Because of the sinfulness of humanity and its suffering, he was incarnate and came upon earth to save humans. Only in his suffering does love have hope to be found. He became human to become their savior; no one but he alone can help. He constantly watches over and helps all who trust in him (cf. Davis 1997, 84).

The concept of suffering and self-sacrifice for others can even be found in many Theravada Buddhist cultures. Merit-making on behalf of another is common to many religions. In fact most religions require the guilty one to transfer their guilt to another by means of a ritual of substitution. The banana leaf float ceremony in many countries in Asia incorporates this concept. This involves a ceremonial house cleaning followed by the whole village proceeding to the local river that evening with a banana leaf float. Each person then vicariously places upon the float all the uncleanness of house and heart believing it will be taken down river as the float disappears. In some parts of Thailand, there is an expression used of a goat which takes away sin suggesting spiritual cleansing through the shedding of animal blood in place of the human concerned. In Tibetan Buddhism, there is an actual scapegoat ritual. A goat is selected and symbolically loaded with guilt, and then sent out to be killed by whoever finds it.

Logically, the Buddhist interpretation of Christ's death on the cross would be that it was an ignominious death, which is neither a voluntary self-sacrificial deed nor an example of heroism. It would be seen as the just retribution of karmic causation. Christ's horrific, torturous death could only mean one thing, that in his previous existence he must have been a very wicked person to have acquired such bad karma (Davis 1997, 85). Yet Buddhist cultures have incorporated popular or secular understandings of redemptive suffering. Many legends and histories among Buddhist peoples do record the concept of sacrificing for others where one person has voluntarily died in place of another.

> Buddhism knows much of sacrifice for others, both in the conception of the Bodhi-sat in Northern Buddhism who defers his entry into Nirvana for the sake of men and in the spiritual fables of the Jatakas, the Birth Stories, which picture often in a childlike way, but sometimes with telling maturity, the sacrifices undergone by the Buddha in earlier lives. Neither Bodhisatts—nor Jatakas—may be historical, but they are evidence of a conviction within Buddhism that a sacrifice is both right and effective. (Appleton 1961, 51)

One famous historical tradition of a vicarious substitutionary death was that of Queen Sri Suriyothai of Siam. In ancient Siamese culture where the death of the king in battle would mean the taking over of his country, the queen sacrificed her life as she received the blow of the Burmese general's sword in the place of her husband King Chakraphat. This heroic deed showed that she willingly sacrificed her life for the king and her country. A memorial *chedi* was built to commemorate her heroic deed.

Modern people have considered martyrdom a heroic act, especially in regard to those who risked their lives and died on behalf of their nations. No matter how horrific the circumstances may have been, their deaths are now extolled as being self-sacrificial, substitutionary bravery. Such deaths are not interpreted in the Buddhist fashion as being the result of karmic predestination. On the contrary, these are the deaths of heroes—those who died sacrificially on behalf of others (Davis 1997, 85–86). The concepts of substitution, vicarious suffering, and liberation through the intervention of and alleviation by another are attractive to modern Buddhists. Using them more in evangelism and teaching may be most effective, for in fact, these concepts directly undermine the Theravada Buddhist ideas of self-determinism, fatalism, and karma.

This theology of religious contextualization promotes common ground instead of merely seeking points of contact (cf. Lim 1983, 195–97). There are both continuities and discontinuities between the Buddhist and Christian faiths, but in evangelism we must start and focus on the continuities and allow the discontinuities to be corrected bit by bit later. Moreover, we must consider these continuities to be real truths (common ground), for God has left revelations of his truth among all peoples and their cultures (Acts 10:38, 14:17, 17:22–31). Therefore, we can start with whatever light a people already have and connect them with Jesus and his teachings.

Most evangelical missiologists have come to believe that religions can confirm biblical revelation, that there are aspects of religious traditions and systems of thought that we can appreciate. By looking at Christ through the lens of another faith, we can gain new insights into our own faith. "While commitment to Christ precludes commitment to the finality of other faiths, it does not rule out acceptance of truths that other faiths may contain" (McDermott 2000, 20; cf. Ramachandra 1999, 117; Yong 2003; Cracknell 2006). Willingness to learn from other religions shows respect and sensitivity in our witness. With this stance, we can relate confidently and boldly with other faiths in the context of religious pluralism and not from religious isolationism or theological exclusivism (cf. Coward 1985, 106–7).

Our position is akin to that of Vatican II in its truly historic declaration on non-Christian religions:

> Buddhism, in its various forms, realized the radical insufficiency of this changeable world; it teaches a way by which men, in a devout and confident spirit, may be able either to acquire the state of perfect liberation, or attain, by their own efforts or through higher help, supreme illumination. Likewise, other religions found everywhere try to counter the restlessness of the human heart, each in its own manner, by proposing "ways," comprising teachings, rules of life and sacred rites ... The Catholic Church rejects nothing that is true and holy in these religions. (Paul VI 1965)

We can acknowledge the truths embedded in the issues that people bring up and use them as bridges to talk about the relevance and significance of the embodied truth, Jesus Christ. We can then help them see beyond their current worldview, despite the baggage they may carry from their past encounter with Christians. Encountering Christ, and even following him, will become simpler and more feasible than will our trying to convince them that Christianity is the way to understand their faith and experiences. We can even acknowledge the abuses and failures of Christianity as a religion and appreciate the marks of truth in their religions and worldviews without having our faith in following Jesus threatened.

OTHER FACTORS IN EFFECTIVE EVANGELISM

Getting the message right is not enough. It is necessary but not sufficient. Besides presenting the message with the right words and concepts, effective contextualized evangelism also requires at least three other dimensions: right messenger (being), right manner (doing), and right objective (aiming).

RIGHT MESSENGER

To catalyze church planting movements with a message that will resolve the issue of suffering, the messenger must live in accordance and congruence with the message. He or she must show the suffering love of God who revealed himself in Christ, the Suffering Servant who died on a "blood-stained cross" (Ramachandra 1999, 140, 171). The individual or corporate witness should have a spirituality that includes actual alleviation of suffering through acts of mercy (to heal the painful effects of sin) and of justice (to fight the causes of suffering) and usually with signs and wonders to overcome sufferings supernaturally. In short, their ministries and resultant churches should be centers of transformational development that can even befriend and serve Buddhist monks and monasteries.

Any effort to alleviate suffering (and not just talk about it) conveys love and compassion, the language from God every human being can understand. Yet there are wrong ways of alleviating suffering as practiced by many Christians today which convey manipulation, proselytism, and even hypocrisy. Thus, learning the right ways to represent and model the suffering God may require training and discipling from experienced mission practitioners.

RIGHT MANNER

Effective evangelism may be done by amateurs as long as they have the right attitude: to be learners and simply witnesses. There is no need to master interreligious dialogue unless they are to join a formal session with Buddhist monks and educated lay leaders. The best teacher may just be any Buddhist, and we can start by asking questions about his or her faith: Why do people suffer? Why do the innocent suffer? Do you believe in God? What kind of God do you believe in? Where do you get information about your faith? What difference does your religion make in your life? How important are spirituality and morality in your life? Why do we and the world exist? What's our purpose on earth? And so forth. In turn, our own faith will be strengthened as we wrestle with their answers as well as the questions that they ask.

As we engage them in a truly dialogic conversation, we acknowledge our common humanity as people who are equally needy, equally sinful, and equally dependent on God's grace. We listen attentively and sensitively and thus rid our evangelism of any stereotypes or fixed formulae, which are barriers to true dialogue. In this way, the discipling process actually starts from our first encounter with the person. The more time we spend with the disciple before and after the conversion experience, the faster and more effective will be the discipleship to Christlike thinking and living.

Changing someone's worldview is tough, but it is best done through affectionate relationships and informal storytelling (Hiebert 2008, 84; Strauss and Steffen 2009, 462–63). Hence, establishing a friendly or intimate relationship is perhaps the most important factor in effective evangelism. As we share confidently, we must beware of appearing offensive by sending the message "You're wrong; I'm right," thereby turning our friend away from the opportunity to hear the gospel. We do not need to attack or condemn others by rejecting or belittling the good in their religion. In fact, all criticism of their religion must be avoided until that person has converted to Christ. There is hardly any use in trying to convince someone whose mind is still in the dark (Eph. 2:1–3, 4:17–18; John 3:19–21). Corrections can come later and usually are the work of the Holy Spirit who guides believers into all truth (John 16:13).

RIGHT OBJECTIVE

What if they receive Christ? Most evangelism ends with baptizing and incorporating the convert in a church that aims at church growth rather than church multiplication. Instead of starting new contextualized churches or house fellowships with the new believers, they are inducted and added to a Christendom church which usually alienates them from their family and friends.

Instead, they should be taught and encouraged to stay in their religious community and start witnessing to their own people to follow Jesus and start making disciples. As far as possible, they should continue to use their external forms and practices to remain in good relations within their community. As they are discipled to answer life issues by direct communion with Jesus Christ through personal meditation and communal reflection on the scriptures, they will soon develop their own personalized and contextualized spirituality. This is what contextualized disciple-making for church multiplication and Christward people movements is all about.

They will then be able to grow an indigenous church movement that is self-governing, self-supporting (with local resources), self-propagating, and self-theologizing. They will gradually learn how to get rid of anything that is sinful: idolatry, individualism/self-centeredness, immorality, and injustice. This will not occur all at once. None of us have been totally rid of such sins. Elisha permitted Naaman to do ceremonial worship to pagan gods (2 Kings 5:17–19) and Paul permitted the Corinthians to eat foods offered to idols (1 Cor. 6–8) (cf. Ramachandra 1999, 139–40). Almost all of our present Christian church practices (in liturgies; weddings; Christmas, Easter, Halloween, and other celebrations) were adapted from the pagan customs of pre-Christian European tribes anyway.

Hereby, we can see the development of new rituals and theologies (new interpretations and understandings of the biblical faith) enriched by our open interaction and dialogue with people of other faiths. We confidently know Jesus Christ is the Light that enlightens all human beings and their worldviews, including religious beliefs (John 1:9, 16, 18). In humility we acknowledge that we do not have the full and final truth ourselves, though we live and think in the Light. After all, no Christian genius nor perfectly trained theologian up to this day has fully explained the manifold mysteries of God nor given a complete systematic theology, much less a satisfactory theodicy to explain the mystery of suffering and the existence of eternal hell (the ultimate suffering) in the hands of a powerful and loving God. Thanks be to God that we do not need to master any good theology before we can bear witness (often so weakly and imperfectly) to the Light revealed in the Suffering Servant.

May more Christians follow this theological contextualization approach so that, combined with the incarnational or friendly approach, many more Buddhists can be brought effectively to accept and worship Jesus Christ to be the one who offers them the truly full release from all suffering in this life and in the life to come—with words and ways that are meaningful for them, yet may seem strange for us.

PART II

MINISTRY IN THE MIDST
OF SUFFERING

CHAPTER 6

SUFFERING, DEATH, AND FUNERALS IN THAILAND

Jane Barlow

I thought my heart was breaking. As I sat on the ground by the simple funeral pyre and watched the flames consume the coffin, the tears fell. I was not alone. The sisters of the young woman we were saying good-bye to also wept, and my tears meant we were one in our pain. She had killed herself. She had not actively taken her life, but ever since the day she found out she was HIV positive, she had willed herself to die. I always knew Dee was a spunky young woman who could do anything she put her mind to, and she had put her mind to this. She made the decision she wanted to die and told me with no apology. She saw her brother suffer greatly (his funeral was just three weeks earlier), so instead of fighting the disease, she chose to fight life. She actively turned her back on God and accepted that this was her karma. In a matter of weeks, she faded away. As together we washed and prepared her body for the cremation, her sisters carefully did her makeup and nails and filled her pockets with coins and bank notes so that she would have a good journey and do well in her next life. They were desperate for hope for her, even though she herself had none. Over the next few weeks, the family was constantly bothered by banging doors and strange phone calls, and the monks at the temple complained that ever since her funeral they were disturbed by the spirits. The family eventually went to a spirit doctor who invoked Dee's spirit, and her voice spoke through him telling them she was in torment. For months after her death, this family suffered and found no comfort or hope in their faith or their community. And as a Christian who had loved Dee and become a part of that family, I suffered with them.

Death and funerals have been a part of my life for many years as I have lived in small village communities in Northeast Thailand and on the Thai-Burma border and worked with the dying in a large prison hospital in Bangkok.

I remember all of the funerals I have attended, but some, like the one described above, particularly stand out in my mind. As a Christian Westerner, I have had the incredible privilege of accompanying many people in Thailand on their journey to death, both Buddhists and Christians. As I have attempted to be the light of Christ in the midst of suffering and death, I have asked many questions. How do Buddhists understand death and its rituals? How do Western Christians understand death and their own rituals associated with suffering and death? How, as a minority church in a predominantly Buddhist culture, can Thai believers find a way to be Christian and Thai in the face of suffering and death? And how can the love of Christ be seen in all of this? This chapter will, through the light of my experiences and reflections over twenty years of living in Thailand, attempt to answer some of these questions.

Thais usually identify themselves as being Buddhist. I will refer to Thai Buddhists with the understanding that few adhere to a pure Buddhist faith, but rather one which incorporates elements of Buddhism, Hinduism, animism, and Brahmanism. Within each of the four geographical areas of Thailand, there are numerous languages spoken and many tribal groups. Among Thais there is no standard set of rituals for any rite of passage in life. The forms used for funerals vary throughout the country. Some of the funeral rites and practices mentioned may only take place in certain areas; other rituals and ceremonies may be omitted completely: it is impossible to provide a comprehensive description of all the funeral practices known in Thailand. Where funerals are mentioned, unless stated specifically, they are normal everyday rural funerals. City funerals are different because of practicalities such as travel, space, and time. Funerals of nobility or royalty are much more elaborate and include many more symbols and rituals which cannot be explored in this chapter. Occasionally, they will be referred to when relevant.

SUFFERING IN CONTEXT

The Christian faith comes alive within the context of a narrative or story. This is how God has chosen to reveal himself. His word tells the story of a God who creates to redeem, and how that has worked itself out in history and continues to work itself out today (Wright 2008, 68–69). He uses the lives of real people in real places to bring the truth. In the same way, I believe that suffering and death only make sense within the context of narrative or story. We cannot theorize about the whys and wherefores of suffering, for when we do, we rarely get satisfactory answers. Job's story is not primarily about the "why" of his desperate grief and suffering. It is much more about how this particular man at this particular time handles his particular suffering. In fact, his well-meaning friends are reprimanded for their theorizing and efforts to explain what is happening (Hauerwas 1990, 3, 45, 112). Therefore, as I examine the issue of suffering and death in a Buddhist context, I believe it should be done in the context of stories. I will refer to scholars and historians, but my primary sources are the real lives of real people in real situations.

DEATH

Death and its stories are found in every place on earth, as it is the one unavoidable certainty faced by all people in every age. Some people seem to be protected from death and can go through life hardly touched by it. Others are touched by death daily because of the situations they encounter. It is often within the context of poverty that death is more common. These encounters with death affect each individual differently. How we and our cultures deal with dying and death has an impact on our lives.

Richard Smith believes that "death gives life meaning. Without death every life would be a tragedy" (2000, 169). Death affects families, communities, and whole societies. Milton Cohen writes that "when a person dies, the society loses in him much more than a unit; it is stricken in the very principle of its life, in the faith it has in itself" (2002, 9). He adds that the funeral ritual is "a collective response to this attack where society can look death squarely in the eye and reaffirm its own will and resolve" (9). Funeral rituals are "an expression of a cultural blueprint, of attitudes, values and ideals passed down by parents, which an individual learns as a member of society. It is religion in action" (1). My fifteen-year-old daughter expressed her understanding of this passing down of attitudes through funeral ritual very vividly in a school essay. She wrote,

> At one funeral I attended I watched my mother cry with her colleague over the death of one of her AIDS patients. I knew from then on that it was OK to feel and express grief, to share and trust with friends and to embrace death as what I believe it is, a new beginning (Personal correspondence).

The meaning that death gives to life, and the understanding of what is beyond, in any one culture or era is reflected in the rituals associated with death. These vary enormously across the world and through the ages and are closely connected to belief systems and worldview.

The death rituals performed for different individuals in society also reflect the meaning given to that particular life by society. These vary depending on the status accorded to the person by society. On one occasion, I attended the very simple funeral of a small child in rural Thailand. On returning her body home from the hospital, I was not surprised when the village elders arrived. I had thought they had come to discuss funeral arrangements at the local temple. However I was in for a shock. They simply walked in, ignored the grieving mother, rolled the child's body up in a mat, and along with the father took her away. I accompanied them to a place in the forest, far outside the village, where they dug a hole and placed her body in it, filled it in, and left. She had not yet celebrated her third birthday, so in their eyes was not yet fully human and so not deserving of "proper" burial rites. Not even a marked grave. She had to be buried in the forest because of the belief that when death is untimely the spirit or *pii* is unnaturally disturbed. Therefore, there is the fear that it might find its way back to bother villagers if it is too close by. The family was devastated, and their religion provided nothing through which their personal loss and grief was recognized or comforted. In this case, the love expressed by the church in their sadness eventually drew them to Christ, the great comforter. Their child was worth nothing in society's eyes, but they gained great comfort when they met the God who made that child in his own image and for whom she had great value and worth. In stark contrast, the funeral of someone high ranking in society or a religious leader will involve up to a year of lying in state, processions, and elaborate rituals. The more elaborate the ritual, the more important the person must have been. The manner of death and her rituals are a reflection on life.

However different these rituals are from one place to another, they are essential in all cultures from one person to another. They mark the most important rite of passage in life and give meaning to life for the living as well as the deceased. The funeral rite, according to Hugh James, "appears to be something very basic to human dignity that indicates that something very important has happened and interprets that event" (2004, 50). It also gives opportunity for individuals and the community to truly realize that the deceased has gone. One funeral I attended provided a strikingly blunt illustration of this. When I lived on the Thai border, many of the people I cared for came from Burma. One man had been a worker at the electricity board in his town in Burma. He had become a Christian during his illness, and when he died, we arranged a Christian funeral. We were delighted to receive a message saying that some of his fellow workers from his old job would attend. As the service ended and the coffin was about to be closed and buried, they stepped forward and asked for permission to speak. Much to our amazement, they proceeded to read out an official document from the electricity board releasing the deceased from his work commitments, which they carefully and ceremoniously placed in the coffin. Everyone in his workplace and at that service was in no doubt that the deceased would not be going back to work and had now officially gone.

THAI BUDDHIST UNDERSTANDING
AND BELIEF ABOUT DEATH

"To be Thai is to be Buddhist is to be Thai" is a well-known saying in Thailand, and it is estimated that ninety-five percent of the population consider themselves Buddhist. Religion is integrated into every sphere of life. Buddhism is closely linked with patriotism, and conversion to any other faith is often seen not only as a religious betrayal, but a rejection of country and king as well.

Buddhism originated in Northern India in the sixth century BC. Monks carried Buddhism along the trade routes to China, and by the third century BC, Theravada Buddhism reached Burma. From there it spread to the Mon and Khmer people, who occupied Siam. Once established, it proved "such a durable and pervasive force that some ethnic groups who migrated into that area readily adopted it as their state religion" (Mahidol University 1996). However, it was never pure Buddhism, but Buddhism intertwined with religion with the already present Brahmanism and animism. King Ramkhamhaeng (1275–1317 AD) established Theravada Buddhism as Thailand's dominant religion. James Gustafson notes that despite establishing Buddhism, "he continued to pay respect to the spirit of the hill" (1970, 25), in keeping with his previous animistic practices. Animism and Buddhism existed comfortably together and continue to do so today.

John Davis writes, "The Thai Buddhist perceives his worldview as essentially supernaturalistic. He 'sees' all phenomena as an integrated whole, in a 'sacred' rather than 'secular' world" (1993, 35). The emphasis is on making merit; faith is placed in the protection offered by charms, amulets, and tattoos. Every property, from a small shack to a multinational corporation, has a spirit house to house the resident spirit, which is kept appeased with regular offerings of food, drink, and incense. People rely on astrologers to pick auspicious dates for important occasions. Merit making and appeasing the spirits are associated with every rite of passage or important event in life (e.g., birth, marriage, and death). Religious belief and daily life are inseparable. Buddhism, animism, and Brahmanism together play a large role in how people live and die. Paul De Neui notes that "it is a syncretistic mix that is flexible, accommodating and dynamic" (2003, 122) and effects every area of life.

As with every other aspect of life, the understanding of death and the response to it has come about through a mixture of Buddhist and animist beliefs. Stanley Tambiah states that "death is the most important rite of passage" (1970, 179). Funeral rites are the most elaborate and prescribed of all the rites of passage. In Buddhism, all existence is suffering, but especially when death occurs. It is possible that the reason Buddhism became popular in Thailand is that it had more to say about death and the afterlife than animism did.

The highest goal for a Buddhist is to reach nirvana (Sanskrit for "blowing out as of a flame"). Nirvana is a state where all craving or desire ceases. The "evil which is the source of all the sufferings of continued mortal existence" (Ling 1970, 19) is extinguished, and the constant cycle of birth, death, and rebirth is broken forever. For the majority of Thai Buddhists, their daily goal is to make merit in order to gain good karma. Making merit is done largely for the future, "either for the benefit of future reincarnations of the living or to benefit those already dead" (De Neui 2002). This looking forward beyond death becomes "the core of their practice" (Johnson 2002, 11), and so preparation for death is part of their daily lives. There is also the belief that if you do good, you will receive good in the here-and-now, giving the making of merit a two-pronged advantage.

Thai Buddhists believe in rebirth. The cycle of birth, death, and rebirth is repetitive and inescapable. Death is the doorway into rebirth, which leads again to death. In pure Buddhist understanding, rebirth occurs the instant death happens. "As long as there is a clinging to life, a desire to go on existing, the current of consciousness does not come to a stop with the body's loss of life" (Dhammananda 1998, 98).

The state into which one is reborn depends on karma: "one's fund of merit accumulated in this life will ensure a rebirth blessed with happiness, prosperity and wealth" (Tambiah 1970, 53). There is a commonly held animist belief in an "in-between" place where the spirit goes before rebirth. This is known as "heaven" or "hell" and has levels of bliss or torment. Tambiah continues to explain that if one has a large balance of merit over demerit, then one's *winyan* (soul or good spirit) will go to heaven until the merit is exhausted, at which point rebirth occurs. If one has more demerit than merit, then the soul goes to hell until the demerit is expiated. Only then will one go to heaven before being reborn. If there is no merit accumulated in life, then the soul becomes a disembodied spirit (*pii*) left to wander the earth until rebirth. In common folk Buddhism or animism, it is believed possible to transfer merit to another, including the dead. The transfer of merit by others may help to release the deceased from torment in hell, or assist in obtaining a "better" rebirth. This belief makes what happens at death and funerals very important to a Buddhist.

Traditionally, when a Buddhist is dying, the family gathers and an effort is made to help the dying person concentrate solely on the Buddha in order to prepare the path to heaven. Monks chant the Buddhist scriptures in Pali. Crying is forbidden as this will upset the dying person and make it harder for them to depart peacefully. The Venerable Suvanno in his instructions on how a Theravadin Buddhist funeral should be conducted explains this by saying that "undue clinging and attachment will only conduce to more suffering" (1996, 10). As soon as death takes place, mourners wail loudly—a sign of grief and a signal to the village that someone has died. Continued weeping is not approved or, as Denis Segeller writes, "the spirit will have to swim through your tears" (1995, 45). The monks continue to chant after death in order to help the dead one's good energies be released from their fading personality.

In the Thai supernaturalistic worldview, the spirit world is the "unseen other world which pervades everything from cradle to cremation" (Davis 1993, 34). The *pii* (malevolent spirits) must be kept happy at all times; otherwise, bad things will happen. The existence of this spirit world is unquestionable for most Thai. Many of the rituals and ceremonies performed by Buddhists stem from the need to appease the spirits, as well as being social events which bind the community together. If these rituals are stopped or forbidden, "dysfunction and disintegration of the social structures that keep the community together ... result" (1993, 36) and people are left with a spiritual vacuum, which is immediately open to abuse by the supernatural world. So much of what is done at funerals is a response to fear—fear of what will happen to the deceased, but also, what is often articulated more, fear of what the deceased's *pii* will come back and do to the living. So when death occurs, rituals and ceremonies are performed with two main goals based on these fears: (1) to improve the merit status of the deceased and so enable the *winyan* (spirit) to go to heaven and (2) to protect the household and community from the return of the *pii* of the deceased.

Merit is made for the deceased through the giving of gifts, food, and money and through the chanting of the monks. It is believed that if monks eat the food, it is then transmitted through them to the dead person's spirit. During the funeral procession, a long piece of white cloth or thread is attached to the coffin and is held by the monks. The monks thus lead the deceased to their next life. Money is placed in the deceased's pockets or mouth for the journey ahead and to pay the fee which allows access to the next world and the ability to buy property there. Personal belongings are placed in the coffin for use in the next world.

From the moment of death, precautions are taken to contain the *pii*. The eyes and mouth are closed and sometimes sealed with wax. The person closing them invites the spirit to quit its abode, and the wax prevents reentry. The ankles and hands are bound to bind the *pii* so it cannot cause trouble. Once the coffin has left the house, the staircase (usually rural houses are built on stilts with stairs leading to the main living area) is removed or disguised in order to confuse the *pii* and prevent it from returning. Water jars are smashed and loud fire crackers are set off or guns fired to frighten the *pii* away. From the moment of death, everything that happens has religious significance. Sometimes there is more than one interpretation for rituals, and sometimes the interpretation has been forgotten and it has become unexplainable tradition.

Death is a social event, particularly in rural Thailand, and as well as serving to make merit and provide protection, as described above, the funeral brings the community together. The whole community gathers at the house or temple and remains there at least until the cremation. They provide support and practical help: building the coffin, arranging flowers, preparing food. People donate food and money to help the family, but also to make merit for themselves and the deceased. The corpse remains in the center of the house until the day of the cremation. As long as the body is present it can receive merit from the gifts and chanting. The coffin is surrounded by wreaths, flowers, fairy lights, and usually a large framed photograph of the deceased. Entertainment is provided round the clock (gambling, cock fighting, boxing, and music); laughing, chatting, and noise is encouraged to keep the *pii* away. Lillian Curtis observes that merit is gained not from being miserable but by the respect shown "in the splendor of the occasion" (1903, 156). A funeral draws together community, but can also be a great financial burden for the family, causing further suffering in the future as they cope with debts incurred.

CHURCH HISTORY IN THAILAND PARTICULARLY
RELATING TO DEATH

In order to understand the Thai church today, one should examine the history and missionary heritage which shaped it. Thai church historian Herbert Swanson emphasizes that "it is impossible to understand the church apart from its past, its accumulation of experiences" (1984, ii). The history of Protestant missions in Thailand, from the early nineteenth century, was fraught with difficulty, danger, and death. There were few missionaries and they saw little fruit from their work. Swanson writes, "The mission believed that the animist/Buddhist faith of traditional society was idolatrous and therefore an affront to the holiness of God" (1984, 22). As faith is at the core of society, the missionaries were isolated from society. New converts to Christianity were cut off from their own society. The missions often enforced their Western forms of church government, which were legalistic and alien to the Thai: "the mission simply tried to transplant the church institutions of the missionaries' own childhood and culture" (1984, 26).

The transplantation of Western church culture included the transplantation of belief and ritual surrounding death. Even before there were Christian converts, the Siamese witnessed Western Christian death rites because so many missionaries died and were buried in Thailand. In 1853, King Mongkut made a royal grant of land in Bangkok for a Protestant cemetery. As there were very few converts by then, this was given primarily because of the high number of foreigners who died and because the missionaries insisted on burial rather than what they saw as the Buddhist practice of cremation.

The Bible does not command Christians to bury their dead. Old Testament Jews practiced burial in caves while surrounding cultures used cremation, mummification, and other death rituals. The early Christian church also buried their dead. Timothy George suggests four reasons for Christian burial: being created in the image of God, the human body deserves respect; through the incarnation the Word became flesh and God uniquely hallowed human life and bodily existence; the body is the temple of the Holy Spirit and should not therefore be destroyed; as Jesus was buried and raised bodily, so Christians believe that burial is a witness to future resurrection. The Latin word for cemetery means "sleeping places," indicating a belief in future resurrection (2002, 66). In the context of the early church, cremation had strong associations with pagan religions and so was unimaginable for a Christian. However, cremation is never condemned biblically. As Christianity spread, Christian burial practices went with it. Elesha Coffman, in her article "The Cremation Question," notes that the adoption of Christian burial "became a sign of changed allegiance" (2002), making it unthinkable that a Christian would cremate.

The practice of burial introduced by the missionaries separated the Christians from the Thai Buddhists. However, more than that, they were separated by the missionaries' attitude towards death. According to Tony Walter, from as early as the twelfth century, the English were seen as "the most individualistic of peoples" (2003, 219). This has "profoundly influenced how English culture and its colonial child, American culture approach both life and death" (219). Christian funerals were private family experiences, in contrast to the public community funerals of Thailand. During the eighteenth century, scientific advances in the Western world changed the definition of death as a spiritual process to a single medical bureaucratic event. The separation of religion and science, which took place during the Enlightenment, eroded the supernatural worldview and undermined the centrality of religion to death ritual. Funerals were somber with black clothes, vestments, and altar hangings. Hugh James writes that biblical passages chosen "emphasized fear of judgment, terror of death and need for mercy" (2004, 27). He also quotes Gorer, who wrote of modern Western funeral rites: "the drastic simplification of mourning customs during the twentieth century was symptomatic of a desire to ignore death" (2004, 17).

With this cultural background, the early missionaries to Thailand inevitably introduced what they knew and experienced of a funeral ritual as "the Christian way." In 1907, Marion Palmer wrote, following a Buddhist funeral, "at such a time as this when we desire quiet and rest, the people here enjoy big crowds and noise" (1907, 67). Curtis expressed disapproval in her comment that "no ceremony is looked forward to with more genuine interest and pleasure than a cremation where there is boxing, cock fights, music, dance, giggling, side shows and other such displays of anything but a funereal nature" (1903, 156). The missionaries were not only critical of the social aspects of the funeral, but also the spiritual aspects. In 1886, Mary Cort noted, "all sorts of deceptions are practiced at a funeral ... the natives think we are very cruel to bury our dear friends and then leave them in the grave forever" (1886, 65, 71). Henry White was condescending in his comment about Thai Buddhist funeral ritual, saying, "One must have plenty of imagination and a minimum of reasoning when dealing with their old customs, else their charm and delightful simplicity is lost" (1912, 103).

It is this attitude that was taught to new believers. Today most Thai Protestant churches conduct funerals using a Western form. There is a dread of syncretism or a reemergence of deeply buried Buddhist concepts related to death. In his study on funerals in Thailand, Banjop Kusawadee writes, "the Protestant Church is afraid of including Thai culture in their pastoral care to the sick, the dying person and in the funeral rite. They try their best to avoid using Thai culture and even terminology which is used by Buddhism" (2001, 138). As a result, Tongpan Prometta says, "when outsiders see what happens when a Christian dies they don't want to have anything to do with Jesus" (2000).

This thinking was confirmed in my own experience. During the seven years in which I lived in a rural community in Northeast Thailand, there was considerable church growth. This was for many reasons, but one particular factor was an attempt by the church to find ways to use local music, language, symbols, and rituals in worship and church life. Jesus became incarnate in the lives of people where they were. However, many new believers carried a deep-rooted concern about what Christians did with their dead. This was articulated by some villagers as the reason for not becoming a Christian. Death and the rituals associated with it are very important for Thai Buddhists. These villagers had many felt needs associated with death that they could not abandon. They were also concerned that if they became Christians, then the religious and pastoral needs of their relatives would not be met at their funeral. It was therefore up to the small church in Thailand to show they did take death and her rituals seriously. They did want to bring comfort and hope to the bereaved, they did want to show respect to the dead, and they did want to live in the absence of fear. Christian funerals should show all of this, but in a new way that points people to Christ and yet does not compromise the gospel.

MINISTERING TO THE SICK AND DYING

However, Christian care and witness does not have to wait until after death. The journey leading towards death is often one of great suffering. One thing I have observed over the last twenty years is something that seems to cross cultures. People often want to avoid death and are reluctant to face up to it when it is lurking close by, whether for themselves or for people they love. In Thailand, despite the Buddhist belief in "preparing the path to heaven" described earlier, this avoidance of the subject of imminent death seems to be the norm in both Buddhist and Christian communities. Sadly, this often means that the dying, when near their time of death, are not able to talk about their fears or wishes as far as death is concerned because others leave them alone, trying to avoid the issue. I believe one of the key roles of Christians at this time is to be present—present in expressing love, present in practical care, present in a willingness to listen and talk. In my limited experience, this is radical in Thai society, but when we are present there is opportunity for Christ to transform lives. I remember one occasion in the prison hospital. A Thai Christian friend and I had been visiting one Buddhist man regularly. He was very sick. He was a criminal. He was alone. He was dying. Usually he was asleep and latterly unconscious when we visited, and when he was awake conversations were limited and fairly superficial. However we prayed for him, either aloud or in our hearts as we sat by his bed. We were present. The last day we visited him, he was unconscious, clearly dying. We sat holding his hands, praying. Suddenly, he sat bolt upright, held his hand up and said, "Stop worrying about me, today I will see Jesus." We have no idea exactly what had happened in his heart or mind, but I believe because of our presence on his journey to death, Jesus met him and that day he, like a well-known criminal on a cross, entered His presence.

CONTEXTUALIZATION VERSUS SYNCRETISM
IN DEATH RITUAL

Alan Johnson writes that in the Thai context, "Buddhist concepts inform the speech and thought forms and feelings of the great majority, if not all Thai society" (2002). For many who become Christians after being Buddhist, the inward transformation of these deeply ingrained thought forms and feelings by Christ can take many years. The missionaries "planted within the Thai church a Western style dualism, deeply concerned with protecting Christian purity from any defilement by heathen practices" (De Neui 2005). Christians were forbidden from attending or participating in local rituals because of fear of syncretism. Protestant missionaries were already biased against many of the Buddhist rituals, which involved showing physical obeisance (kneeling, prostration), because they associated this with the Catholic worship of saints and statues. This sort of obeisance was linked with both idolatry and low class servitude (Swanson 2004). There was a fear of anything related to the supernatural or spirits. According to Philip Hughes, new converts "had to give up all those religious activities which had given their lives meaning, and through which they had hope for the future" (1982, 13). In Thailand, many new converts in the early days of missions readily accepted the forms of worship and laws given to them by missionaries. Without ever understanding the concept of grace or experiencing an inner transformation, deep down they could not give up what they had known before. Their new religion was domesticated (often at a subconscious level) in order to make it acceptable to the old. Christianity became a new vehicle by which they could still live out their old understanding of karma and the need to make merit. Although the forms of their faith seemed Christian, it was actually a syncretistic mishmash of old and new. It is at times of stress or grief, such as death, that the old ways of thinking sometimes reemerge, causing confusion, syncretism, and even a turning away from Christ.

The term contextualization was first used publicly by Shoki Coe in 1972 (Hesselgrave and Rommen 1989, 29–32). He wrote that contextualization, while "responding to the Gospel in terms of a traditional culture" (what had been called indigenization), also "takes into account the process of secularization, technology and the struggle for human justice" (Neely 1995, 26). Contextualization is the indwelling and radical impacting of a culture by the gospel at every level. The culture determines the forms which are then used to communicate and celebrate the core message of the gospel—grace. This adaptation or contextualization of forms risks compromise, and many missionaries have preferred the easier route of sticking to the forms they know, even if this means the core message of the gospel has not been communicated effectively. However, there are some who see the urgency in making the truth of the gospel a reality within Thai culture. For example, Prometta urges the Thai church to consider contextualization.

> Thai Christians have been taught to believe that the ways imported into the church from Europe are the ways of God. These ways had meaning back in the places where they came from. The problem was when they came to us we didn't know the meaning. The meaning didn't transfer. I want you to understand just how important it is for Jesus to come in the cultural forms that *our* people can understand. (2000)

The forms traditionally used in Christian funerals are alien to a Thai Buddhist. Some churches in Thailand have attempted to look at how they can adopt culturally appropriate forms which will convey the true message of a Christian funeral and at the same time meet some of the needs of non-Christian relatives of the deceased. I will therefore now look at what some churches have decided to do as they have grappled with the issue of how to be both Christian and Thai in the face of death. The following suggestions come from research I carried out as well as discussions with three groups of Thai Christians: firstly, a group of fairly traditional church leaders in central Thailand; secondly, the Center for Church Planting and Church Growth (CCPCG), which is seeking to plant contextualized dynamic equivalent churches in Northeast Thailand; and thirdly, the small rural church in Northeast Thailand where I lived for eight years. The discussion about funerals in this third group, where contextualization was being attempted at many levels, started because an elderly woman expressed interest in Christianity but also genuine fear about what would happen when she died. Despite her fears, she became a Christian; she was the only Christian in her family. Before she died, she explained that her family would insist on a Buddhist funeral; she knew she was going to the heaven that Christianity preached, so she felt it did not really matter. To everyone's surprise, when she died, her son (the Buddhist village headman) asked the pastor to arrange a Christian funeral, because of his respect for both the Christian ways and for his mother. This would have never happened in the past when Christians were not trusted to do a proper funeral. So what was the church doing that made the difference? I believe it was the fact that they were thinking through how to behave in a Buddhist community in the context of death.

WHAT SHOULD CHRISTIANS DO AT BUDDHIST FUNERALS?

Most funerals in a Thai community are Buddhist because the majority of the population is Buddhist. The church is a small minority. So what should Christians do when their Buddhist neighbors die? As I have said, in the past, Christians were taught to have nothing to do with Buddhist rites or rituals. They separated themselves from the communities in which they lived and therefore were not trusted. However, the overwhelming opinion of the three groups I researched is that Christians should attend Buddhist funerals in order to show love. Some of the Christians who discussed funerals came up with a list of things they felt should or should not be done. Others will have more to add—this is just a sample of their thoughts. (For a detailed description of rituals and symbols common at Buddhist funerals, see the appendix.)

- Christians should not light incense at the house, but could bring flowers instead as a sign of respect.
- Christians can and should be involved in helping in practical ways such as making food for the family and guests. They should take

opportunities to explain that they are not making merit when they do this, but expressing their love and concern for the bereaved.

- Christians can be in the house when the monks chant, but they should not *wai* as if praying, but sit quietly with their hands in their laps.
- Christians should not drink alcohol or gamble at a funeral.
- Christians should not join in any of the religious ceremonies at the house (e.g., washing the hands of the deceased, circling the house with the coffin).
- Christians may join the procession to the temple. They should not hold onto the white cord or scatter rice.
- Christians should not circle the pyre.
- Christians should not give robes to monks.
- Christians can accept the bundle of candles, incense, and flowers distributed by the hosts and place it on the pyre as this just shows a participation in the burning and nothing significantly religious. Some choose to prepare their own without the incense to enable them to take part but to take away any suggestion of worship

Despite all these suggestions of things Christians should or should not do, the overwhelming sense was that Christians must be present in order to show God's love at this time of grief

WHAT SHOULD CHRISTIAN FUNERALS BE LIKE IN A BUDDHIST CONTEXT?

Buddhists should feel welcomed and not alienated by Christian funerals. Ceremonies and rituals in Thai life can be natural bridges within the environment of Thai culture for explaining God's grace. The Christian funeral should therefore give support to grieving relatives (whether Christian or Buddhist), celebrate the life of the deceased, demonstrate love, and preach the gospel.

In the rural church where I lived, funerals are a very important part of Christian witness. The church helps the family by providing food; people bring rice and money as well as helping to prepare food. They do this not to make merit but to show practical love and care. No alcohol is served in contrast to a rural Buddhist funeral, where it is expected that alcohol will be available. The coffin is lavishly decorated with flowers, fairy lights, and a large photo of the deceased.

As with a Buddhist funeral, the family often hires large speaker systems to play loud music day and night. At times when the monks would normally come to a Buddhist funeral (morning and evening), there are Christian services each day leading up to the burial or cremation and continuing on for several days afterwards. Funerals are considered to be evangelistic opportunities. I once heard my husband issuing an invitation to believe—and I was sitting in our house half a kilometer away! This is considered completely acceptable behavior for a funeral, even though such obvious Christian proselytizing would normally be unacceptable in a major Buddhist community. Church members stay with the family through the night, as they do at a Buddhist funeral, singing, talking, and laughing together, not to keep the evil spirits away, but to show love. On the day of the burial (most Christians still bury, although the CCPCG feels that cremation is more culturally appropriate and perfectly acceptable), a special service is held at the house. As many church leaders as possible are invited. The coffin is led to the graveyard by a large wooden cross followed by church leaders in robes. This is to indicate that the cross is the way to heaven, and the respected leaders are there to give honor to the deceased. A band is hired to play music and people dance behind the coffin, not to lead the way to heaven but to show respect and celebrate the resurrection in Christ. Before burial, a short history of the deceased's life is read. These would also be distributed in much the same way as happens at Buddhist funerals. The purpose is to give honor to the deceased rather than to make merit on his or her behalf. The burial service is very similar to a Western service as it includes prayers and Bible verses or a short evangelistic sermon, but it differs in that at the end the hosts throw coins or sweets into the crowd—not to make merit, but as a fun way to thank people for coming, and to break any emotional tension. This church has actively looked for the traditional symbols they can incorporate without being syncretistic (e.g., the food, the community event going over days, the decorations, the loud music, and the procession). In places where this is happening, Buddhists notice and barriers are broken down. Prometta quotes villagers saying, "If this is what happens when Christians die I want to die! Dying this way is great. Heaven must be more fun than this. Those who die in God are really happy" (2000).

HOW CAN THE LOVE OF CHRIST BE SEEN IN ALL OF THIS?

On one occasion, I was called to the hospital to collect the body of a woman who had died. She lived in a small village where there was a new young church. She was the first Christian to die in her village. Christians had been active and present in caring for her when she was sick, even when others refused to have anything to do with her. I drove to the hospital to pick up her body, already worried about how we could arrange a Christian funeral in this predominantly Buddhist village. We took Mrs. Tom to her mother's house in the center of the village. We laid her body in the middle of the room and, respectfully and gently, I helped her brother wash and dress her, quietly explaining to him what to do and answering his questions. When we finished, I looked up and was amazed. Standing in front of the house, squashed into the narrow lane, were about a hundred people in complete silence just watching. When I stood up, the questions started—what do Christians believe about death? Why wasn't I doing anything to keep away the *pii*? Wasn't I frightened they would come after me? Can you gamble at a Christian funeral? And then eventually—didn't I know this woman had AIDS? Why wasn't I afraid? Why did I show such love and respect? It was an amazing opportunity to challenge people's prejudices and help them overcome their fears. The Buddhist village headman agreed to a Christian funeral and gave land for burial; the whole village came, not afraid of the dreaded disease that had killed this woman or the fact that nothing was done to appease the spirits or make merit for her; her daughter was accepted and cared for by members of the family who had previously rejected her, and the village allowed her to go to school. The example that was seen in the way Christians cared for this woman when she was sick, even in death, helped to transform attitudes in that village.

Suffering, pain, and death are a reality of the world in which we live, whether in a predominantly Buddhist context or some other context. The role of Christians is to answer this question: how can the love of Christ be seen in all of this? This is our goal, that Christ's love is seen. We cannot do that by alienating people, by judging people, or by ignoring their practical, emotional, or spiritual needs when they are suffering. Neither can we do it by giving in to the fear that drives so much of what many Buddhists need in relation to death. As Christians, we should be walking with people in dying and death, present in their suffering and demonstrating the love of Christ, the one who can meet all our needs.

I would like to finish with a poem I wrote following the death of Dee's brother from the introduction.

I just watched a man die

I just watched a man die.

He was young, in the prime of life
So much to live for.
This morning he died.

I just watched a young man die.
I wasn't with him when he took his last breath
But I have held him and comforted him for painful weeks
As he screamed in agony and longed for death.

I just watched a young man die.
I walked with his family as they watched him suffer
And I mourn with them now as they grieve
And I ask why must we watch young men die.

I just watched a young man die.
And it made me think of another woman who watched a young man
die.
She watched a young man in the prime of his life
As he died in agony on a cross.

I just watched a young man die
Because Jesus, who died on that cross, but is now alive,
Has called me to walk with these young men who die
And show them Christ's love.

I just watched a young man die.
There will be more, and women too.
Help me Lord, to walk with them through their journey of suffering
And point them to you, the one who understands their pain.
(Feb. 1998)

APPENDIX

The following tables show some of the Buddhist or animist rites and rituals observed by the author primarily at rural funerals in Northeast Thailand. Many of these rituals are done in order to make merit or prevent the *pii* from causing problems. Most are therefore unnecessary or inappropriate for Christians. However, I believe it is important that we understand why our Buddhist neighbors do what they do at funerals, so we can help meet their needs in different ways that point them away from fear and to Christ.

FROM THE TIME OF DEATH TO THE TIME OF CREMATION OR BURIAL

The corpse is laid to face west.	This is the direction of the dead and will speed the journey to the next world.
It is washed and covered with talcum powder or tumeric.	This is physical cleansing, but also spiritual cleansing for the journey to heaven. The powder may just be aesthetic, but tumeric is believed to have spiritual cleansing properties.
The corpse is dressed in new clothes (if poor, wrapped in a clean white cloth instead). Sometimes dressed with clothes inside out.	The new clothes smooth the way into heaven. *Pii* wear their clothes inside out, and so this will keep the *pii* happy. For some, dressing the corpse nicely is simply a sign of respect and a final practical gesture of filial piety. White is the traditional color of mourning. Until around 1884, it was compulsory for mourners to wear white and also to shave one's head.
The dressed corpse is covered with a white cloth exposing nothing but the head and right hand, which is left hanging outwards and downwards. Relatives then ritually pour perfumed water over the hand.	The ritual cleansing shows respect and asking forgiveness from the corpse for wrongs done.
A coin is placed in the mouth of the corpse and sometimes bank notes in pockets.	This is to pay the "spirit fine" (Bock 1884, 261) in order to be able to enter the next world and buy property there.
The eyes and mouth are closed and sometimes sealed with beeswax.	The person closing them invites the spirit to quit its abode first, "leaving behind every anxiety" (Bock 1884, 261). The wax prevents "re-entry."
Ankles (sometimes big toes) and hands are bound, and a cord is fastened around the waist. Sometimes white cords are also placed around the ankles, wrists, and neck.	This is to bind the *pii* so it cannot cause trouble. The cords symbolize "the worldly ties of responsibility: bound ankles mean attachment to property, wrists attachment to spouse and the neck, the children" (Segaller 1995, 40).

The hands are placed in the *wai* position on the chest with flowers, joss sticks, and candles put between the fingers.	The *wai* is a sign of respect. The incense is used to worship Buddha on arrival in heaven, and the flowers are "an offering to the sacred hairs of Buddha" (White 1912, 102). The candles light the way to heaven.
A jar of water, the deceased's favorite food, and lit candles or a lamp are placed at the head.	The candles light the way to heaven; the food and water provide nourishment for the journey. The lamp also allows the *pii* "to see what is going on in the room, including the gifts placed near the body for making merit" (Kingshill 1991, 162). The same lamp may be used to light the pyre.
A rope is tied between two of the house posts. A white cloth is thrown across this and draped over the corpse like a tent until the coffin is ready.	This provides "housing" for the spirit and keeps it contained.
A wicker framework is hung across the doorway in some places. In others, a string encircles the house.	This is to prevent evil *pii* from entering the house.
The coffin is made of bamboo or wood. Food is placed nearby. When the coffin is finished, the body is placed in it and a palm leaf is wafted over it.	The food keeps the spirits happy while the coffin is built, and so protects the builders. The palm leaf drives back any of the workmen's own good spirits (*kwan*) which may have fled. It also forces the *kwan* of the deceased into the coffin, as "it would never do to have them running around unattached" (White 1912, 104).
Monks chant every evening. They are given gifts and special food.	Merit is gained for the deceased and the bereaved through listening to the chanting and giving gifts. It is believed that "food taken by the monks is transmitted through them to the dead person's spirit" (Segaller 1995, 41).
A supply of incense is kept close to the coffin. As visitors arrive, they *wai* the coffin, light incense, and sometimes prostrate themselves in front of the coffin.	This is known as *wai sop*—paying respect, or some interpret it as worshipping the corpse. Some say the lighting of the incense is a way of asking forgiveness from the corpse for wrongs done.

CREMATION

A long ribbon or piece of white cloth, known as the thread of life, is attached to the front of the coffin. It is held by the monks when they chant in the house and as they lead the coffin out of the house.	The deceased has contact with the monks through the ribbon and so gains merit. The monks lead the deceased to heaven.
Before the coffin leaves the house, the stairs are replaced, disguised with banana leaves, or turned upside down. Sometimes a hole is cut in the bamboo wall to take the coffin through. The water jar outside the house is overturned or smashed. The coffin is carried out feet first and circles the house three times. As the coffin leaves, fire crackers are set off or guns fired.	This is all to confuse the *pii* so that it cannot find its way back to the house. Another interpretation is that the turning upside down of the stairs and water jar represents the wheel of life. The loud noises are to frighten the *pii* away from the house.
A young male relative is ordained for the period of the funeral and walks with the monks.	Ordination is one of the best ways of earning merit. This merit is "given" to the deceased and is one of the most honorable things a son or grandson can do for his deceased relative.
The funeral procession consists of the monks leading, followed by the coffin carried by pall bearers, an ox cart or a pickup truck, musicians, the men, and finally, the women. People laugh and joke and often carry knives.	The monks lead the way to heaven; the musicians drive away sorrow and fear of the spirits. Traditionally, the knives were used to cut the wood in the forest for the funeral pyre and so earn merit. The wood is already cut these days, but the knives represent the merit earned.
Puffed or roast rice is strewn along the path of the procession.	This is done to lure the *pii* to the cemetery rather than having it enter the coffin and making it too heavy to carry. This is also seen as a symbol that "just as a person dies he will never be reborn the same person again, so the rice cannot grow again" (Tambiah 1970, 183). Another interpretation sees it as "the symbols of blessings falling upon the multitude" (Perkin 1923, 219).
The site of the pyre is decided by throwing an egg on the ground, although usually these days there is a permanent crematorium.	Where the egg breaks is where the *pii* wishes the pyre to be.
The coffin is carried around the pyre three times. Guests walk round the pyre "in an attitude of supplication begging forgiveness from the deceased for all offences committed against him while alive" (White 1912, 106).	Walking round the pyre represents the circle of life. It suggests the "soul's pilgrimages in the earth, hell and heaven" (White 1912, 106). It is also done to confuse the *pii* again.
The coffin is opened, and the hands and feet are cut lose from the bindings. The body is turned over face down.	The *pii* is released in a "safe" place or to prevent the escape of the spirit. These two contradict each other—an indication of the many different interpretations of funeral traditions. Turning the body also prevents the unpleasant "sitting up" of a body as it starts to burn which can be very distressing on an open pyre.

A young green coconut is cut open and the milk poured over the face.	Coconut milk represents purity and is used to ritually cleanse once more. Others say it is to ensure beauty in the next life.
Personal belongings are placed in the coffin.	These will be used by the deceased in the next world.
Other clothes belonging to the deceased are tied in a bundle and thrown back and forth over the coffin three times.	This purifies the clothes and makes it possible for them to be worn by others.
Coins are thrown on the ground or out amongst the guests. There is always lots of laughter as people scramble to get them.	This is done to pay the spirit masters of the ground. It is also seen as a sign of blessing the people and of generosity on the part of the hosts.
The monks chant in Pali one more time. People usually sit and *wai* respectfully as they chant.	This is done to earn more merit. People don't actually understand what is said, but the merit is gained by the words washing over you.
Monk's robes are laid on top of the coffin. Important people in the community are then called upon to present the robes to the monks.	This is another way of the deceased gaining merit. This is frequently a problem for Christians attending Buddhist funerals who are asked to participate, as a sign of status, by the hosts. To refuse is to refuse the status and honor being shown. Segaller traced the practice back to the old days when the very poor, destitute monks would take the cloth covering the corpse before cremation in order to make themselves new robes (1995, 44).
The pyre is lit. The host distributes incense, flowers, and candles, which the guests add to the pyre.	Incense and flowers represent worship; candles "speed the departed on the way to his next re-incarnation" (Le May 1986, 122). Participation is taking part in the burning and so showing respect and earning merit.

CHAPTER 7

HOPE AND SUFFERING AMONG SOUTH ASIAN BUDDHISTS: OBSERVATIONS FROM THE FIELD

Anton Francis[3]

I have asked several Christian youth from Buddhist backgrounds, "What was it about the Christian gospel that attracted you?" Almost every youth answered with a similar answer: "The hope which Christianity offered." With both youth and adults, we have seen that one of the greatest attractions of Christianity has been how we address various issues relating to suffering. If we are to understand this better, we need to first look at the attitude to suffering that they had when they were Buddhists.

THE PROBLEM OF SUFFERING

Everyone in my sample said they felt that the Buddhist approach to the problem of suffering left them without hope. When people spoke of the misfortunes of life, they often said, "This is my *karumē*." They meant that it is the inescapable consequence of the karma they have accumulated in their past lives. They have had this since birth and, although they have tried to overcome it by doing meritorious deeds, they sense that there is no hope of escaping it. They cited examples of even good people who suffered in this way. The Buddha's key disciple Mugalan was an arhat (in the Theravada sense), but he died under tragic circumstances because of what he had done in a previous life. The impression is that Buddhism has a negative attitude to life without much hope because basic reality is the presence of *dukkha*.

---

3   Anton Francis is a pseudonym of a Christian youth worker living in South Asia.

The scholarly Buddhist community generally has a different understanding of *dukkha*. They would say that it "would be appropriate to describe Buddhism not as 'pessimistic' but as 'realistic,' since it begins, quite simply, with the common facts of experience" (Bowker 1970, 237). John Bowker explains that "awareness of suffering is not symptomatic of gloom or despondency; it is, rather, the realistic observation of the way things happen to be" (238). Buddhist scholars even speak of people living in happiness and bliss here and now. Narada Maha Thera says, "Real happiness is found within, and is not to be defined in terms of wealth, power, honors or happiness. ... According to the Buddha, non-attachment (*viragātā*) or the transcending of material pleasures is a greater bliss" (1980, 321). Thera says that such attitudes are characteristic of an *Ariya*. "Average men are only surface-seers. An Ariya sees things as they truly are" (320). He defines an *Ariya* as "one who is far removed from passions" (82).

TEMPLES AND SHRINES AS PLACES OF RELIEF FROM SUFFERING

A common scenario emerged from my discussions with youth who had come to Christ from Buddhism. Typically, the father was inconsiderate and sometimes an alcoholic. The mother suffered much, and this triggered an interest in religion. Seeking refuge from her troubles, the mother began to go regularly to the Buddhist temple and sometimes to the shrine of a god. Often, one or more children would go with the mother to the temple. Those who ended up coming under the influence of the gospel were the ones who had gone to the temple in this way. A majority of the Buddhist youth who come to our programs come from relatively unhappy homes. This is not the same as saying that all Buddhist families are unhappy. I know of many wholesome families that do not fit into the above categorization. Our program seems to attract people from dysfunctional backgrounds.

The youth who went to the temple had been taught that they go to the temple to meditate on the Buddha and the Dharma, and that they are to find salvation through their own strength. They had been taught that the original reason for going to the Buddha, the Dharma, and the *sangha* for refuge (*sarana*) was to help them along the path towards nirvana. But now they were going to look for relief from their earthly problems. They sensed that this was not the original idea behind going for refuge. It seemed to them that they were looking for salvation through the help of someone else.

The sense of contradiction appears in the habit of going to shrines for refuge too. There are many Buddhist temples in our country[4] with a shrine to a god just beside them. Usually the shrine is to the god who is said to protect the geographical region in which the temple is found. Even if there is no shrine beside each temple, most Buddhists revere the gods and follow Buddhism with these two paths kept side by side without a conflict. They have been taught that the role of the gods is to protect the *sāsana* (religion) and to superintend over their particular regions. They were taught that the gods depend on the provisions and meritorious deeds of the people for their subsistence. But now the gods have this new function of protecting and providing for individuals. Buddhist reformers regularly arise to protest against the use of these shrines as places of refuge. They continue to say that people have created their own gods to fit their particular needs.

DISILLUSIONMENT WITH RELIGION

One of the most significant discoveries I made in my conversations in preparation of this paper was that almost all the people I talked to had formerly been devout Buddhists. Most of them said that they were the most devout of all their siblings. Most of them said that a major factor that led to their openness to the Christian message was disillusionment with what they saw in the temple. Generally, a Buddhist would not want to expose the wrongdoing of the monk because that would be to bring disrepute upon the *sangha*. This is in keeping with our shame-oriented culture where people do not like to bring shame to those whom they respect. They describe it in terms of respect for the robe, which, of course, represents the institution of the *sangha*—one of the three gems of Buddhism. The robe is also revered because it is what the Buddha wore.

Stories abound of how priests guilty of serious wrongdoing are assaulted after their robes are removed and of monks who wear slacks when they go to do illicit acts. One person told me that he was once assaulted by a monk but decided not to hit back. However, he told himself, "The day he removes his robes, I will kill him!" A former monk told me that he entered his chief priest's room and found him in bed with a woman. He said he immediately bowed in worship, explaining that he was not worshipping the monk himself but his robe—the institution of the *sangha*.

---

4   Country not named for security purposes.

People who are loyal to Buddhism primarily because it is the key to their cultural identity more readily act to protect the reputation of the monks without much inner turmoil. Those who sincerely seek to follow the precepts of Buddhism are more troubled by such contradictory behavior. Their sincere quest for pure religion may make them open to non-Buddhist influences. An authority on evangelism among Asian Muslims urges Christians not to think of devout Muslims, who seek to conscientiously follow the precepts of their faith, as unreachable. They may be more receptive than others are to the gospel because of their quest for an authentic religious experience[5]. This quest could overcome the cultural barriers to their being open to Christianity. This would be particularly marked in the case of young people who, given their idealism, tend to revolt against what they see as signs of hypocrisy.

I need to mention that some Christians from Buddhist backgrounds have told me that the fact that most Christian clergy do not wear a robe that distinguishes them as clergy is a hindrance to their being accepted as clergy in a nation where there is high respect for the religious robe. Pastors in Buddhist areas would do well to consider this when deciding what to wear. On the other hand, in our ministry, one of the things that attracted young people to Christ was the fact that those who preached the gospel wore shorts and joined them in the playing field. They saw that Christianity was a life religion, that one could be religious and have fun. This agrees with the appeal to youth in Ecclesiastes to remember the creator when they are young so that they can enjoy life while they still have the strength to have fun. The Bible recognizes that youth enjoy fun, and appeals to them to come to God must include having the best kind of fun (Eccles. 11:9–12:7).

Whatever one wears, there can be no compromise when it comes to the holiness of life within the church. One of the most urgent needs in Asia is for a revival of holiness that must characterize those engaged in evangelism. Some people with prominent evangelistic ministries are known to have serious character flaws that should have disqualified them from public ministry. Holiness seems to have been relegated to a relatively unimportant place in the quest for quick results and the overemphasis on power. Contradictory behavior is ignored because of giftedness. When those disillusioned with the temple join the Christian community and see this, they could end up with serious inner turmoil resulting in the rejection of Christianity. If the church does not adequately address this need, the Buddhist populations in Asia will not hold Christianity in high esteem. Individuals will

---

5   Source withheld for security reasons.

come to the church attracted by the prospect of meeting urgent personal needs. But before significant populations of our nations are attracted to the Christian gospel, they will have to see Christians demonstrating the high moral values that Buddhists regard highly but often fall short of practicing themselves.

Related to the need for holiness among Christian leaders is the advisability of adopting a simple lifestyle. The Buddhist ideal of detachment from earthly encumbrances has resulted in the expectation that those advanced in religion divest themselves of material extravagance. Thus they expect Christian leaders also to live simply. Some Christian leaders who see material prosperity as an essential result of faith in God tend to flaunt their wealth. Buddhists seeking material prosperity would be among those attracted to their churches. However, this will not help commend Christianity to Buddhist nations as a whole. The majority of the people would see this as self-indulgence.

Many Buddhists claim that these evangelists' funding comes from the West. This could unnecessarily cause people to be antagonistic towards Christian evangelism. They would accuse Christians of buying up converts through material inducements. I have heard people say, "We cannot compete with the dollars they get from Western countries. In their plans to control us, once they came with the gun, and now they come with their dollars and their religion. They are attracting our people through their affluence and through bribing them with gifts."

It could be that some of the attacks against Christians doing evangelism are because Buddhists feel weak and fear that they would be overwhelmed by the power of Western dollars. Could this be a situation where we should follow Paul's example of being weak to win the weak (1 Cor. 9:22)? The incarnational model of ministry involves going to people and getting close to them. If you display the trappings of affluence, it will be difficult to get close to relatively poor people. Those who come to the church through this means may come attracted primarily by the affluence of the Christians. It seems more biblical to go to where Buddhists are and become one with them rather than having them come to us.

EXPERIENCING THE HOPE OF THE GOSPEL

The average Buddhist young person usually does not have the attitudes attributed to an *Ariya* as described by Thera. He or she does not think that Buddhism associates life on earth with things like happiness and bliss. For those I interviewed, Christianity seemed to give a hope they did not find in Buddhism. One person said, "I didn't know what I was suffering for. I did not know what I had done to merit such a fate.

That was very unsettling to me." When I asked a girl why she became a Christian, she said, "I did not want to go to nirvana." She was attracted to the hope of heaven as opposed to what she saw as the nothingness of nirvana. It seemed to her that nirvana was an unworthy goal to strive for over so many lives.

A majority of adults who have come to Christ in recent years in our context have come attracted by the power of God to meet urgent physical needs. The majority of the youth, however, have come to Christ because they were attracted to the relational Christian message. I must clarify that I believe that God uses miraculous manifestations of power in meeting human need to open the minds of people once resistant to the gospel. That is clearly demonstrated in the book of Acts. However, I am claiming that in addition to this, the content of the gospel, especially its understanding of the relational nature of the Christian life, is often the primary attraction to Buddhist youth who respond to the gospel.

Specifically, these youth were attracted by the idea of living life with hope through a relationship with a God who cared for them. Several people told me that they were attracted to Christianity because it seemed to give the hope of overcoming their suffering through the intervention of God in their lives. Whereas once they had resigned themselves to their fate, now they felt that with God they could look at the future with hope. They could look at their life positively as a higher power had come in to guide them through life. Particularly attractive was the idea that God had a plan for their life. Most had fathers who had been bad examples. Now, there was the prospect of a father who would get involved in their lives and lead them to a bright future.

Unlike the adults in our church, hardly any of the youth that I talked to told me that they came to Christ attracted by the power of God. Rather, what attracted them was the idea that God is for them and cares for them. One young person told me, "If you tell a problem to a Buddhist, he will tell you, 'This is your karma.' If you tell a Christian, he will say, 'Let's tell God about it. He can help you come out of this.'" Youth generally said that the prospect of having a community that would care for them was one of the first attractions of Christianity. They felt that earlier they had no one to tell their problems to.

The story of Ashok is one example. He was the son of a dealer in illicit liquor. His mother resorted to the temple for relief from her difficult experiences, and Ashok was the member of the family who went most with her to the temple. While Ashok was in his mid-teens, his father died. A few years later, his mother's health began to deteriorate. Ashok wondered who would care for him if his mother died. He also decided to seek protection from the gods of the same shrine. Around this time, he was invited to programs of our ministry. He was not eager to attend a Christian meeting and initially rejected the invitations. But persistence by the young Christians resulted in his eventually going to an evangelistic camp. He debated with the leaders on many issues and returned home unconvinced about the validity of the Christian faith. Some months later, he went to another camp and there too debated with the leaders. One of the speakers at this camp, when describing God, quoted Isaiah 49:15: "Can a woman forget her nursing child, that she should have no compassion on the son of her womb? Even these may forget, yet I will not forget you." Ashok realized that this was the God he was searching for, and he committed his life to Christ at that camp. Today he is an effective youth evangelist.

Sachin became a Christian in university. He told me, "I suffered before I became a Christian. And I suffered after I became a Christian. But now there is a meaning to my suffering. I realized that suffering in the Christian approach to life has meaning for me and for others." He was impressed by the life of the campus ministry worker who led him to Christ. He said that there was a clear sense that this worker's life was lived for the sake of others. He suffered for the sake of others and did so gladly because of a passion for his work. Suffering seemed to be meaningful to this campus worker.

Another thing that attracted Sachin to Christ was that he sensed that "the messenger and his message were in harmony with each other." He sensed that the Christians he met practiced what they preached, that religion was a daily, hourly reality to them. Later, he saw that many Christians also did not practice their faith. But he had come to understand the power of the gospel by then, and this blow did not cause him to give up the faith. According to his understanding, Buddhism came to the fore during times of devotion such as in the morning and evening when the lamps were lit and the *pancha sila* were recited or when they went to the temple. But the *pancha sila* were not practiced by most people during the rest of the day. Even after becoming a Christian, Sachin felt that the Buddhist explanation of suffering, especially in the *abidharma* (the higher teaching), was more intellectually satisfying than the Christian one. While he was a Buddhist, he did not want to say that it was not practical, because if he did that he would betray his religion. He considered giving up on society and going into the jungle to practice pure Buddhism in solitude. He was troubled by the fact that most Buddhists did not practice Buddhism. When he saw Christians practicing their religion in their daily lives, he was attracted to Christianity.

BIBLICAL REFLECTIONS ON THE GOSPEL OF HOPE

What we see here is an alternate approach to the popular prosperity theology approach to Christian mission. Prosperity theology has attracted people with the promise of material and physical prosperity especially in poorer communities. There are many problems with this approach. Firstly, it does not do justice to the strong biblical insistence that suffering is the lot of every Christian. Consequently, people could get disillusioned when they discover that being a Christian brings suffering and the reversal of material and physical fortunes. Secondly, the promise of prosperity is not a key feature of the apostolic gospel presented in the New Testament. An overemphasis on this masks the heart of the gospel—that is, of Jesus Christ being the savior who saves us from sin and its consequences to give us eternal life. This could result in the unhealthy growth of the believer who takes a long time to imbibe the message of salvation from sin. An alternative approach is to bring into their first understanding of Christianity the teaching that suffering is inevitable for Christians and that God will use this suffering to bring victory to our lives. As Jesus said, "In the world you will have tribulation. But take heart; I have overcome the world" (John 16:33). The idea that suffering can be a meaningful blessing under God is closer to the biblical message and is more likely to help nurture stable Christians.

Romans 8:24 says, "For in this hope we were saved." Hope was a part of the basic gospel that resulted in the Romans receiving salvation. The verses that precede verse 24 describe the hope that formed a key to the gospel the Romans heard. Verse 20 says, "For the creation was subjected to futility, not willingly, but because of him who subjected it, in hope." "Futility" or "frustration" here has some similarity to the Buddhist understanding of *dukkha* in that it describes all of life as tainted by emptiness. This could be an effective point of contact in the presentation of the gospel. The cause of this futility, according to the Bible, is the curse ("subjected" by implication by God) that resulted from the fall of humanity. But the subjection was made "in hope." Pain is a reality, but its experience is tinged with hope. This hope is described as "the glory that is to be revealed to us" (8:18); as "the revealing of the sons of God" (8:19); as the "freedom of the glory of the children of God" (8:20); and as the "adoption as sons, the redemption of our bodies" (8:23). The attitude of hope is described using the language of the labor at childbirth: "groaning together in the pains of childbirth" (8:22). This is a realistic approach that accepts the reality of the pain of futility and expresses it in groaning. But in this approach, the groaning is done so with the anticipation of the birth of the new age, which will soon come.

This hope enables us to approach our problems with patience. "But if we hope for what we do not see, we wait for it with patience" (Rom. 8:25). Paul's idea of patience (*hupomonē*) is not the negative bearing up with hardship that we often associated with patience. It is a positive perseverance in the midst of hardship with the prospect of a positive result coming out of the hardship. Paul says, "And we know that for those who love God all things work together for good, for those who are called according to his purpose" (8:28). A key reason why we have this confidence is the knowledge that God is for us. "What then shall we say to these things? If God is for us, who can be against us?" (Rom. 8:31). Because God is greater than all the problems we face, we are assured of victory. "No, in all these things we are more than conquerors through him who loved us" (8:37). In the midst of the pain, we do not lose the most precious thing in life, our love relationship with God, "for I am sure that neither death nor life, nor angels nor rulers, nor things present nor things to come, nor powers, nor height nor depth, nor anything else in all creation, will be able to separate us from the love of God in Christ Jesus our Lord" (8:38–39).

We have already said that the Christian idea of patience is not resignation to one's fate but a means of working with God to bring good out of the situation. This positive approach to suffering has resulted in Christians throughout history being devoted to the alleviation of human suffering. This is seen in one's responses to a variety of physical, mental, and other disabilities. Buddhists are now active in programs to deal with a number of these issues. This may have been influenced by the worldwide push to overcome disabilities which, I believe, could be traced back to Christian activism. Still, many Buddhists regard all handicaps as an aspect of one's fate (karma) that leaves one in a hopeless situation.

E. Stanley Jones tells the story of a Japanese Buddhist university professor who went blind in mid-career because of a detached retina. He could not agree with what his religion taught about this tragedy, that it happened because of what he had done in a previous life. He was encouraged to look at the Christian answer to this problem, and he found the story about Jesus and the man who had been born blind (John 9:1–3). Here Jesus refused to accept the typical karmic explanation for suffering and said that the works of God would be manifested through the man's blindness. The professor said, "Could the works of God be manifest through my blindness? Then that is the answer: I'll use this blindness." Not only did this man become a Christian, but also he became an effective evangelist. He studied theology in Scotland and then taught theology in Kobe Theological College in Japan (Jones 1968, 182).

The hope approach to futility taught by Paul in Romans 8 looks to a positive end without denying the reality and the prospect of ongoing pain. It differs from the instant gratification approach of evangelism which majors on immediate eradication of problems as advocated by prosperity theology. This approach seems to be more popular in evangelism today. I submit that the hope approach is more biblical and more effective in the long run.

THE CHRISTIAN COMMUNITY AS A PLACE OF HEALING

The positive hope-filled feature of Christianity is expressed in Christian community life. Though there is a strong sense of community solidarity in Buddhist communities, there isn't much caring extended in connection with personal needs such as emotional needs and the wounds one has received in life. Recently, there has been a move to start small groups practicing such community life but this has not yet become very popular. Most of the youth who came to us have been greatly attracted to the fellowship and care that they experienced.

The fact that the poor are treated equally in the Christian community has been a special source of attraction to youth from relatively poor backgrounds who are angry with the class distinctions that exist in our society. In fact, when significant numbers of poorer youth first came to Christ in our ministry, they first reacted to the class problem with a newfound anger. Earlier, they had resigned themselves to the fact that they were inferior to the wealthy. When they realized their equality in Christ, they were angry about the way they had been treated, and they misdirected their anger at our leaders. Thankfully, that was a temporary stage. Once they knew that they were treated equal, they knew that they had no reason to be angry with us.

One of the significant theological discoveries I made during this process was that the New Testament speaks very often about how, as a result of his work on the cross, Christ breaks barriers that separate people. In John 10, after speaking about how he as the good shepherd will die for the sheep, Jesus describes how he will bring other sheep that are not of the fold. His audience would have known that he was talking about Gentiles. Then he made the revolutionary statement: "So there will be one flock, one shepherd" (John 10:16). After describing Christ's work of dying for "all" in 2 Corinthians 5:14–15, Paul says, "From now on, therefore, we regard no one according to the flesh. Even though we once regarded Christ according to the flesh, we regard him thus no longer" (5:16). Class and race distinctions are no longer significant. Now what matters is whether a person is a new creation in Christ (5:17). In Ephesians 2:11–22, Paul vividly describes how through the work of Christ, peace was made. Jews and Gentiles were brought near through the breaking down of the dividing wall of hostility resulting in one new person. Galatians 3:28 summarizes this teaching, saying, "There is neither Jew nor Greek, there is neither slave nor free, there is no male and female, for you are all one in Christ Jesus."

Because all of us are prejudiced by nature, it has been necessary for us to preach and teach the doctrine of the breaking down of barriers through the work of Christ regularly. We insist that no prejudice of any kind will be tolerated in our movement. At different times, this issue resurfaces and must be dealt with decisively so that a corporate culture which does not tolerate prejudice is forged and maintained. Those who think in ways that reflect prejudice are challenged to change their ways. It has been necessary for us to discuss issues of race and class with the youth, especially when something serious in this area is experienced in the society around us.

Another feature which the youth find very attractive about the Christian community is our concern for meeting human need. When one of our workers or volunteers finds out that the young person or his family has a need, they will go to his or her house to see whether they can help in any way. This is in contrast to getting the services of a monk. The urban youth I talked to believed that the monks were more attracted to serving the rich donors of the temple. They complained about having to provide a car if they wanted the monk to come for an alms-giving, a funeral, or any other ceremony. Monks are not supposed to own material things. They have to depend on the alms of people for their subsistence. The people, in turn, attain merit through this alms-giving. Thus arose the practice of giving alms to monks when they came to serve people at funerals and other family functions. This led to services being offered only if monks were supplied with their needs. Then came the current practice of monks giving a list of the things they want. This has become a burden especially for the economically deprived.

I was conducting a memorial service for a member of our church a week after she died. She was a convert from Buddhism and most of her relatives were Buddhist. The house was very modest with only one room. On one end of the room, the son of the deceased was smoking heroin. After the service, my wife and I were having a meal with the family when a person under the influence of alcohol came into the room. He sat down and in the course of the conversation told me how the monk would have sent his menu ahead of time and required an air-conditioned car for his transport. He said, "You have just come here to be with these people." He then asked for the times of our Sunday worship service. This incident gives evidence of the power of Christianity in addressing the needs of individuals.

The above attitude that we described towards monks in urban areas is not generally found among youth from rural backgrounds. In the villages, the monk is usually a beloved person with much closer contact with the people. He intervenes often in matters relating to the lives of the people. They can go to him with their problems with confidence that he cares for them. There is such a close link between the temple and the people in the village that often, if the temple is handling an issue, the police cannot interfere.

A major feature of a Christian theodicy is God's call to his people to participate with him in alleviating human suffering. Christians look forward to the new heavens and the new earth and do what they can to see the principles of that kingdom applied on earth. When a need is seen, it is natural for Christians to respond—not with the hope of gaining merit, but because it is an essential part of the Christian lifestyle. Christian involvement in human need has often attracted Buddhists to the Christian community. Some come because they have needs that we can meet. Others come to participate with us in the social work that we do. The desire to serve humanity is a felt need that is often neglected. Providing ways of meaningful involvement in alleviating suffering to youth could be an effective means of opening their minds to the Christian message.

BETRAYING ONE'S RELIGION FOR A PACK OF PROVISIONS

The opportunity that Christians have to help in situations of need also brings with it a special problem. Buddhists gain merit when they help people. The question arises in their minds why Christians would help people of another religion. As mentioned previously, they might see an ulterior motive in this. They could interpret this help as bribes to convert people. Almost all the young converts from Buddhism I talked to told me that other Buddhists asked them what they had been given by the Christians to make them change their religion. They often heard statements like, "You betrayed your religion for a pack of provisions." The Buddhist editor of a newspaper which had published several damaging articles about the church and Christian organizations, told a Christian minister that it was impossible for him to believe that any Buddhist would become a Christian unless he or she was offered some physical incentives. Even giving a scripture portion to a patient in a hospital is interpreted as an allurement that could result in an "unethical conversion."

In response to this challenge, we have adopted the approach of having a clear separation between evangelism and giving help to youth. We have a lot of education programs for youth, but no mention is made of Christianity during the tuition classes or when giving scholarship assistance. Rejecting or opposing the Christian gospel does not reduce the chances of receiving this aid. The young people know that this help is given by Christians, but there is no mention of Christianity during the carrying out of the program. The youth know we organize youth meetings that are of a religious nature, and some of them come to these meetings and accept Christ. But there is no compulsion to come for such meetings.

Despite making a distinction between evangelism and physical and other assistance so that one is not tied to the other, this continues to be a complex issue. People will misunderstand. On one hand, Christians cannot turn a blind eye to the physical needs that would not be met in the lives of the youth unless we help them. On the other hand, if those who help people with physical need also do evangelism, the accusation of using unethical allurements to convert people is almost inevitable. There are no quick answers to this problem. In the first half of the twentieth century, many who were committed to evangelism saw social concern as an enemy of evangelism. In the second half of that century, evangelicals realized that evangelism and social concern are partners in fulfilling the mission of the church. Now in the twenty-first century, in a few places, people may find it expedient to do evangelism distinct from social concern. Our church does both but does not tie the two together too closely. This is not for theological reasons, but in order to reduce the hostility to evangelism that we are facing. Each situation requires a carefully thought-out solution. All those who do evangelism in Asia today must grapple with this issue.

DOES KILLING ANIMALS RESULT IN SUFFERING?

Buddhists say that suffering is the consequence of wrong deeds, and we have found that the most commonly mentioned wrong deed said to cause suffering is killing animals. Christians are often caricatured by Buddhists as those who slaughter animals. Buddhists have responded in different ways to this issue. Some are thoroughgoing vegetarians. Others say that it is acceptable to eat some meats so long as the animal has been killed by someone else. To these people, the killing of animals is wrong. They will not eat beef because the cow gives us milk and does work for us. To kill a cow would be like killing your mother. They would be more open to eating fish or chicken. When the government introduced an aggressive program that encouraged inland fisheries to use the lakes found in rural areas, some monks strongly opposed it. This was not because they objected to the eating of fish but because they felt non-Buddhists would come to work in this industry and live in the Buddhist villages. These outsiders would upset the equilibrium of the community where the lake and the temple were the key markers.

In view of this antipathy to fishing and the slaughter of animals, we need to be careful about how we approach the topic of eating meat. Some Christians feel their context requires adopting a vegetarian lifestyle. It would be wise for all to avoid involvement in the slaughter of animals and in hunting as a recreational activity. The members of our church reacted very negatively to an illustration a preacher gave from his experience of working as a butcher. Ashok, mentioned above, said that even fifteen years after becoming a Christian, he still felt a tinge of guilt when he killed an ant. Christians should be known as advocates for the humane treatment of animals. A biblical understanding of the stewardship of creation does not lead to a connection between the killing of animals and resultant suffering in the human condition.

PROCLAIMING THE MESSAGE OF A SUFFERING SAVIOR

A leading Buddhist writer once told me that even though he respected Jesus, he regarded the Buddha as superior to Jesus because Jesus was killed as a young man in his battle for righteousness whereas the Buddha was able to carry out his campaign up to a ripe old age. The rationale is that people suffer for the karmic wrong they have done. Therefore, Jesus must have done some really bad things in order to suffer such a brutal and humiliating death. Because it is a stumbling block to the Buddhists, some have given less emphasis to the message of the cross in their gospel presentation. This is not an acceptable solution because the cross is basic to Christianity (1 Cor. 2:2, 15:1–4). The solution is to give it extra attention so that even though it is a culturally distant message, we will find effective ways to get the message of the cross across to Buddhist audiences. As we shall see, the Bible uses many different figures to communicate this idea.

I will make a few brief observations regarding the communication of the culturally distant message of the suffering of Christ to the Buddhist mind. First, the early Christian evangelists also encountered the objection that Jesus should not have died the kind of death he died. Therefore, we should look at how the biblical writers and preachers respond to this objection. The Gospels and Acts present the death of Christ as something carefully planned by God and predicted by the prophets, as a triumph and not as a defeat (see Fernando, 1995, 149–53). As Jesus said, "For this reason the Father loves me, because I lay down my life that I may take it up again. No one takes it from me, but I lay it down of my own accord. I have authority to lay it down, and I have authority to take it up again. This charge I have received from my Father" (John 10:17–18).

Second, the New Testament creatively employs conceptual imagery to get the message of the cross through to the minds of its readers. It uses the image of blood to refer to the violent way in which Christ died as a punishment for our sins. This is the most common image used in the New Testament for the death of Christ. The New Testament uses the image of purification where dirty things are cleaned (1 John 1:7, 9; Hebrews 9:14). It uses the image of propitiation from the temple ritual to express how Christ bore God's wrath for our sin (1 John 2:2, 4:10; Rom. 3:25; Hebrews 2:17). It uses the images of redemption and ransom from the marketplace where slaves were purchased for a price to show how Christ paid the price for our redemption from sin (Eph. 1:7; Col. 1:14; Mark 10:45). From the legal courts comes the concept of justification expressing how we are acquitted and counted righteous in Christ (Rom. 4:25, 5:16, 18). From family life and friendship comes the idea of reconciliation which describes how people who are alienated from God are brought into relationship with God (reconciled) through Christ's death (2 Cor. 5:19; Rom. 5:10). This suggests that we too should use our creativity in order to ensure that the message of the cross is understood by our audience.

Third, the idea of one dying for another is not as alien to our cultures as we might think at first. Sacrifice for another is a major value in every culture. There are stories in Buddhist folklore of heroes who died in order to save their countries. Here is one such story from Sri Lanka:

> Queen Viharamaha Devi was the daughter of King Kelanitissa who ruled Kelaniya. ... The king punished a monk once by boiling him alive in a cauldron of oil. It is said that the gods, angered over this cruel deed, made the ocean rush inland and flood the land. Soothsayers said that if a princess is sacrificed to the sea, the raging waves will stop. The young princess paid the ultimate sacrifice to atone for the sins of her father. She was placed inside a beautifully decorated boat and set adrift on the

sea. As soon as she was set off, it is said, the sea suddenly turned calm again and the water receded. (Lanka Library Forum 2007)

These stories and ideas could be used to good effect in proclaiming the gospel (see Fernando 1995, 141–48). The idea of one dying for another is not as strange as we might think. Given that it is the answer of the creator of the universe who made humans in his image, it should not surprise us that the cross agrees with the deepest instincts of all human beings.

Fourth, while guilt before God is not an immediately recognizable felt need in many Buddhists, shame before the community and the fear of evil spirits are very relevant needs. There is a strong emphasis on Jesus bearing our shame in the New Testament record of the death of Christ and in the exposition of it. It also presents the gospel as a victory over demonic forces. Paul says, "He disarmed the rulers and authorities [probably demonic rulers and authorities] and put them to open shame, by triumphing over them in him" (Col. 2:15). The idea that Christ bore our shame and defeated evil spirits on the cross could be the initial message that orients the hearer towards a more positive approach to the cross. The opening afforded by these truths could make the hearer more receptive to the message of Christ bearing the guilt of our sin.

Fifth, there is great appeal in the message of Jesus loving people enough to die for them to free them from the dreary cycle of samsara. As one formerly Buddhist youth told me, "The Buddha did all that he did for his salvation though, of course, he did preach his message to people. Jesus, on the other hand, died to save us from our sin because he loved us." People who scoff at the idea of needing a savior are sometimes moved to tears when they see the portrayal of the death of Christ in a film.

Sixth, the appeal of the cross is enhanced when one recognizes that it was the creator of the universe who died on the cross. A university student who was a convinced Buddhist first heard the message of Christ dying on the cross for our sins at a Christian student gathering. He found this idea repulsive and debated about it with the Christians who invited him for the meeting. His point was that no one can pay for his wrong deeds other than himself. When he realized that it was the creator of the universe who had died, it began to make sense to him. He reasoned that if there is a creator and if he is the one who set the moral laws in motion, then he can do what he wants in satisfying the demands of the laws he created (see Fernando 1995, 156–62).

Seventh, while the Christian message does not delve into the causes of suffering with the philosophical rigor that Buddhism does, it presents a way for liberation from suffering, a key aspect of which is that the God of the universe also suffers. He identified with suffering humanity as he took our pain upon himself, and he will come to us and be with us in our present pain (Kitamori 1965; Stott 1986, 329–37). This is because he loves us. This good shepherd died for the sheep unlike the hired hand who ran away when his life was at risk (John 10:11–14). This is a generation yearning for true love and for leaders who can be trusted. Many today have been hurt by people they have trusted but who failed to be committed to them when they were in real need. To such a generation this is indeed refreshingly good news.

CONCLUSION

The appeal of any religion is directly connected to how it handles the problem of suffering. The Christian answer to this can have great appeal to a Buddhist with its message of a God who suffered for humanity and opened the way to a life that does not deny suffering but approaches it positively with an attitude of hope.

CHAPTER 8

THREE RESPONSES TO SUFFERING: A CAMBODIAN CHRISTIAN PERSPECTIVE[6]

Barnabas Mam as told to Bruce Hutchinson

Suffering has not been an easy road for us in Cambodia. Like someone facing an oncoming storm, I have learned to respond in three ways—rest in God, resist it, or run away from it.

Born into a Cambodian Buddhist family, raised by my devout Buddhist parents, trained as a Buddhist temple boy by a senior monk who was my uncle, and then recruited and coached by a communist mentor for two years, I found it difficult to rest in times of suffering. But through my trials, experience of God's deliverance and provision, and the love shown by others, I learned the secret of yielding to God's will and discovering the inner strength needed to accept my circumstances. It took time to digest and submit to the will of God. Most times I resisted and didn't rest. The more I strived, the more it hurt, and the more broken and depressed I became.

A former communist activist, I was converted at a Christian rally in Phnom Penh where I was sent as a spy for three years before the city fell to Khmer Rouge forces under Pol Pot on April 17, 1975. I survived the horrors of the four year reign of terror and killing and hardship millions of my fellow countrymen and women and children suffered.

The church in Cambodia and the Christian refugees from the former Cambodian camps in Thailand count it a privilege to be co-partakers with Christ in his suffering. My church in Phnom Penh prepared me for suffering before the Khmer Rouge arrived. I recall the last sermon given by Taing Chhirc. A former Cambodian navy major who returned from Scotland to stand with the growing church, he would eventually face martyrdom along with most Cambodian believers after the time of great harvest. In his sermon, he compared the young

---

Cambodian church to the prophet Elisha, and the foreign missionaries to Elijah. All the foreign missionaries were told to leave, and only the Cambodian believers were left behind. Major Chhirc challenged the church to cry out for a double portion of the spirit of Elijah. He gave me a personal word of exhortation on that fateful morning of April 17, 1975, the words of Romans 13:1, "Submit to all authorities."

The Khmer Rouge then ordered the evacuation of the entire swollen population of Phnom Penh, almost three million persons. I was among them and, by the grace of God, survived the Pol Pot years out in the country in what became a giant slave labor camp and killing field. I went on to join an underground church in occupied Cambodia under communist Vietnamese control, then fled out of fear for my family's life to a refugee camp in Thailand where I taught and ministered to fellow refugees. God sent Mark Erickson, a YWAM spiritual leader, to spend thirty minutes a day with me praying. He counseled me to rest and allow God to fight the battles for me. The love and commitment Mark showed to my family melted my heart. I learned the secret of yielding to God's will and discovered inner strength to accept the situation. I was freed from self-condemnation and of being judgmental of others. Only then was I able to forgive those who had offended me. I experienced a breakthrough, and then preached the gospel with anointing, conviction, and results.

God used me to write and translate hundreds of worship songs. I eventually returned to Cambodia to pastor a church, disciple hundreds of church planters, and become one of the leaders in the rapidly growing Cambodian church. I established several ministries including helping establish a Cambodian prayer network that gave birth to a regional network. Now, as the Asian director of a local international ministry, God has enabled me to train national church planters and pastors in their respective countries.

I have seen the church in Cambodia grow in the midst of adversity. Some of this adversity was caused by people in the community and restrictive policies of previous government ministers towards church registrations. This adversity has helped to point the church in good and healthy directions of church models rather than a church with fancy buildings. The church has continued to grow in spite of persecution and hardship. Suffering cannot stop growth but only refines and strengthens it. It unites the church to pray, to accelerate the spread of the gospel, and to promote the exponential growth of the house church movement.

In 1979, after much of the country was liberated from Khmer Rouge rule, only about two hundred Christians survived the Killing Fields. Informal statistics obtained from a trusted source in the Ministry of Cult and Religion disclose that village heads throughout Cambodia have reported a total of around five thousand "places of worship" or dwellings where Christians (including various cults in Cambodia) meet regularly—in other words, house churches.

What do Cambodians see as the cause of the suffering of the Pol Pot era? Some blame former King and Head of State Norodom Sihanouk. Some blame Marshal Lon Nol (installed in a military coup that deposed Sihanouk). Others blame the passivity of Theravada Buddhism or the weakness and corruption of the Vietnamese. Some see suffering as the fruit of evil but don't look within themselves. Some Buddhists accept suffering as their karma—"Let's just swallow the gravel dinner." Fatalism is strong in Cambodia.

Some Cambodians have learned the lessons of the Pol Pot era but some have not. Those who are rich have learned to forget. Those who still suffer in their poverty learn to remember. There is a Khmer saying, "The gourd sinks and the broken glass floats," which means the strong will sink lower while the weak will rise up higher. The gourd represents nobility, the rich and the intellectuals, while the broken glass represents the poor and unschooled. So the Khmer Rouge was seen as the broken glass that floats. This concept has a scriptural counterpart in Matthew 23:12 where Jesus says, "Whoever exalts himself will be humbled, and whoever humbles himself will be exalted" and in 1 Peter 5:5b, "God opposes the proud but gives grace to the humble," where the apostle is assuring believers that Christ the good shepherd will lift those up who humble themselves even in the midst of suffering. If we admit we are weak and can't face suffering on our own, we have a chance to rise up as we depend on God. But if we think we are strong enough in our own strength and worldly resources to survive and overcome suffering, we will sink.

Among the population evacuated from Phnom Penh on that April day, I remember seeing some rich Chinese. When the Khmer Rouge government announced that it had abolished currency, some of these wealthy people jumped into the Bassac River near Phnom Penh to drown themselves out of despair. The poor, who carried food and cooking utensils, had a better chance of survival.

BUDDHISM AND CHRISTIANITY

The difference between the Buddhist and Christian approach to suffering is that Christians are instructed and empowered to depend on and rest in God in the midst of the suffering so that we can endure. Buddhists seek to escape suffering through dependence on oneself. The Buddha said, "No god, no Brahma can be called the Maker of this Wheel of Life: Just empty phenomena roll on, dependent on conditions all" (Visuddhi-Magga, ch. XIX). The Buddha even accused God of being "stained": "If God directs the lives of all that live, karma, good and evil, fortune, ruin too, then humans are but servants of his will. God is stained by what he's done as well" (Mahabodhi Jataka 528:19).

Christian teaching provides us with an understanding of suffering, the willingness and ability to share in Christ's suffering, and an insight into our own suffering as a means to bless others who suffer. We should not despise Buddhists for emphasizing escape from suffering, but should help them face suffering with the power of God's love and the promise of his comfort and the prayer support of other believers.

The weakness of the modern Christian church is that we don't prepare people to face suffering. We allow people to become overwhelmed by suffering when it comes. If we don't prepare the church to withstand suffering as "more than conquerors," then the church will be taken by surprise when suffering comes and will lose ground. Suffering is a blessing if we accept it with the clear understanding that God is there with us when we walk in the valley of suffering. Those who emphasize the prosperity aspect of the gospel can be helped to see that suffering is a part of character building. Those who are pious are called to suffer with Christ, not for Christ. If we suffer for Christ, we suffer for our own work, which is legalism, but if we suffer with Christ we co-operate with him. It is our privilege. Some churches in the West pray for persecution to come. We should instead pray for an understanding of suffering with Christ and the ability to share in it. Persecution will come soon enough to all those who love the Lord. Jesus said he would send us out as lambs among wolves (Luke 10:3).

Most of our local Cambodian pastors are not salaried. They are often misunderstood or persecuted by their own unsaved extended family members, but have found joy in serving God among their own people. Like Peter in Mark 10:29–30, they can rejoice in hundredfold blessings. Some even give up their positions as village heads or commune leaders. They travel long, bumpy, difficult, and often slippery roads to take the good news to people in other villages with joy. Some of them don't have good homes to live in; they don't have big church buildings for congregations to meet and worship together in, but they enjoy fellowship in homes as the early church did, and they have planted many churches. When I call pastors to our leadership and discipleship training sessions, they bring their own food, mosquito nets, and sleeping mats just to ensure they have a place to sleep on the floor of the training room at night. They pay half their travel expenses—some pay all—as well as their registration fees so they have a sense of ownership of the training program.

Suffering is not a means to justify or defend oneself, but for us to see who God really is, what he does for us, and how to respond to his goodness and mercy in times of suffering. I thank God that he sent someone to show me when not to resist or fight those who had offended me. In 1989, I was falsely accused by some evangelical leaders who wrote letters against my boss and me when I was a ministry leader in Campus Crusade for Christ. I chose not to defend myself, and the regional director of the ministry dealt gently and wisely in my absence with those who had brought the allegations. While attending a Christian conference in Bangkok in 1992, a well-respected missionary leader from America asked me if the situation had been dealt with, and he was able to bring some of those brothers who accused me to meet me at the lunch table so they could say sorry to me and do something to restore my reputation so I could be accepted for ministry.

I can cope as a result of this and see fruit now as the director of an Asian ministry. Higher promotion brings greater attack, but when promotion comes from the Lord, he also equips you to handle it as long as you sincerely cooperate with him. Suffering works endurance, hope, and character.

THREE RESPONSES TO SUFFERING

Suffering is a school of endurance. I have learned it is like a storm. There is a time to rest in God, a time to resist it, and a time to run away from it.

The first response to suffering is resting in God when storms come. During the Killing Fields, a lot of educated people survived by hiding their identities and acting as common people. David ran away from King Saul and then pretended to be crazy in the presence of an enemy king to hide his identity. As a believer, God taught me not to hide but to completely rest in him and let him fight the storm for me. I can do this only when I trust God's word, as in 2 Chronicles 20:15: "Do not be afraid and do not be dismayed at this great horde, for the battle is not yours but God's." Paul refers to this act of trust as our being seated with Christ in the heavenly places in Ephesians 2:6 and our standing with Christ in Ephesians 6.

The second response to suffering is resisting it. This demands a lot of boldness, discernment, and support. The cause of the suffering could be sickness or a system—that is, political, which in Cambodia meant they did something other than what they said. At one time during my time in a Khmer Rouge labor camp, I suffered for months from malaria without any medication, so I could not run away but had to resist and fight the situation. This produced in me a lot of perseverance, endurance, and hope; it drew me closer to God as I needed his help to fight it. As a form of treatment, my Khmer Rouge captors burned my wrists to kill the nerves by igniting small balls of dried bamboo fiber tied on to my skin. I still have scars on my wrists today, also around my navel from the same treatment for stomach upset. Another time when I had sore eyes, they held my head over a steaming pot of boiling rice and forced me to open my eyelids. I couldn't even cry out for the pain as this would have been a sign of weakness which at that time could have resulted in severe punishment.

I also learned a valuable lesson about positively responding to suffering from a woman by the name of Somaly Mam, who was sold to a brothel by her grandfather at the age of twelve. She endured hardship as a young prostitute until she managed to escape. She ended up in France, got educated, and then came back to Cambodia to lead a fight against sex exploitation, founding the non-governmental organization AFESIP (a French acronym) which acts on behalf of women in distressing situations. Through her ministry, thousands of young women from out of the sex trade have been cared for and reeducated through vocational training. Her fourteen-year-old daughter was kidnapped and raped in revenge. In Mam's life, she endured, ran away, then resisted by returning to fight.

The third response to suffering is running away from it. There are times when we need to run away from the storm, which can be caused by politics when some people decide to flee and migrate to other countries. Hundreds of thousands of Cambodians fled the Killing Fields and lived crowded together in refugee camps in Thailand, finally ending up in third countries such as the United States. Paul ran away from the Jews who plotted to kill him in Damascus.

So what was the good in running away—what were the pros and cons? For the Cambodian refugees, there was the chance to raise a family in a new culture with better education, better economic conditions, and living in a democracy. The disadvantages included separation from their own culture and extended family.

PERSONAL RESPONSE TO SUFFERING

In my own situation, I experienced all three responses to suffering. Sometimes I hid my identity and abilities (especially the ability to understand English) so I could completely rest in God and trust him to protect me and fight for me.

While in a reeducation (labor) camp in 1976 and 1977, I forced myself to learn from every task I was told to do, such as making fertilizer by mixing human feces with mud, then drying and pounding it to a powder. Like Job, my circumstances became one of my good teachers. Another of my tasks was to wrap dead friends in sleeping mats and bury them in shallow graves.

I survived my time in the camp by my wits and faith in God to see me through dangerous situations, experiencing many times the protection and provision of God while many others around me either died, tried unsuccessfully to escape, or were taken away to be executed. The words of Psalm 23 became very real and relevant to me. I knew Jesus as my shepherd, provider, and comforter through the valley of the shadow of death. In those darks days, I learned how to worship and thank God in every circumstance. In the ensuing years, God enabled me to write and translate many worship songs that have brought comfort and hope to many in their own suffering. Some of those songs are well received by prisoners in state prisons in Cambodia. I have been invited to preach the gospel to prisoners in a number of places, disciple some of the new believers, and baptize those who commit their lives to follow Jesus.

My conviction of the need to tell the truth probably saved my life under one of my twice-weekly interrogation sessions when I felt my time was up. The prisoner count had dropped from 300 to 127. The incident is recorded in a 2005 interview:

The Lord had told me that many of my close friends in the camp would die and only seven of them would survive with me, so when the eighth friend passed away,I knew I would soon be released. At midnight, my name was called. Normally, those who were called out at midnight never returned. They were interrogated and tortured ... often to death. I told a close friend to inform my home village that I had died. I gave him my shirt and pants and went out with only my *krama* (scarf) tied around my waist. At that time my detention camp was under the Eastern Zone Party, which had become increasingly pro-Vietnamese and would eventually overthrow Pol Pot. I was brought to the military headquarters and had to face ten top officers. They asked me whether I spoke English. I said yes. They asked whether I was a Christian. I said yes. They had all the reasons to kill me. However, they said instead, "Give him a generous supper". I thought they were fooling me with their generosity. Then I remembered Psalm 23: "You prepare a table before me in the presence of my enemies." After that the officers tuned their radios to BBC World and asked me to translate the news for them. Then they gave instructions for the guards to take better care of me and to protect my life. A few days later I was released, together with the remaining one hundred and twenty six prisoners.

I was evacuated together with hundreds of people from the east to an area near the Thai border, where I experienced the Killing Fields. The young people had to undergo a forced mass wedding, about three hundred at a time, and were killed after that. Miraculously, my life was spared. I became the personal assistant to a Khmer Rouge leader.

In February 1979, after liberation, I returned to Phnom Penh and joined an underground church. There I met Boury, a widow with 6 children. Her late husband was killed by the Khmer Rouge a few years earlier. We got married in 1980, and a year later the Lord blessed us with a baby girl whom we named Shalom (peace in time of trouble). In January 1985, I fled to a Thai refugee camp with my wife and three daughters (in fear of my life under the Vietnamese-installed communist government of the time) and remained there until March 1993. During that time, we planted fifteen churches, equipped 50 Christian leaders, and helped pastor a Vietnamese church in Ban Thad, another nearby camp in Thailand. When the Paris Peace Accord was signed, we were welcomed back to Cambodia. (Sze 2005)

By fleeing to Thailand, I was able to minister to my fellow countrymen in Site II camp, home to around 150,000 refugees. God also taught me to fight against the system and suffering by not just doing churches and running English language schools but by counseling and teaching counseling to those who had suffered so much, as the apostle Paul says in 1 Corinthians 1.

I have a story to tell of the traumatic experience of a young former Buddhist abbot from Wat Obok in Site II camp whom I was mentoring at the time: He had left the monkhood and become engaged to a beautiful Cambodian girl when a group of bandits in the camp came at night to rob her family of the dowry gifts and money he had given them, and tied them all up. All, that is, except for the ex-monk, who had hidden with his fiancé's younger brother in a secret place in the house. Through a crack in the wall, he saw one of the bandits attempting to rape his fiancé. The brave girl struggled and fought back, hitting him with a piece of wood, but the other two bandits jumped in to help their friend to try to overpower the girl. The young man could not stand it anymore, found an axe, and rushed out of his hiding place and struck the bandits, who ran off badly wounded vowing to get revenge. The family was rescued by his brave actions, yet the conscience of the young man—who had been brought up under the Buddhist teaching for so many years that killing any living creature was wrong according to one of the *panca sila* (the five precepts of Buddhism)—was so tormented that he could not sleep. The next morning, he was behaving strangely, could no longer control himself, and was gripped with fear—the fear of going to hell for his sin and of the bandits coming back to take revenge.

Through UN contacts in the camp, a place was found for the family to live under the protection of a Thai military unit, but the charm of the young women in the family soon attracted the soldiers' attention to the alarm of the parents, and negotiations were made through the International Red Cross to have the family repatriated. How could I safely follow the family through their journey of suffering? I could not reveal myself to the Thais as a Christian minister, but I could act as a translator for the UN officer.

LOVING THE ENEMY

My family accommodation was a typical bamboo and palm leaf building, situated in the compound of a camp church and surrounded by the homes of the families of Cambodian soldiers of the resistance army of the Khmer People's National Liberation Front. We were in the habit of praising God and praying together every morning and evening. Our children's ministry and English education were very effective and attracted a lot of children and young people to our church. I trained the teachers not only in English but also in singing Christian songs, counseling from a Christian perspective, first aid, and in hostage negotiation. The singing from the children, English students, and congregation brought hope to five Vietnamese hostages being held nearby.

One dawn when I was lying in bed, sick with bleeding hemorrhoids and a high fever, I heard the sound of strangers running up to the bamboo windows calling for help in English with Vietnamese accents, "Help! Help! We are Christians too!" and hanging onto the bars. I had to ask myself, "Do I ignore the plight of the Vietnamese because of whom I had to escape from Cambodia, or be obedient to Christ's command to love my enemy and help them?"

At my bedside were some young leaders and teachers who were visiting me, so I told them to offer help to the Vietnamese, who turned out to be a Catholic priest and four professionals. We were threatened by the Cambodian soldiers and told it was none of our business and that we would be killed along with the Vietnamese if we interfered. At that time, the Vietnamese and Cambodians were like Jews and Samaritans. We were not on good terms. The Cambodian soldiers punched the hostages and dragged them away towards the Cambodian border to release them into the hands of the army across the border, as they could not come up with the ransom demanded for them. But my people contacted the UN security officers, who arrived at the site fifteen minutes later. We discussed what to do next and were able to identify the soldiers' families, who pleaded with the soldiers by two-way radio to return the Vietnamese. After a few hours of negotiations, the soldiers agreed to bring the men back across the border and they were brought to a safe place where they were visited by a Spanish Catholic priest. He came to thank us for two reasons: for caring for the men, who were regarded as the enemy by many Cambodians, and for the love shown by the evangelical believers to the Catholic captives. This became a powerful testimony to the camp of Christian care and love.

STANDING AND RESISTING

One day at Site II camp, our daughter Poj failed to return home at her usual time from the evening Bible study group she was teaching. I became alarmed when Poj's sister Moj and mother reported her overdue, fearing she had been abducted. I asked everyone to start praying for her protection and for divine guidance for me. My faith was shattered. I found myself like John the Baptist who, having pointed people to Christ as the Lamb of God, sent disciples to check to see if Jesus was the promised Messiah. I also asked our young worship leader, Borin, if he had the faith to believe that Poj would be found. When he said yes, I asked him to pray for me. Pastors from other churches who heard what had happened came and I asked them to pray for my wife, and Borin and I left to search one camp after another in the darkness. At the border of our camp, Thai soldiers on night duty allowed us to go through to the north site to search. After an hour of wandering about, I sensed this was not the best way to continue, so we stood still and prayed for guidance. Hearing Cambodian soldiers talking to each other at a nearby outpost, we walked over towards them and I introduced myself in Khmer, asking if we could approach. We were welcomed warmly and I shared my dilemma. They took me to the headquarters of the police unit, where I met the chief operations officer, who then passionately contacted the other outposts around the camp by radio to find out if anyone had seen Poj, giving them a description of her and what she was wearing. Even while he was talking to the other outposts, I could hear voices on the radio saying, "We see her now, on a bicycle. She has a yellow blouse and three-color skirt. She's being taken by a man. We are so sorry now; she's being taken into the KISA (Khmer Intelligence and Security Agency) compound." They were sorry because they were not allowed into the security compound, and the chief police officer said, "This is all we can do for you. You need to seek help from others who have the authority to search there."

Borin and I prayed for more guidance and sensed God saying that we should not rely on military people, but on a civilian who was the closest friend of the KISA commander—a man who would speak peace. The name of Mr. Van Roeun, the director of the School of Fine Arts who lived in the camp, came to mind, so we found him at 11:30 pm. Though he was sick with a high fever, he was good enough to take us to see a Mr. Ta, a teacher of English and the principal of a camp high school and a very good friend of the KISA camp commander. Mr. Ta had heard of my reputation as a teacher of English as a second language and was also willing to take me then and there to see the commander.

When he heard my story about Poj being abducted, the commander denied that anything like that would happen in his camp, but with soft, persuasive words from Mr. Ta, he finally agreed to have his entire camp searched for my daughter. I thank God for my second role as an ESL teacher, for the commander also knew that I had taught many of his staff how to read and write good reports in English, which may have been another reason why he agreed to help.

The commander sent me to an outpost with an escort of six armed soldiers, suspecting that the kidnapper may have taken Poj there, and at 3 a.m., Poj was found and brought back to the camp commander. I walked back with my team in the pre-dawn darkness to find Poj safe and unharmed.

When Borin and I returned to our home with Poj, we were overwhelmed to see many Christians there who had been praying for us through the night, and there was great joy when they saw their prayers being answered before their own eyes. Later that morning, the chief UN officer visited me and collected information about my daughter's abduction, then called a meeting of all the camp commanders and administrators to raise a standard against sex trafficking. As a result, many sex traffickers were identified and arrested and the sex traffic system in the camp was demolished. I thank God that he allowed my daughter to be part of this.

Once again, suffering is shown to be a great teacher—a teacher of endurance under trial. We need to discern when to rest during the storm, when to resist it, and when to run away from it.

SUFFERING WITH CHRIST

It is appropriate that the Cambodian language discipleship series I have developed includes a module on suffering from a biblical perspective. In my teaching, "Sharing the Sufferings of Christ," the objective is to understand God's purpose in allowing us to suffer with Christ, to take benefit from the suffering and strengthen Christian character. The Apostle Peter tells us not to be surprised that we participate in the sufferings of Christ, and to rejoice (1 Pet. 4:12–13). Reflect on Matthew 10:22 and Matthew 24:9. Here, Jesus tells his disciples that suffering comes before rejoicing. John 16:20, 22. Suffering is like a cross and joy is like a crown. No cross, no crown; no suffering, no glory. The Apostle Paul encourages us to expect good things out of suffering (Rom. 8: 18, 28).

Suffering opens our hearts to see God's sovereignty (2 Cor. 1:3) so we can comfort those who suffer (1:4). This allows us to be even further comforted through Christ (1:5) as we endure more suffering (1:6). Today's suffering trains us to endure tomorrow's. Therefore, we can no longer rely on ourselves but on God (1:8–9). The hope of suffering is more deliverance. We can look back to what God has delivered us from, and forward to what he will deliver us from (1:10).

Suffering makes a way for us to receive prayer support (2 Cor. 1:11). God will raise up prayer support like a shield, even from those you do not know. Paul exhorts the Roman and Corinthian churches to pray for him (Rom. 15:30–31; Eph. 6:19–20). We need three levels of intercessors: very intimate intercessors whom we can trust with the depth of our suffering, such as that we can experience in our emotional and moral life; those we can trust with specific issues; and those we can trust with general issues.

Suffering makes a way to test and refine our character as is stated in I Pet. 4:12: "the fiery trial that is to test you." 1 Peter 1:7 states that faith is proved genuine like gold through suffering and results in godly character (cf. Rom. 5:3–4). Suffering makes a way for us to rejoice (1 Pet. 4:13). Freedom means a lot for captives; joy means a lot for those who suffer; food means a lot for those who are hungry. An English proverb says hunger is the best sauce.

Suffering makes a way for us to be blessed (1 Pet. 4:14). We don't need to run away from suffering, especially that which would make a way for us to be blessed. Suffering makes a way for us to glorify God (1 Pet. 4:15–16). We can suffer persecution for no other reason than because we are Christians, and if we learn to cope with it, suffering and hardship will become a stepping stone to higher ground so we can glorify God with understanding.

Suffering makes a way for us to receive the "crown of life" (James 1:12). The crown (not honor and glory on earth, but eternal life) is for those who have withstood the tests of hardship and suffering and have remained faithful to the end.

God's glory will be revealed in us, and all things we experience work together for the good of those who love Him and who have been called according to His purpose. When we suffer, we should not just look at the negatives but expect good to come from it.

CHAPTER 9

INVESTIGATING LAYPEOPLE'S CONCEPTIONS OF *DUKKHA*: GROUNDWORK FOR CONTEXT-SENSITIVE WITNESS

Alan R. Johnson

For most people growing up in a religious system, the natural assumption is that their particular group's practice of that religion is directly connected to specific teachings from their sacred books or traditions. The reality, of course, is that specific practices may have only a tenuous connection to specific textual teachings. The term "folk religion" is used to describe the configuration of actual practice versus the formal beliefs and teachings that grow from the religious texts. The folk religion focus is on everyday issues, a pragmatic orientation, and elements of local traditions mixed with the formal religion (Moreau, Corwin, and McGee 2004, 304). Cross-cultural workers who are interested in communicating the gospel to people in a specific social system, blind to their own folk practice of the Christian faith, often proceed as if the religion of the texts is the religion of the average person. This manifests itself in the study of religion as a system of doctrine and teaching rather than paying close attention to learning about the actual practices of people. Such study, while important and foundational, may not be that helpful in communicating the good news because local people's concerns and issues lie in other places than specific doctrinal positions.

Basham's work on merit and power in the Thai setting illustrates the complexity of understanding how people appropriate key religious concepts and draw upon them in different fashions depending on the situation (1989). He notes the central role of merit in the literature on Thailand and its connection to Buddhist notions of karma and hierarchy (1989, 126). Basham's problem is not that merit and power do not exist in Thai culture; rather, it is the tendency to give them too much explanatory power instead of seeing them as part of Thai official culture (1989, 128). His own interview data shows a significant minority of people that express disbelief in merit, while others give it lukewarm endorsement (1989, 129). He discovered that people who would "comport themselves in public as if they subscribed wholly to merit [including reporting belief to stranger-interviewers], express skepticism concerning merit in more private contexts" (1989, 129). His work shows that many people who really do believe in merit "find its explanatory value dwarfed by more mundane explanations for events which signal fortune or misfortune for those they know personally" (1989, 129).

I want to suggest that a more ethnographically informed approach to learning how people conceive and practice their religion and the kinds of worldviews that are connected to that practice will be more productive in developing ways to communicate Christ in a given context. In my view, the issue is not one of trying to find a one-to-one correspondence between a religious concept from the local religion and one from the Christian faith. The issue is more complex than that, and in most instances, there is no such direct conceptual mapping possible. Instead, we are looking for a configuration of concepts that relate to and move beyond local worldview so that the message of Jesus becomes meaningful in a particular social setting. Terminology is not unimportant, but of even greater import is finding ways in which the good news is actually heard as good in the Buddhist worldview and social system.

The problem of the foreignness of the Christian faith among many Buddhist populations, whose ethnic identity and Buddhist faith are intimately linked, is exacerbated by the presentation of the gospel in terms of a completely foreign worldview for them. They have to leave all of their frames of reference in order to understand the message. When coupled with foreign forms of church and social life as well, the result is that instead of equating conversion with a change of allegiance to Christ, people equate it with selling or betraying one's own identity. This is very much bad news and not good news.

The road to developing a more context-sensitive method for sharing the message of Jesus includes both a solid understanding of the classic doctrinal positions of the religious system as well as an incorporation of ethnographically derived insights about actual practice and salient worldviews. The focus of this paper is on the First Noble Truth of *dukkha*, commonly translated as suffering. My interest is to examine how laypeople in Thailand conceive of *dukkha* and how they deal with their suffering. I begin with some preliminary considerations first, laying a foundation for the importance of the ethnographic approach and its practical significance. Then I will look at formal definitions of *dukkha*, introduce the interview data, and conclude with a discussion of applications from this material to sharing the gospel in the Thai setting.

PRELIMINARY THOUGHTS
ON CONTEXT-SENSITIVE WITNESS

Before I look at the First Noble Truth, I want to argue with some conventional wisdom as it relates to sharing the gospel in the Buddhist world in order to show the practical significance of a context-sensitive approach. The first piece of conventional wisdom among many Christians working as missionaries or local believers in Buddhist contexts is that you do not need to learn anything about Buddhism; you just have to preach the gospel. The reasoning goes like this: since people are not really good Buddhists, in the sense that they do not go to the temple and they know very little about the actual doctrines of their religion, all we need to do is proclaim Christ and not worry about their worldview.

The problem with this is that we all experience our religion, to use a phrase from Tambiah, as an "interpenetrating totality" (1985, 257). So while for analytical purposes we can separate things and say that the Thai incorporate elements of Brahmanism, traditional religion, and Theravada Buddhism, people experience it simply as a whole, as their religion. Although the average Buddhist may not have formal doctrinal knowledge of their religion, they are deeply influenced by the goals, values, and worldviews of the folk version of Buddhism in their society. In our zeal to get the gospel out, we have forgotten to take into consideration the nature of communication, that it not only has to do with encoding the message, but also with the filters that receivers use to decode that message. Simply finding Thai terms to use does not guarantee understanding when those receiving the message are interpreting things in light of their Buddhist informed worldview.

One factor that has slowed down a dialogue on context-sensitive methods in the Buddhist world, as compared to say the Muslim world, is the fact of the existence of non-contextualized Buddhist-background believer churches. The presence of local churches that are visible, legally recognized entities with a long history, their own traditions and subculture, and various institutions such as schools, hospitals, and Bible training centers associated with them, makes it possible to live inside a Christian "bubble." In places like Taiwan, Japan, or Thailand with very Western-style churches, there are examples of individual growing congregations inside the insular Christian subculture. It lends the sense that the Christian message is working and having an impact to some degree. However, when we stand back and look at the total percentage of the population that adheres to the Christian faith in these places, it remains very small. The macro picture makes it very apparent that the bulk of the population is not easily responding to the mode of Christian faith being offered. Once we stand outside the bubble of the Westernized Christian subculture, it becomes hard to argue that we don't need more context-sensitive approaches. At the very least, issues of message contextualization need to be explored to determine variables in low responsiveness to the gospel.

A second piece of conventional wisdom that I have encountered is the notion that local people will automatically be context-sensitive. My personal observations that this is not the case in Thailand received empirical backing from the research of Nantachai Mejudhon (1997). He found that Thai believers emulated the practices of westerners in the way they shared the gospel (1997, 314, 283–318). In my own work, I have always been a bit surprised at how the majority of Thai Christians and churches I have encountered do not explore methodologies that would be more "Thai" in terms of both the message content and the style of communication.

A third piece of conventional wisdom has to do with the strategy to reach young people, particularly those who are in college. The logic is that if we reach this potentially influential group now, we will be able to share the gospel with many more people in the educated classes in the future. While it is true that college-age people in Thailand are the most open and responsive group, the fallacy is that after being turned into good Thai Christians in normal churches, they will be able to witness back into the Buddhist world. Helping them to become Christians is critical, but turning them into Christians who are socially and conceptually foreign to their fellow ethnic group members wipes out the very base of gospel ambassadors that this strategy hopes to create.

I want to argue that strategically we need to work both at the level of those who are most open and responsive, as well as finding ways of communicating the message to the core of the society. The possibility exists that those who do not respond from that age group can become even stronger in their Buddhist orientation in the future. Thus, if a foreign form of the Christian faith continues to be propagated, it will mean the ongoing isolation of the existing church in the society and the inability of the church to communicate meaningfully to the core members of that society. Duangduen Bhanthumnavin of the National Institute of Development Administration along with a team of researchers looked at religious characteristics along different age groups from ages ten through sixty-four with a sample of 3,450 people. They found that Buddhist religious practice increased with age, particularly among women, that religious lifestyle increased with age in adults, particularly in Bangkok, and that the relationship between belief and practice was greatest in adults aged forty-five through sixty-four years and university students, while it was lowest among secondary students (1997, 9–10). This empirical evidence of change in religious practice with age serves as a warning to strategies that are postulated on the assumption that Buddhist faith is unimportant to the target group.

I believe there are potentially vast consequences that can follow from a more context-sensitive approach from existing local churches and Christians in a place like Thailand. Recent statistics show that somewhere around 0.3 percent of the ethnic Thai are Protestant Christians (Thailand Evangelism and Church Growth Committee 2006). While there are multiple variables that are part of this slow response to the Christian faith, one factor is no doubt the forms in which the good news is normally communicated to people. If a concerted effort were made widely across the Protestant movement to endeavor to seriously engage folk Buddhists within their worldview with the gospel, it would play a major role in opening the door for large numbers of people to respond positively to becoming Christ followers.

DOCTRINAL BUDDHISM AND *DUKKHA*

In the context-sensitive approach I am advocating, the first step is to develop a solid understanding of the particular doctrine or concept under consideration, which in this case is *dukkha*. The goal at this point is to develop a baseline for comparison with the ethnographic data by endeavoring to understand the formal nature of suffering and its role within the broader worldview and metaphysics of Buddha's thought. The second step is to move from this definitional material to develop working hypotheses of how these formal doctrinal understandings might play out in the lives of people. This will then allow for comparison with the interview data and help to reveal the actual worldview structure and concerns of regular Buddhist people. Other chapters in this volume provide us with detailed treatment of the classical doctrinal formulations of the Buddhist concept of *dukkha*, so I will move directly to the next step of setting up some tentative hypotheses.

Moving from the classic definitions of *dukkha* we have seen elsewhere, what might be the implications for Buddhist practice? Looking from the outside at the concept of *dukkha* and what drives it philosophically, we can speculate on how this doctrine might impact actual practice. This can then become comparative material for what is discovered about actual practice from the interview data. It is reasonable to ask the question, what lay behind the Buddha's quest? He sought liberation from the cycle of birth-death-rebirth, and his enlightenment experience showed him that the human condition was an undesirable one, as well as showing him how to help people achieve a more desirable state. It would be safe to assume that at least some Buddhist practitioners would be motivated by this desire to alleviate their condition of suffering. It would also seem that Buddhist practitioners would be very familiar with the concept of suffering since it is so central to the Four Noble Truths and forms the essential foundation for the practice of the Eightfold Path.

Finally, because *dukkha* is so intimately tied to the notion of impermanence, it would seem that people would be very familiar with the notion of dependent origination, impermanence, and the no-soul doctrine as well. In the section that follows, I will examine interview data from both monks and laypeople to see how their views of suffering and their responses to suffering connect with the formal doctrine and assumptions I have made here.

INTERVIEW DATA

With formal definitions as a base, it is now time to turn to interview data to see how regular people and monks view *dukkha*. Between June and October 2009, I and a research assistant talked with twenty-two different people from a variety of walks of life. All of them were residents of Bangkok, except for one monk I spoke to in Surin. As is normal when asking people about things that are key cultural values, most laypeople and monks upon finding out that I had a question about Buddhism suggested that I talk with an abbot at a temple who had knowledge about this. However, I assured them that what I was really interested in was just how regular people thought about *dukkha*.

We talked with eight monks, all who were in their twenties, except for one in his thirties who was a recent convert to Christianity from the monkhood. I interviewed six people (three monks and three laypeople), asking general questions relating to *dukkha*, and tried to expand on items of interest. I then asked my research assistant, Prayun Maiwong, to conduct interviews with people using a structured question set.

Five monks were asked two questions:

How do you extinguish suffering?

What do you recommend to others in regards to how to extinguish suffering?

Eleven people were asked four questions and then were asked to rate how strict they were in their practice on a scale of one (low, not strict at all) to five (high, very strict). The four questions were:

What is the definition of suffering in Buddhism?

When suffering happens in your life, what do you do?

Do you ever bring this approach to suffering into your everyday life?

Why do you think people in general practice dharma?

Ten of the eleven interviewees rated the strictness of their practice.

Rating of Strictness of Practice	Number of People Responding
5 very strict	0
4	3
3	3
2.5	1
2	2
1 not strict at all	1

This small number of interviews was a good exercise in exploring the way in which people think about *dukkha*, and serves as a kind of preparatory exercise for more in-depth interviews and survey questionnaire work in the future. What was of interest is that even though the number of interviewees was small and the question sets quite limited, at certain points there was a very high level of agreement in the material and a definite clustering of ideas.

After I had collected my own interview data, I was connected with Geoffrey Wheeler of Udon Thani, Thailand, who was doing his own study on suffering and had talked with several Thai people on the subject of happiness and suffering. He captured interview material from seven people that he ran into in the course of his everyday life—at the post office, waiting in a hospital, personal acquaintances. The line of questioning that he used did not have a focus on Buddhist concepts but allowed people to talk about happiness and suffering. He asked questions about happiness and suffering in their life and let people describe it.

Here is a summary of the sources for the ethnographic data gathered from twenty-nine people:

Interviewer	Type of Interview	Interviewees
Alan Johnson	Open-ended interviews on suffering	three monks three laypeople
Prayun Maiwong	Structured interviews	five monks eleven laypeople
Geoffrey Wheeler	Interviews with people on happiness and suffering	seven laypeople

DEFINING *DUKKHA*

For the definition of *dukkha* we focused on what Thai laypeople think. There was a great deal of similarity in the answers in that they all contained one or both of the ideas of not getting what we hope for or desire and things that make us *mai sabaai jai* (unwell in our heart, upset). There often was an acknowledgement that *dukkha* included mental, emotional, and physical realms, but in general the answers focused more on mental and emotional states. This included anxious thinking about things and the emotional state of being upset. The range of terms besides not getting what we hope for and being *mai sabaai jai* included being lonely, stressed, disappointed, not becoming rich, sick, afraid, tired, depressed, anxious in thoughts, hot-hearted, and uncertain (*mai tiang tae*).

What is of interest here is the very concrete way that *dukkha* is described versus the philosophic stance that sees even pleasure due to its impermanence as a source of suffering. No one in our interviews ever connected *dukkha* to the doctrine of impermanence, which is so critical to the formal meaning of the term in Buddhism. In the way described by the interviewees, their notion of suffering is the same as that of suffering and pain at the mental, emotional, and physical levels.

DEALING WITH *DUKKHA*

In this question, we had two sets of information, one from laypeople and the other from monks. There was both overlap and some differences. What was striking about this material was the recipe kind of fashion in which strategies for dealing with suffering were listed, and the fact that the vast majority had nothing to do with Buddhist practice. Answers included crying, being alone, going out for fun, watching movies, looking for an answer to the problem, trying not to think about it too much, talking with friends, and yelling out loud. Monks overlapped with the laypeople in that they too recommended common sense types of solutions such as not thinking about things too much, trying to think of your own part in the problem, trying to use wisdom to fix the problem, releasing things, and not getting stuck on what happened. The big difference was that their solution sets were much more focused on Buddhist practices, which included reading Buddhist literature, remembering one's karma, meditating, controlling and quieting your heart, holding on to Buddhist precepts, and extinguishing desire. The concreteness of the description of suffering was followed by a similar concreteness in terms of dealing with suffering. While monks were more prone to advise Buddhist practices as a solution, they still advocated common sense approaches as well.

WHY PEOPLE PRACTICE DHARMA

I wanted to ask laypeople this question because I was curious to see how they framed Buddhist practice. Was it related in any way to the notion of suffering? What did they see as the ultimates of Buddhism? This question helps point in the direction of their worldview as to the reason for the practice of their religion. Even if it turns out that they live out their lives differently, nonetheless their thoughts on this question indicate how they frame their world.

Only two of the eleven interviewees said that Buddhist practice had to do with the relief of or deliverance from suffering. However, six of them said that it was for peacefulness and tranquility (*khwaam sangob suk*). It seems to me that the prevalence of this term provides the analog to the condition of suffering that is defined as being unhappy, no joy, or no pleasure (*mai sabaai jai*). If life is suffering, and that takes the form of being unwell in one's heart, the practice of Buddhism then provides the answer to help one have a quiet happiness. Other answers had to do with making merit, finding a place of rest for your heart, finding a way out, and avoiding evil.

What is of great interest here is the fact that only three of the eleven interviewees rated themselves as being a strict practitioner; the rest of the group was from the middle down. Yet their answers to this question were all couched in major Buddhist concepts having to do with tranquility, a cool heart, merit, walking the middle way, finding a way out, and relief / becoming free from suffering. This means that when they think in broad terms of their religion, they frame it in terms of major concepts from Buddhism, while in their actual practice they can, at points, as with *dukkha*, hold a view that is more practical, concrete, and this-worldly than actual Buddhist doctrine.

APPLICATIONS TOWARDS CONTEXT-SENSITIVE WITNESS

With both the interview data and formal definitions in view, it is time to reflect on some of the implications of this material for sharing the gospel in the Thai context. I hypothesized above based on formal definitions of *dukkha* that it would be reasonable to expect that the relief of suffering should be a major motive for practice, that people would be very familiar with the formal definitions due to *dukkha*'s importance as the First Noble Truth, and that there would be some connection to the notion of impermanence since the concept of *dukkha* derives from that. This preliminary interview data focusing on average laypeople and monks, rather than those who are highly trained, points in a direction away from connection to formal definition towards more concrete definitions of suffering and common sense methods for dealing with it. If further research confirms this as a general perspective among the average Thai Buddhist, then this material provides us with some direction for shaping our witness and discipleship content.

The context for the discussion in this section is formed by two positions which form the contrasts to what I am advocating as a more context-sensitive approach. The first is based on the research of Mejudhon that I cited earlier which shows that expatriate cross-cultural workers as well as Thai Christians in general use Western strategies in sharing the gospel with Thai people (1997, 310–11). His Buddhist interviewees indicated a frustration with these methods and felt that both would benefit by learning and listening from Buddhists (1997, 312). The second is the naïve notion that is a reaction to findings like Mejudhon's that the solution to the problem is to embrace Buddhist terminology in one of two fashions. The first is to, in essence, reinterpret Buddhism in light of Christian concepts, while the second is to go the other direction and say more or less that Buddhist terms are pointing to the same thing and thus there is no need to really stop being Buddhist.

Both sides of this continuum are problematic. The overly Western approach is so because it has patently not worked well in bringing a response to the gospel in Thailand. The approach which embraces Buddhist terminology and reinterprets it around Christian themes is unfair to Buddhism; Christians do not like this when the tables are turned and monks tell us what our Christian terms actually mean in terms of Buddhist concepts (such as God really is karma or dharma). The farthest out of these approaches, which levels everything off to being the same, syncretizes to the point of losing the gospel and Jesus altogether. Context-sensitive, ethnographically informed witness is something much different than either of these polarities. The foundation point is to be faithful to the gospel and relevant to the context, and its starting point is in listening versus coming up with pre-planned answers.

My first observation here is that this brief exercise in listening on the subject of *dukkha* points us to a starting place that is rooted in the psycho-social needs of Buddhist people. The interviewee's world is the experience of *dukkha* as the concrete problem of being unhappy (*mai sabaai jai*), and the goal in their understanding of Buddhist practice is to seek for its opposite, peace and tranquility (*khwaam sangob suk*). To start at either the notions of sin and separation from God, or the formal definitions of *dukkha* is to miss where much of our audience begins their quest.

One of Mejudhon's questions to Buddhist interviewees was, "What way of presenting the gospel would most appeal to Buddhists?" The answer was very revealing and is in harmony with my interviewees' thoughts.

> Buddhists mentioned that Christians should demonstrate the gospel in such a way that Buddhists experience the power of quietness and peace in their hearts. A Buddhist said, "If the gospel helped Buddhists to gain what they seek in Buddhism, it would be communicable and reasonable. Buddhists seek an escape from suffering, quiet minds, and *Kham Loom Yen* (cooled shade of life), happiness." (1997, 308)

We hear from Buddhists themselves that casting the good news of Jesus in terms of what they are seeking, while at the same time demonstrating this in our own lives, makes sense to them. Here again we see the contrast of the concrete, here-and-now experience for the average Buddhist versus the future-focused ultimates of escaping suffering by extinguishing desire and achieving nirvana.

In practice, this means starting in the terminology of their experience, being unhappy (*mai sabaai jai*) and pursuing peace and tranquility (*khwaam sangob suk*), and showing how the living God, interested in redeeming his creation, can bring what we are longing for. The interview findings point to an area for further study in that people commonly frame the purpose of their merit-making as helping them become *sabaai jai*. The notion of *sabaa jai / mai sabaai jai* needs to be explored in more detail as a place for talking about developing a relationship with God.

A second point is that, having made this argument about an appropriate starting point and frame for sharing the gospel, I need to hasten to say that a context-sensitive approach does not essentialize cultural systems and assert that everyone thinks the same way. We need to realize that there are people who understand the formal definitions and do practice their religion in a strict fashion. Christian witnesses need to be aware of the meanings of major concepts like *dukkha* and be prepared to talk intelligently with people who take their Buddhist practice seriously. At this level, there is also hard work to be done. We need to show our understanding of their conceptual world, be versed in its terminology, and make a clear presentation of where biblical concepts intersect with Buddhist concepts. It is interesting that one of the themes that emerged from Mejudhon's interviewees was the desire on the part of Buddhists that Thai Christians and missionaries should find good things in Thai culture and Buddhism as contact points (1997, 312). Perhaps one of the areas that can be appreciated is Buddha's role as one who diagnosed the human condition, helping us to see that something is awry. This can lead to a discussion of Christian views of the human problem, using the entire Bible as a tool rather than simply using sin terminology, as is the case in normal canned gospel presentations.

In my experience, Buddhist people expect there to be different things about the Christian faith. Even though the most common statement the Christian witness will receive in Thailand is "All religions are equally good, they teach us to be good people," at the detail level, people do not assume everything to be identical. Given a chance to dialogue, they are often curious about what the Christian view is on a given issue. To appreciate Buddha's insight about *dukkha* and the human condition and then be able to articulate a scriptural view of humanity's condition with contact points in Buddhist terminology is to follow an approach that biblical authors used. The authors of the New Testament frequently took terms commonly used in their social setting and invested them with new meaning that moved beyond the original use to bring an enlarged understanding of what God has done through Jesus. This was certainly the case with terms like gospel (*euangelion*), love (*agape*), adoption (*huiothesia*), ransom and redemption (*lytron* and *apolytrosis*), the triumphal procession (*thriambeuo*), and others (Flemming 2005, 144–46). Flemming reminds us that Paul was not afraid to transform and "convert" language from pagan belief systems (2005, 145). He illustrates with words like transformation (*metamorphosis*), mystery, and liberation, all of which had associations with Greek mystery religions. Flemming notes that "Paul seems quite willing to risk misunderstanding by co-opting language from the religious culture of his readers and infusing these forms with new meaning that in part alters and in part replaces the old" (2005, 145).

My third point has to do with some potential objections to my suggestion of using the common notion of *dukkha* as a starting point. The first is the question as to how this approach is different from current approaches. In my view, one of the strengths of the method of sharing that Thai Christians use is their emphasis on the experiential element. Thai Christians share their own personal experience of God's help, pray for people to have their own experience, and encourage them to pray for themselves. Thus, witness is not simply sharing content, but also creating an opportunity for people to meet God's power in their personal needs. This takes the form of answered prayers, healings, dreams and visions, and other personal visitations. It is these experiences that either create the initial opening for a person to move towards faith in Christ, or provide the confirmation for that decision. If many Thai Christians already begin their witness on the premise of God's power to help people with their personal needs, how is starting with the concrete experience of *dukkha* as unhappiness different?

Using these concepts as a starting point is different not because of its focus on personal need, but because of the way it is framed. The popular way to witness brings together a focus on the experience of God's power by the listener (which is good), but is connected with a method of sharing content that, as I have noted above, is not appreciated by Buddhists. This approach reinforces the notion that the Christian faith is a foreign one because many people's first exposure to the message of Jesus and the life of God's people is one that has very few connections to their lives as Buddhists. What I am suggesting is that the focus on personal needs be retained and that the initial framing be shifted to notions of the experience of *dukkha* as unhappiness, and God's ability to bring about tranquility in the midst of our circumstances. The gospel then becomes something that answers a longing already present in the listener's practice of Buddhism. Changing the starting point can help in lessening the sense that the Christian faith is foreign to Thai people.

The second objection is that we truncate the gospel to start inside such a worldview. It is important to keep in mind that starting points are just that— starting points to dialogue with a Buddhist listener. This does not mean that we stop there, but that we use that as a place to help people open themselves to a relationship with the living God and then move to an understanding of the fracturing of that relationship and how it can be healed through the cross and resurrection of Jesus. The third problem area has to do with discipleship and is not something new. When we cast the gospel and a relationship with Christ in terms of what it does for us, we are in danger of creating a version of faith that is self-centered and inward-focused. The gospel has to do with a change of allegiance; it is a turning from idols to the living God (1 Thess. 1:9–10) and following Christ as Lord (Rom. 10:9–10).

If we do not help seekers and converts move beyond the experience of God meeting their needs and giving them peace and tranquility, we are in danger of creating a sterile version of faith that is unable to connect people with God's redemptive mission. Context-sensitive witness does not mean that we abandon the scripture and work out of local conceptions alone. Paul's sense of his apostolic calling to bring people to the obedience of faith (Rom. 1:5, 15:26) indicates "that the apostle has in view the believer's total response to the gospel, not simply his or her initial conversion" (Köstenberger and O'Brien 2001, 182). Köstenberger and O'Brien show that Paul's use of the *euangelion* word group covers not just evangelistic preaching but teaching as well and includes bringing people to faith as well as grounding them (2001, 183). What this means is that there will be a necessary wrestling with how to understand both the local concepts and new ones from the Bible that is not capitulation to the old thought world or simply arguing for the new in completely foreign ideas. Building a new biblical worldview in converts must include more than simply repudiation of the past.

A final observation that I want to make from the interview data is the way in which respondents rated themselves as being not very strict in their Buddhist practice while framing the pursuit of that practice in very Buddhist terms. This is a reminder to us that even when the bulk of the populace does not appear to participate widely in formal religious practices, they are still shaped by the worldview of that religion. People in Thailand, strict or not in their practice, knowledgeable or not in their understanding of Buddhism, still identify themselves as Buddhist.

What the interview data points us to is that there is likely a configuration of key concepts through which average people view the world and frame their own and others' practice of religion. My own observations and Mejudhon's interview data show that the usual methods of telling the story of Jesus are cast completely outside of this thought world of seeking peace and tranquility, a cool heart, making merit, relief from *dukkha*, and finding a means of escape. Context-sensitive witness does not just appropriate Buddhist terms and reinterpret them or invest them with a different meaning; rather, it engages in dialogue to help people see how Jesus is meaningful in their own worldview. This is a much more complicated task. It means doing the hard, labor-intensive work of understanding the context and helping people understand Jesus in that context while moving them towards the worldview of the Bible. This involves much more than dressing up canned gospel presentations in new Buddhist terms; it is the longer and more difficult task of helping entire communities of believers learn how to live and communicate across two thought worlds so that they can love their Buddhist neighbors in word and deed.

One other point needs to be remembered as it relates to context-sensitive witness. Most of us as local pastors and missionaries are used to looking at techniques or methods that will bring church growth results as fast as possible. Context-sensitivity is not a method; rather, it is an all-encompassing perspective that influences everything we do. At the level of message contextualization, we are aiming for creating more understanding as the gospel is shared so that people have the chance to truly assess it and make an informed decision. It does not mean that people will instantly respond to any given presentation of the good news. The effects of context-sensitive witness need time in order to be seen within a particular setting.

CONCLUSION

My argument here has been that a context-sensitive and ethnographically informed approach to sharing the gospel has the potential to be more fruitful at several levels. It can help Buddhist people make better sense of the gospel initially, help reduce the sense of foreignness of the Christian faith, and open the doors for a wider response to the gospel. After exploring formal definitions of *dukkha*, I introduced interview data that suggests average laypeople have their own concrete view of *dukkha* and do not define it or shape their practice around it in the way of classical doctrinal Buddhism. Moving from the interview data and its contrast to the formal definitions, I then suggest that laypeople's understanding of *dukkha* can be a fruitful place to start sharing about what God has done in Jesus. My final point draws upon the interview data, which points to the influence of Buddhist concepts in the worldview of average lay practitioners. I advocate that Christian witnesses consider developing an explanation of the message of the Bible and God's redemption and its impact on humans with these concepts.

The interview work here is preliminary and needs to be developed further and checked in a broader audience to see if views are similar in different places in Thai society. Similarly, my suggestions regarding approaches in Christian witness are nothing more than an initial sketch that sets an agenda and direction. There is a great deal of hard work and discussion among Christians that needs to be done. While the approach advocated here can be used on an individual basis in personal witness, its most powerful implementation is at the level of churches and entire movements. This is because, at its heart, a context-sensitive approach seeks to address the issue of identity and the perception of foreignness. Exposing people to a vision of the Christian faith that is conceptually familiar to them could have a powerful and multiplicative impact that opens up large numbers of people to see Jesus as a legitimate life option for them.

AN EVANGELICAL CHRISTIAN OBSERVATION OF THE CORRELATION BETWEEN THE BUDDHIST VIEW OF SORROW (*DUKKHA*) AND SUICIDE IN SRI LANKA

G. P. V. *Somaratna*

Buddhism constitutes the religious faith of about seventy percent of the population in Sri Lanka and is primarily of the Theravada school. According to traditional Sri Lankan chronicles, Buddhism was introduced to Sri Lanka in the third century BC. Sri Lanka has the longest continuous history of Buddhism of any Buddhist nation, with the *sangha* having existed in a largely unbroken lineage since its introduction. Theravada Buddhist institutions in Sri Lanka have nourished the Sinhalese culture for over two thousand years. The character, traditions, art, literature, architecture, language, and other aspects of Sinhalese culture have a heavy influence of Buddhist teachings.

Buddhism practiced in Sri Lanka is complex and varied. One can notice two forms of Buddhism which Milford E. Spiro refers to as nirvanic and karmic Buddhism. According to nirvanic Buddhism, it is a religious way of life: avoiding all evil deeds, promoting life by doing good deeds, and purifying the mind from mental impurities. The concept of a supreme creator God is rejected or at least considered irrelevant to Theravada Buddhism. Buddha is regarded as supreme sage, the model of a fully enlightened person. As there is no belief in God, no incarnations of God are worshipped. Dharma without a personal divine being does not have a relational aspect, although worshippers offer flowers at the statues of the Buddha—which they know are inanimate objects.

HUMAN LIFE

Human life is the most difficult to achieve in the cycle of samsara and is considered a rare and priceless privilege because the human mentality presents a distinctive capacity to choose and to change its karma. Buddhism extols the value of human life, for birth as a human being is the culmination of the individual's efforts through many previous cycles of birth and an upward step on the way to ultimate enlightenment. Humans have a very special status in Buddhism—for only a human can attain full enlightenment as Buddha. Although a bodhisattva can take many different types of lives (for instance, as an animal or a deva), Buddhas are always human (Dhirasekera 5:545). Humans can be seen as highly favored because only they have the ability to seek out the Dharma and the means to listen to it and follow it. Buddhists believe that human rebirth is extremely rare in the cycle of samsara (Guenther 1959, 17). Its likelihood is expressed in terms of a half-blind turtle rising from the depths of the ocean to the surface once in hundreds of years and putting its head through the hole of a cattle yoke tossed about by the winds and currents on the waves of the ocean—all this being greater than that of achieving rebirth as a human (Bodhi 1995, 129).

Among the lower realms, *pretas* (spirits) and dwellers in the netherworlds are gripped by pain and fear and have to endure their lot but cannot better themselves. Animals are intellectually unable to understand the Dharma in full. The way of life of the demons is dominated by violence and is antithetical to the teachings of the Dharma, while most of the gods simply enjoy reaping the fruits of their past actions and do not concern themselves with the future. The teaching of the *Balapandita Sutta* was given by the Buddha at Savatthi on the topic of the characteristic behavior of fools (Bodhi 1995, 129). It shows how evil thoughts, words, deeds, and actions lead fools to states of misery and anguish. The Mahayana Sanskrit text *Bodhicaryavatara* of the seventh century also repeats this story. The Sinhala work *Lovadasangara* written in the fifteenth century repeats the idea expressed in the sutra for the ordinary Sinhala reader. When their past *kusal karma* have all had their result, these devas will fall into lower worlds and suffer again. The Sinhalese Buddhists are aware of all these facts. However, it is ironic that the highest rate of suicide in the world exists in this society where human life is considered so rare.

SUICIDE

Suicide is the act of killing oneself. It is deliberately initiated and performed by a person with full knowledge of its fatal outcome. Self-inflicted violence can be considered as a specific act of violence where both the perpetrator and the victim are the same. This is essentially a phenomenon peculiar to mankind. While self-inflicted violence can result in death, suicide is only a part of this serious problem; many more survive attempts to take their own lives and live to suffer the consequences.

This act of self-harm remains a serious social problem and is the eighth leading cause of death in Sri Lanka. Studies have shown that as much as forty-one percent of the intensive care units of rural hospitals are occupied by victims of self-inflicted injuries. The heaviest concentration is among teenagers and young adults. This signifies personal distress among individuals and strains in the fabric of rural communities. Suicide victims have overburdened the country's medical resources. Suicide creates a profound sense of loss for both those close to the event and for the wider community (National Report 2008, 69).

Sri Lanka had the highest rate of suicide in the world in 1995, with an estimated 47 suicides for every 100,000 persons. There was a fifteen percent increase in suicides over all age groups between 1990 and 1995, and the number of suicides among people aged sixty years and above increased by fifty percent in the same period. Three times as many men as women killed themselves. Seventy-five percent of the suicides have occurred in rural areas.

BUDDHISM AND SUICIDE

Suicidal behavior is a major health concern in many countries, developed and developing alike. At least one million people are estimated to die annually from suicide worldwide. Many more people, especially the young and middle-aged, attempt suicide. Sri Lanka is among the thirteen countries with suicide rates fifty percent or more above the mean in the world. In societies where Buddhism and Hinduism dominate, suicide has been higher than the rest. Japan, China, and South Korea are among the countries where the suicide rate is increasing. The exception is Thailand, where the rate is 6.3 per 100,000, and where taking one's own life is believed to lead to condemnation to hell for 500 lifetimes. Sri Lanka, which has a predominantly Buddhist population, reveals that a large number of suicides are among Buddhists even though their religion does not favor suicide.

However, the belief in rebirth and the lack of definite statements on suicide by Buddha make suicide much less "sinful" than killing another person.

HIGH RATE OF SUICIDE IN SRI LANKA

According to a hospital-based study in 2000, an average of one percent of hospital admissions were related to suicide attempts (H. J. De Silva et al. 2000, 17–24). The WHO report ranks Sri Lanka among the four Asian countries with estimated suicide rates at over 20 self-inflicted deaths per 100,000 people. According to the Institute for Research and Development, a Sri Lankan nonprofit forum of professionals and academics, the island, in 2007, had a rate of about 21 suicides per 100,000 people. Although the rate has dropped since 1995 (when it peaked at 46.6 suicides per 100,000 people), the figure still remains high. The rate of female suicide in Sri Lanka being 18.9 to 100,000 makes it the highest rate of female suicide in the world (Kearney 1985, 81; World Health Organization 2003).

Police records also show a plunge in the number of suicides over the past few years from a peak of 8,449 in 1995 to 4,504 in 2006 and 4,225 in 2007. However, these figures also reveal that of the deaths recorded as suicides in 2006, more than half were due to poison, with some 2,268 men and 519 women consuming toxic substances (primarily readily available pesticides). The accurate number of suicides is likely to be higher as some deaths that are thought to be accidents, like single car accidents, overdoses, or shootings, are not recognized as suicide. Suicide is the eighth leading cause of death in males and the sixteenth leading cause of death in females. It is the third leading cause of death for the age group ten to twenty-four years. Trends in rates of suicides for teens fifteen to nineteen years of age are even higher. It indicates that from 1950 to 1990, the frequency of suicides increased by three hundred percent, and from 1990 to 2003, the rate decreased by thirty-five percent.

DECREASE

Sri Lanka's recent decreasing suicide trend is the result of the proposals of the presidential task force appointed in 1996. The recommendations made by this committee were instrumental in amending the penal code in 1998, which made suicide no longer a crime. The lethality of pesticide was reduced and accessibility to highly lethal products curtailed. The dramatic publicizing of suicide in the mass media also discouraged it.

ATTEMPTED SUICIDE

Most acts of self-harm do not end in death. Some studies have shown as many as twelve to thirteen unsuccessful acts of self-harm for each death (H. J. De Silva et al. 2000). A moderate number of six to eight has also been suggested (Morcek and Ratnayake 2001). The National Health Bulletin states that the main cause of death in the age group fifteen to twenty-five in Sri Lanka is suicide. The districts in Sri Lanka which show records of a high incidence of suicide have experienced high rates of population growth as a result of migration. Owing to variable standards in certifying deaths, the legal and social consequences of suicide, and the difficulty of identifying a suicide, the reported rates of suicide in some parts of rural Sri Lanka are low. Many of these are "protest suicides." They are only semi-serious, but up to ten percent of them turn out to be fatal.

A suicide attempt is sometimes interpreted as a "cry for help" and attention, or to express despair and the wish to escape, rather than a genuine intent to die. Most people who attempt suicide do not complete suicide on a first attempt; those who gain a history of repetition have a significantly higher probability of completing suicide.

DUKKHA

The nucleus of the Buddhist teaching lies in the Four Noble Truths, which were expounded in the Buddha's very first sermon entitled "The Great Discourse on the Turning of the Wheel of Dharma" (Bodhi 2003, 56.11). They are: suffering, the origin of suffering, the cessation of suffering, and the way leading to the cessation of suffering.

> Now this, monks, is the Noble Truth of stress: birth is stressful, aging is stressful, death is stressful; sorrow, lamentation, pain, distress, and despair are stressful; association with the unbeloved is stressful, separation from the loved is stressful, not getting what is wanted is stressful. In short, the five clinging-aggregates are stressful. (Dhammacakkappavattana 2003, 56.11)

According to the Buddha's Noble Truths, one cannot run away from suffering—it is there in everything one experiences in the world. "It is as though there is nothing left to do about our suffering except to go, as it were, straight to Nirvana. There is no other hope" (Sangharakshita 1996, 78–9).

The foremost truth about the human condition, according to Buddhism, is the reality of *dukkha*. The term *dukkha* indicates all frustrations, discontents, unhappiness, disappointments, and all unsatisfactory states of affairs characteristic of the world's mental and material environment. The prevalence of *dukkha* in all its different forms is dependent on the activity of unwholesome (*akusal*) mental processes. All inner psychological conflicts as well as conflicts produced in society are traced in Buddhism to these causes. The behavior of the large majority of living beings is determined by the mental processes referred to in Buddhism as unskilled or unwholesome. Conflict in society is therefore considered in Buddhism to be endemic (Premasiri 2006, 78–85).

Depressed people often report feelings of diminished self-esteem which, according to Buddhism, is *dukkha*. *Dukkha* is a part of a more global emotional state when an individual withdraws from other activities and seemingly reinvests them inward. Certain events that occur as a part of life carry *dukkha* as a component. Endings, separations, losses, and death elicit strong emotional reactions in those who are experiencing them; *dukkha* is often a part. More specifically, divorce, moving to a new place, graduations, the end of a romantic relationship, a good friend moving away, the completion of a major project, and the death of a loved one are examples of normal events that can evoke strong, reactive *dukkha*.

The Buddhist *bana* preaching often resorts to *dukkha*, which forms an important part in the exposition of the dharma. Any response to the human condition is an attempt to deal with the ills, sufferings, unhappiness, and disconnectedness of human life (Halverson 1978, 221). All these terms have been used to convey the meaning of the Pali word *dukkha* as Buddha identifies the Four Noble Truths. These conceptions are fundamental to all levels of the Sinhalese religious complex. The Buddhist system of the Sinhalese involves apparent anomalies and contradictions of belief which are connected by the common thread of *dukkha*.

The view that life is sorrowful is imbedded in the Sinhalese worldview. A village woman who fails in a mundane affair would say "*aniccan, dukkhan*" as a kind of exclamation. Some popular modern Sinhalese songs also carry a melancholic nature and convey the idea of *dukkha*.

CAUSES

A number of factors are associated with the risk of suicide, including: mental illness, drug addiction, and socioeconomic factors. Although psychiatrists see psychopathology as the underlying cause for suicide, there is a wide range of causes which contribute to suicide. Demographic, social, environmental, generic, and religious factors increase the risk of suicidal behavior. In any case, suicidal behavior may be multifaceted. It is often hard to find the cause of the sorrow which leads a person to commit suicide. Our attention, in this article, will be focused on sociological factors relating to the Buddhist teaching of *dukkha* where the Christian church can intervene positively.

Economic and social hardship faced by families, and physical and psychological abuse of women in the domestic environment (especially women living with in-laws, with no social contact and support) may trigger thoughts of suicide. While external circumstances, such as a traumatic event, may prompt suicide, it does not seem to be an independent cause. Individuals from dysfunctional family backgrounds and high residential mobility are seen to be at high risk for suicidal behavior (Ferguson 2001, 747–753). Thus, suicides are likely to occur during periods of socioeconomic, family, and individual crises. According to four psychiatrists who worked in hospitals in Sri Lanka, suicide is not an indication of depression or other serious psychopathological ailments. Suicide in "Sri Lanka is just an impulsive act."

IMPERMANENCE *(VIPARINAMA-DUKKHA)*

Impermanence (*anicca*) is one of the essential doctrines or three marks of existence in Buddhism. The term expresses the Buddhist notion that all of conditioned existence, without exception, is in a constant state of flux. According to the impermanence doctrine, human life embodies this flux in the aging process, the cycle of birth and rebirth (samsara), and in any experience of loss. This is applicable to all beings. Buddha taught that, because conditioned phenomena are impermanent, attachment to them becomes the cause for future suffering (*dukkha*). Impermanence is intimately associated with the doctrine of *anattā*, according to which things have no fixed nature, essence, or self. The popular singer W. D. Amaradewa sings most of his songs on the *viparinama-dukkha* (suffering from impermanence) in the samsara. The constant teaching of Buddhism is the liberation from *dukkha*. *Dukkha* caused by constant change is reflected in the average person's social circumstances.

THE BUDDHIST CANON ON SUICIDE

Much scholarly writing on suicide presented from a Buddhist viewpoint has an academic or apologetic focus. Suicide is regarded ambiguously in the Pali canon. There are passages in the Buddhist scripture where the Buddha approved the suicide of *bhikkhus* who were struck by pain and sorrow. A short examination of cases of suicide in the Pali canon would be useful, as teachings embodied in them would be used in contemporary Buddhist preaching. According to the *Samyutta Nikaya*, a Buddhist monk named Vakkali fell ill while on his way to visit the Buddha at Rajagrha and, being in great pain, committed suicide by slashing his throat (Bodhi 2003, 938–41). The Buddha went to see his body and declared that he had attained nirvana, and that Mara would be unable to find his departed consciousness (*vijñana*). Similar cases of the suicide of Godhika (Bodhi 2000, 212–15) and Channa (*Channovaada Sutta* 1995, 1114–16) show that the Buddha actually condoned their suicides on the grounds that the three *bhikkhus* were *arahants*. Since *arahants* are regarded as liberated persons, they were in their last birth. Some scholars, using these passages, have indicated that suicide to overcome sorrow is prohibited for the unenlightened but permitted for the enlightened (Lamotte 1975, 106). Similarly, on one occasion, a group of monks meditating on the repulsiveness of the body, without proper guidance, became depressed and killed themselves (Vin. III, 68–70). The Buddha did not comment on their death even though they were not *arahants*. The commentary interprets it as Buddha trying to teach about the effects of karmically inevitable suicide. The idea of a karmically predetermined suicide seems difficult to reconcile with the conception of suicide as a volitionally induced act (CD 1951). In a 1993 monograph on the subject of death in Buddhism, some scholars asserted that the Buddhist tradition, especially in Japan, is very tolerant of suicide and euthanasia. Evidence of this is the Buddha's tolerance of the suicide of monks (Wiltshire 1983) and Sinhala stories praising suicide by monks and laypeople.

HERO

Since Buddhism neither promotes nor prohibits suicide, this has had a grave effect on the Buddhist attitude towards suicide at times of sorrow. This ambiguous attitude has, at times, even led to the appreciation of suicide as a heroic act. The Buddhist chronicle *Mahavamsa* includes narratives about the suicide of Sinhala kings at times of *dukkha*. One such narrative details how when the poet Kalidasa was murdered by a courtesan in Sri Lanka during the reign of Kumaradasa, the king, in his deep sorrow, jumped into the fire of the funeral pyre of his friend, Kalidasa. A contemporary parallel is how, on hearing of the murder of film idol and politician Wijaya Kumaratunga, some of his admirers committed suicide as they could not bear their sorrow. When General Kobbekaduwa was to be removed from office in 1991, three Buddhist monks threatened public self-immolation. As we can see from newspaper reports and suicide notes, this heroic attitude has encouraged people to willfully terminate their lives at times of sorrow.

Although there are no proper records regarding suicide in the past, history shows that Sinhalese Buddhists had an attitude of tolerance towards acts of suicide. An English traveler noticed that suicide was frequent amongst the Sinhalese in the nineteenth century, and it was "frequently committed under such circumstances as show no extraordinary contempt of life, and at the same time a desire of revenge" (D'oyly 1919, 56). Emerson Tennant, Government Agent of Kandy in the 1850s, reported that the Sinhalese had a habit of borrowing money which they were unable to pay back which led them to commit suicide.

ETHICAL

Buddhists live by ethical codes which are both a guideline for action and a catalyst to growing awareness and a deeper understanding of life. The first precept of Buddhism is not to kill. At a simple level, this is interpreted as not killing any creature. Buddhism does not make a great distinction between humans and other sentient beings. Killing is the absolute negation of a being. Killing oneself is one variation of killing a living being and is therefore seen in a negative light as simply another cause of suffering.

The five precepts of Buddhism have intrinsic difficulties. The first precept which prohibits killing has not generally been interpreted as to impose vegetarianism, which was never a norm of Sinhalese Buddhism (Obeyesekere 1990, 28). Similarly, the fact that this precept equals human beings with other beings enables Buddhists to think lightly of killing of a human being, as they are regularly compelled to kill non-human beings either for food or for security. It does not address the consumption of flesh from animals that are already killed. Taking part in killing for food is incompatible with the first precept. This includes hunting, fishing, trapping, butchering, and so on. However, the fact that monks eat meat means that someone else is encouraged to do the killing for them. It therefore allows for someone else to do the "dirty work" while the adherent can feel comfortable with the Buddhist principles of compassion and non-harming. Pesticides that rural people use for suicide are intended to kill insects and rodents which in turn is a violation of the first precept. Therefore, the validity of the first Buddhist precept as a deterrent for killing may in fact work as an encouragement to homicide and suicide, both of which are very high among Buddhists in Sri Lanka.

The themes of impermanence, decay, and death are omnipresent in Buddhist literature. In many Asian cultures, Buddhism is identified as the authority par excellence on matters pertaining to death, and is closely linked to the rites and ceremonies associated with the transition from this life to the next. Buddhist literature emphasizes the importance of *cuti-citta* or "death consciousness" and of meeting death mindfully since the last moment of one's life can be particularly influential in determining the quality of the next rebirth (*prasandi*). Notes left behind by suicides indicate that they have a *cuti-citta* so that they may be reborn in a blissful state (Dhirasekera 1979, 4:273). *Cuti-citta* (death consciousness) in the Theravada tradition is one of the fourteen functions of the life-continuum and is followed immediately by the first moment of consciousness at conception. An individual (*patisandhi-citta*) is the resulting new appearance.

There is no teaching of an everlasting hell in the Buddhist perception of the universe (Jayatilleke 1972, 29). The underlying idea often is that the suicide, though a result of sorrow in this life, is motivated by a belief that a future life may be better. The letters left behind by those who contemplate their suicide have never wished hell to be the destination of their next birth.

KARMA

The doctrine of rebirth is correlated with the principle of karma, which asserts that all morally determinate actions, wholesome and unwholesome, have an inherent power to bring forth fruits that correspond to the moral quality of those deeds. Taken together, the twin teachings of rebirth and karma show that a principle of moral equilibrium balances between the actions and the felt quality of life. Thus, morally good deeds produce agreeable results: bad deeds, disagreeable results. The Buddhist does not believe that any finite bad action, no matter how bad, would warrant eternal damnation. Thus we find in Buddhism no eternal punishment or eternal reward, but rather happiness and sorrow in proportion to one's own thoughts and actions. However, like all realms of rebirth, rebirth in the realms of hell is not permanent, though suffering can persist for eons before being reborn again.

Buddhists do not believe sin can be forgiven by divine grace. Buddhism does not recognize the Christian idea behind sin because in Buddhism there is, instead, the cause and effect theory of karma. Since an individual is in control of his life, he has the ability to terminate it when the *dukkha* is unbearable.

In Buddhism, sin (*akusal*) is largely understood to be ignorance. And, while sin is understood as "moral error," the context in which "evil" and "good" are understood is amorality. Karma is understood as nature's balance and is not personally enforced. Nature is not moral; therefore, karma is not a moral code, and sin is not ultimately immoral. Thus, we can say, by Buddhist thought, that our error is not a moral issue since it is ultimately an impersonal mistake, not an interpersonal violation. The consequences of this understanding are devastating. For the Buddhist, sin is more akin to a misstep than a transgression against the nature of a holy God.

Thus, in Christianity and Buddhism, two different forms of survival are under consideration. On one side, an eternal afterlife in heaven or hell is taught in Christianity. On the other side, Buddhism teaches a sequence of rebirths. Of these alternatives, the hypothesis of rebirth may seem far more compatible with moral justice than an eternal afterlife. The Buddhist does not believe that a finite bad action, no matter how bad, would warrant eternal damnation. When the bond attaching man to life is not determined by the respect to a personal divine being, he can easily willfully terminate it.

Buddhism is not a relational religion. Buddha has attained nirvana and therefore is not a living being. The devotees are fully aware of this. Therefore, they resort to other avenues of help in times of trouble. Hindu priests, devil priests, and astrologers fill the vacuum created by the Buddhist monk who does not intervene in the mundane affairs of the laypeople other than helping them to gain merit.

ALCOHOL

Dependence on liquor and drugs has been identified as a serious health issue and social hazard. It has acted as a major cause for the eroding of human values in the society of Sri Lanka. Males are more likely to commit suicide; alcohol abuse and the resulting domestic violence are reported as contributory factors. Alcoholism and related behaviors are known to cause misery and suicide among women and children as well. Sri Lanka is listed as one of the countries with the highest alcoholism levels in the world. This is ironic in a country where the precept "I undertake to abstain from using intoxicating drinks and drugs, which lead to carelessness" is chanted every day publicly and privately as a promise. Alcohol misuse was directly or indirectly responsible for between five to ten percent of hospital admissions in Sri Lanka. A strong association between alcoholism and suicide has been noted, and there was a serious rise in suicide rates in the 1990s along with the increase in the production and consumption of both licit and illicit alcohol. A high consumption of alcohol has been noted even among Buddhist monks where, interestingly, suicide is not absent.

A sample survey carried out by the Alcohol and Drugs Information Centre (ADIC) in six districts in the southern part of Sri Lanka revealed that sixty-five percent of alcohol users were found mostly among middle-aged men. The rate of increase of alcohol users is highest among those at the threshold of youth. Apparently, every other youngster in the prime age group of fifteen to twenty-four years consumes alcohol. These numbers increased by a disturbing thirty-seven percent in the period between 1998 and 2004 (ADIC 2004). Lone drinkers were predominant (eighty-six percent). Features of psychological interest, such as sleep disturbance (sixty-four percent), emotional problems (forty-two percent), loneliness (thirty-four percent), domestic problems (thirty-six percent), social problems (twenty-four percent), and financial problems (thirty-four percent), were also noted (Ferdinandas and De Silva 2002). *Dukkha* emanating from alcohol abuse has contributed to the high rate of suicide among men in the lower ranks of rural and urban society.

INTERPERSONAL

According to Nalini Ellawela, director at Sri Lanka Sumithrayo, the country's premier counseling center, most suicides are caused by love affairs gone wrong, poverty, parental pressure on marriage, unemployment, unwanted pregnancies, failure at examinations, fear of punishment, inability to pay loans, and, in recent years, women going to the Middle East to work. This can be explained in terms of Buddha's statement on *piyehi vipayogo dukkho* (separation from the loved one is sorrow), a sentiment involved in all these cases.

Interpersonal disputes involving domestic problems and love affairs are the main precipitating factors for suicides. Broken affairs bring about a feeling of rejection (Hettiarachchi 989, 204–8). In the West, the focus has been on individual psychological factors. In contrast, cultures in the East and also in most developing nations tend to view suicide as a social problem, and the emphasis of their research has always been more on various social stressors than on the identification of mental illness. Mental illness is, therefore, seen as one of the less common causes of suicide and is given equal conceptual status with love affairs, family conflict, and social maladjustment.

In Sri Lankan studies, the most common risk factor associated with attempted suicide is family and marital discord. Sociologists have also suggested that Sri Lankan youth have few support systems as a consequence of war and poverty and are unable to cope with societal and cultural demands. A sample survey conducted by Professor Jeanne Marecek of the Swarthmore College in 1998 found that sixty-six percent of the respondents were mostly young people who mentioned a love relationship as the cause of disappointment (Marecek 1998, 75). Others included failure in school or work, and family conflicts as the cause.

Love problems, family conflicts, and achievement-related conflicts have been mentioned. Unwanted pregnancy, rape, and other frustrated sexual urges have also been noted (Marecek 1998, 76). According to Maracek, loving, kind, patient, and understanding behavior towards suicidal individuals bears positive results. This is an aspiration which is not always attained in a religious atmosphere where personal merit-making gains priority.

Love can do many things to people—even drive them to suicide. A broken affair can bring about a feeling of rejection or a desire for revenge to make one's partner feel guilty. These feelings are, in most cases, the reasons for committing suicide. Ultimately the Buddhist view of life is that it generates suffering (*dukkha*), annoyance (*upaghaata*), trouble (*upaayaasa*), and fret (*parilaaha*).

COLONIZATION

A research project conducted by the University of Massachusetts Department of Public Health with Inupiat people in Northwest Alaska found that suicide rates are more than eleven times higher among the migrants than the average Canadian. They also found that colonization can inadvertently contribute to suicide and other behavioral health risks. Similarly, statistics taken by the Department of Census and Statistics since 1950 show an increase of suicides in the areas under colonization schemes in the dry zone of Sri Lanka. The dramatic rise of suicide in Sri Lanka has been attributed in part to the large-scale internal immigration which disrupts family, imposes stress, and limits the support network. Studies in Sri Lankan settlements with high suicide rates found that the insecurity of new settlers coupled with the lack of social controls and social inequity are key determinants of suicidal behavior. These colonizations have been fed by rural to rural migration (Kearney 1987, 86). The dominant pattern since the 1950s has been the migration of rural people from the wet zone to the dry zone in the North Central and Southeastern provinces of Sri Lanka. They settled in the state-supported irrigation and colonization schemes where paddy cultivation is encouraged. The Accelerated Mahaweli Development Scheme since 1981 also encouraged people to move into the newly irrigated areas. According to available reports, more men than women made this move. Therefore, the gender ratio has been unbalanced in many districts.

There has been a remarkable increase in the suicide rate in areas where migration and an imbalanced gender ratio are found. There is some correlation between the incidence of suicide and the presence of a disproportionate number of men. The general disruption of customary habits, practices, and relationships following the rapid pace of social change has had a sweeping impact on the increase of incidence of suicide in Sri Lanka.

The districts of Vavuniya, Polonnaruwa, Kurunegala, and Anuradhapura, which have had high suicide rates, are areas where recent internal migration has occurred. The resulting acculturation stress, identity conflicts, and discontinuities between past and present have been associated with significant social disparities among young people living in these communities (Brass and Tait 2000; Larsen 1992; Bjerregaard 2001). The traditionally valued extended family structure was broken. The older population was left behind in the rural areas. The lifestyle and responsibilities of young people also changed. The increased incidents of suicide indicate that fragmented communities in these colonized areas cannot cope with the stressful life. Even in the comparatively older colonized areas, like Ampara, there is no supporting social network which the traditional unitary-caste farming villages could supply.

High mobilization of rural females to factories in free trade zones and the Middle East have also created a sorrowful atmosphere. Dysfunctional families, extramarital sexual activities, and unwanted pregnancies have aggravated the agonies. The increase in the incidence of suicide indicates that the community cannot cope with the course of change.

SEPARATION FROM LOVED ONES

Marriage has a protective effect on suicidal behavior. Living alone was about twice as common among the suicides as in the general population for both men and women. Connectedness to others, responsibility for dependent children, and fears based on religious beliefs have played a protective role against suicide. Separation, spousal abuse, and divorce were common among those who committed suicide in Sri Lanka (Samaraweera 2003). In some cases, young couples prevented from marrying by family opposition, who face the irresolvable conflict of either living apart or severing ties with their families, choose suicide, together or alone (Vijayakumar1993, 46).

SOCIETY

In his seminal book *Suicide: A Study In Sociology*, Emile Durkheim suggests that one of the main causes of suicide is a failure to connect with other people. Durkheim believes that suicide stems from a lack of identification with a unitary group and postulates that suicide rates should be lower where there is a high level of religious interaction. He argues that with Catholicism there are protective factors against suicide. In Durkheim's terminology, one must strengthen that bond one has with society so that it will become strong, flexible, and robust. To overcome isolation and feeling unloved, one must strive to make that imaginative leap to identify with people. One must go out to people, search one's own experience, and use it to empathize with others. Relational religions like Islam and Christianity have provided that opportunity where Buddhism has failed.

LACK OF SOCIAL LINKS

Sinhala Buddhists worship individually. They do not have the habit of eating together in a religious setting—probably because of caste differences, which were very strong in the past. Their *bodhi puja*, *dana*, and chanting are private affairs, and communal worship is not encouraged. In addition, in the case of colonization, immigrant communities are composed of people from numerous villages who belong to various castes. Therefore, neighborly relationships are not strong. This individualist tendency makes people vulnerable in times of crisis, leaving them to grapple with their negative feelings alone. Buddhist monks, who are renouncers, do not actively take part in social affairs. The religious support that a communal worship can offer is lacking in Theravada Buddhism in Sri Lanka.

THE COPING MECHANISM OF THE SURVIVORS

The Buddhist coping mechanism in the event of a suicide in a family also has a tendency to condone the premature termination of life. Family members have often stated that their child experienced a premature death because of the expiry of life span they brought with their birth. According to them, the karmic forces allowed only a life span up to the time of suicide. Untimely, death, due to the interrupting action of karmic force, is known as *upachhedika karma*. Rural folks say that the time period that he or she is allowed according to karma has ended. The suicide was caused by a powerful evil karma derived from the past. Therefore, suicide is considered to be an untimely death determined by karmic forces, and the family is helpless because the death was karmically unavoidable. This would be further emphasized by their views regarding astrology. It would be interpreted as a bad period which the person had to pass through.

The relatives would resort to religious actions to transfer merit to the dead person so that he or she may be born in a better status. The monks who came to perform ceremonies would quote from the stories of suicide in the sutras to encourage the living relatives.

The belief in rebirth is a comforting factor to a Buddhist. The process of change from one life to the next is called *punabbhava* in Pali. The process is also called samsara and is seen as a universal perspective, affecting all living beings.

Those who try to commit suicide have another method of comforting themselves. Buddhists believe that the superiority of thought that the dying period has at the moment of death will determine the quality of the next life.

COMMUNAL WORSHIP

Researchers have noted that "the lack of a religious base or a life philosophy in the individuals and their immediate environment surfaced many times leading to suicide" (H. J. De Silva et al. 2000, 19). According to Durkheim, suicide rates are lower where there is a high level of religious integration. The religious practices and beliefs which emphasize communal fellowship have been regarded as protective factors against suicide. A study by Simpson and Colin found that in Islamic societies, where communal worship is emphasized, belief in religion reduced suicide rates. Some studies have shown that church attendance and the extended religious network have strong preventive influences. The degree of commitment to an Abrahamic religion acts as an inhibitor of suicide. A study of three ethnic groups in Singapore showed some correlation between religious affiliation and suicide. Hindu Indians and Buddhist Chinese had high rates of suicide while the Islamic Malays, who strongly oppose suicide, had very low rates.

Researchers have found that higher levels of social and national cohesion have a tendency to reduce suicide rates. Suicide levels are highest among the retired, unemployed, impoverished, divorced, childless, urbanites, empty nesters, and other people who live alone. In Durkheim's terminology, one must strengthen—must exercise even—that bond one has with society so that it becomes strong, flexible, and robust. The scholars who empirically tested Durkheim's major assertions using contemporary data for American SMSAs found a potent religious effect. That is, high rates of church membership are associated with low suicide rates, whether those members are mainly Protestants or Catholics.

Suicide is most condemned in Christianity; its doctrinal statements concerning suicide are all negative. If there is a difference between Catholics and Protestants with respect to suicide rates, it must be in some aspect of social organization that differs between the two churches. However, if there is a factor related to suicide, then it is the social organization that is the cause of the difference, not religion in itself. Catholics in Sri Lanka have a low rate of suicide compared to Buddhists and Hindus. Durkheim finds further proof of this in other factors related to social organization—that is, family structure (Giddens 1969, 83). Where there is more integration in family structure, the suicides are lesser in number.

Durkheim argues that the most important aspects of social organization and collective life for explaining differences in suicide rates are the degree of integration into and regulation by society. For Durkheim, integration is the "degree to which collective sentiments are shared," and regulation refers to "the degree of external constraint on people" (Ritzer 1992, 90). Catholicism is a more highly integrated religion than Protestantism, and it is in this that the difference in suicide rates is expressed. It is not the religious doctrines themselves but the different social organization of the two religions that are important. As Giddens notes, the degree of integration of family structure is related in the same way to suicides (1971, 83). Those in larger families are less likely to commit suicide whereas those in smaller families, or who are single, are more likely.

Religious affiliation of any kind is assumed to decrease with modernization, thus causing a rise in suicide. Between 1850 and 1920, Protestants in Europe were more involved in the modern economy than Catholics. Therefore, Durkheim found that Catholics had a lower suicide rate than Protestants. Straus and Straus compared Muslims with Estate Tamils, Sinhalese Buddhists, Ceylon Tamils, and Burghers in Sri Lanka. Their research showed that Muslims had the lowest suicide rate (2.1 per 100,000), which was less than the next lowest group, Christian Burghers (4.8 per 100,000), while the Buddhists had the highest (Straus 1953, 469).

Cultural factors play a major role in suicidal behavior. It is well known that susceptibility to suicide is related to the social relationships that a person has. It is also clear that the greater the number of social relationships, the less susceptibility there is to suicide. Local communities are important for the prevention of suicide.

The church can act as a binding agency and reduce social isolation where traditional endogamous links are broken and society is fragmented because of the multiplicity of castes present.

LACK OF SOCIAL RELATIONSHIPS

Though Sri Lanka is a poor country, the most common motive for suicide is not poverty but disappointment in love. It has contributed to the belief that suicide stems from one's inability to cope with negative feelings, emotions, and urges coupled with poor decision-making skills. Many of those who end their lives or attempt suicide are those who feel unwanted, unloved, victimized, or that they are a burden to others. Depression leads people to focus mostly on failure and disappointment, to emphasize the negative side of their situation, and to downplay their own capabilities or worth. Humans have an immense need to be really listened to, to be taken seriously, and to be understood. Attempted suicides are a cry for help and a sign of desperation. It is a desire for a response from others and the need to end the pain.

INFLUENCE OF ASTROLOGY

Disturbed feelings and actions, and negative events which cause sorrow, are usually attributed to astrological influence. Sorcery, demon possession, and various kinds of black magic are suspected when life becomes sorrowful. Ghosts, spirits, demon possession, magic, and bad astrological periods are common in explaining sorrowful events like suicide. Sorrow caused by astrological calculations and omens is an area where the church could intervene successfully in a fellowship setting.

MEDITATION

Buddhist monks often advise people who are in a stressful state to practice *samadhi bhavana* (concentration meditation) and *vipassana bhavana* (insight meditation) in order to develop calmness, tranquility, and stability of mind. *Maitri bhavana* (loving kindness) is recommended to control anger and aggressive behavior. This practice needs time, discipline, and separation from the family. *Bhavana* practices are normally undertaken alone. A person with suicidal tendencies in a village would not be able to grasp the intricacies of these types of mental exercises. The fundamental virtue of Buddhism is mercy, and in order to practice mercy (*maitri*), a lifetime of training is required. People are attached to their present life, and that is the cause of their suffering. In order to end suffering, one must get rid of such attachments through a lifetime of training. Deliverance from attachments and liberation from suffering are what is understood by "salvation" (*vimukti*) in Buddhism. Through salvation, one enters the state of selflessness and comes to practice true mercy, according to Buddhism.

Buddhists try to reach nirvana by following the Buddha's teaching and by meditating. Meditation means training the mind to empty it all of thoughts. They believe that when this happens, what is important becomes clear. Buddhist meditation is undertaken in solitude.

Pirit chanting and other popular Buddhist practices cover the special needs of the life of a Buddhist. However, such activities are costly. Such events need prior preparation and the support of the family. Special attention of this nature would not arise in a desperate person who is contemplating suicide. In the case of Christianity, where communal worship is emphasized, this kind of preparation for mental training would not be necessary as the social support is capable of smoothing away the pain caused by loneliness.

ANGER

Psychologists believe that angry feelings are often helpful, or even necessary, for some people to grow. This is so because if a person is the victim of destructive actions, or a longer destructive upbringing, hiding feelings caused by those destructive actions can be harmful. The cost can take many forms, including disengagement with the world, having symptoms of depression or guilt, substance abuse, chronic relational problems, and other feelings of sorrow (Aronson 2004,

91). The Buddhist teaching is that one must not be overcome by hatred—and an individual has to do this without any external help.

Buddhism does not provide devotees with a great trust. It does not provide a caring sage that vows to answer or heal broken or lost souls through the medium of prayer. Unlike Christianity that welcomes prayers to God with open arms, Buddhism does not have such a practice. What Buddhism encourages is seeking liberation as a personal endeavor.

The absence of a supreme being that makes them feel like they are cared for or watched over is another area in which Buddhists feel helpless in times of trouble. Abrahamic religions promise the concern of a caring God towards their devotees. The church has the privilege of using prayer cells to help people express even negative feelings without using these feelings against themselves in the form of suicide. Buddhists, who do not believe in a supreme being, have to resort to magic, astrology, and karma.

CHRISTIANITY

In Acts 2:42, we read that one of the four things the early church devoted itself to was "fellowship." Fellowship is first a relationship. Fellowship was a very important part of their reason for meeting together. It was one of their objectives. Luke tells us that these early Christians didn't have fellowship to merely gather together but devoted themselves to it. This means that fellowship was a priority (Bridges 1985, 18). It was a getting together for spiritual purposes: for sharing needs; for prayer; for discussing and sharing the word; for encouraging, comforting, and edifying one another. It is vertical as communion and fellowship with the Lord through the word, prayer, the filling of the Holy Spirit, and the abiding life. It is horizontal as communion and fellowship with other believers. The church can serve as a good partnership as the partners share equally in the privileges and responsibilities, the assets and liabilities, the blessings and burdens. Companionship developed in a religious atmosphere where the presence of God is assumed involves communion or communication, interchange, intimacy, sharing, and receiving.

With their strong social support, life-affirming values, and love, Christians are in a unique position to fight a largely preventable problem. That suicide is unlawful is the teaching of holy scripture and of the church, which condemns the act as a most atrocious crime. In the past, the denial of Christian burial for suicide acted as a deterrent. According to the Catholic Encyclopedia,

For a sane man deliberately to take his own life, he must, as a general rule, first have annihilated in himself all that he possessed of spiritual life, since suicide is in absolute contradiction to everything that the Christian religion teaches us as to the end and object of life and, except in cases of insanity, is usually the natural termination of a life of disorder, weakness, and cowardice.

SOCIAL NETWORKING

Some churches maintain a greater social networking among members of the congregation than others. Fundamentalist churches require greater participation in church activities than churches with liberal tendencies. It is proven that religions marked by structures that promote networking tend to have lower suicide rates (Levinson 2002, 1,599).

A prayer group will be able to identify a person who is experiencing apathy, lethargy, and loss of interest in friends and social activities. Marecek's research among Sri Lankan Buddhists indicated the "value of offering love, kindness, and understanding to the suicidal individual" in preventing a possible destructive action. There is a need to avoid isolation. This tendency for aloneness and isolation is explained in the Sinhalese word *tanikama*, which is not only an aversive emotional state but also one peril of demon possession.

Telling someone who is in extreme physical or mental pain that by "taking poison" they are breaking the precepts, or that they are only hurting themselves, would be unlikely to dissuade them. What seems important is the imaginative identification. If we are able to empathize with others, then we will be more able to face our own suffering and therefore be in a better position to help others face theirs. This is where Christian fellowship can fill the vacuum left by Buddhism in Sri Lanka.

CONCLUSION

Suicide in Sri Lanka is a significant and complex phenomenon. The epidemiological profile of suicide in Sri Lanka differs from the typical profile reported in the scientific literature, because the latter has generally been gathered from studies conducted in the United States and European countries. The complex web of socioeconomic, cultural, and religious factors in Asian countries differs from that of the West. Suicide prevention activities in these countries clearly need to take these contextual issues into account.

According to WHO records, there were thirteen countries with suicide rates 1.5 times or more above the mean. Sri Lanka was leading with the highest suicide rate. Although suicide has occurred in Sri Lanka throughout its history, the extent today is appalling. In most Sri Lankan rural areas, personal and interpersonal difficulties are evidenced as the social compositions change, and serious psychiatric problems are managed within families which are ill-equipped to do so. A simple understanding of recognizing suicidal behavior and the framework of managing it could be provided by the church because of its communality of worship and the fellowship setting.

In an effort to prevent suicide in Sri Lanka, a presidential task force was appointed in 1996 to look into ways of preventing suicide and made several recommendations to the government. Some of these recommendations have been contributory to the sharp decline of suicides.

Mental health services are inadequate to facilitate access for all those who require treatment and counseling facilities. At present, the psychological support that is provided even after an act of attempted suicide is grossly inadequate. There is only one psychiatrist per 500,000 persons in Sri Lanka. Further, out of the total number of psychiatrists available in Sri Lanka, almost sixty-five percent are employed in the western province.

A low value of life is a potential risk factor for suicide in Sri Lanka. Buddhists do not view human beings as the crown of God's creation; they do not believe that man was made in the image of God. Christians in Sri Lanka, who have a comparatively low rate of suicide, have achieved it because of their personal relationship with God and their regular fellowship gatherings. The church has to recognize its capacity to reduce suicide and improve the common valuing of human life.

The chief cause of suicide in Sri Lanka is a lack of interpersonal relationships. However, "there is always a shoulder to cry on in a church environment." In traditional uncommunicative Sinhala Buddhist families, even if one is surrounded by parents, relatives, friends, and acquaintances, a person can still be alone with his or her problems. This leads to the feeling that no one cares for him or her. Placed in such isolation, the lack of control of thoughts could drive young people to make the harsh decision to commit suicide.

Sumithra Ratnayake of Sri Lanka Sumithrayo states, "Unless someone was willing to listen to the person concerned, he or she might well resort to suicide"

(2007, 141). She noted that every individual who committed suicide had actually talked about it, but there was no one willing to listen and empathize with him or her. Relatively minor problems like an unapproved love affair was sufficient to trigger suicide (Sunday Times 29/10/2000). Early identification of mental disorders and persons at risk of suicide can be identified in the fellowship environment of the church.

Through congregational worship, the church can act as a catalyst to offer dignity to individuals who come to worship. The Roman Catholic Church's provision for oral confession to the priest has a therapeutic value (O'Brien 1974, 189). Although Protestants have given up the practice of public confession, the cup of tea which many churches offer after the worship service has a tremendous therapeutic value in a culture where people do not have the inclination to listen to another person's anecdotes. The prayer cells and Bible study groups which meet on Sundays and weekdays also offer opportunities to release the concerns in believers' hearts. This in turn, according to Durkheim's hypothesis, eliminates any inclination to commit suicide.

Man, who is a social being, needs a community to live together for mutual benefit. The church is a body of individuals outlined by the bonds of functional interdependence. The Christian church is an organization which has characteristics of cultural identity and social solidarity. The church helps by providing a pattern of relationships between individuals sharing a distinctive culture of faith. It allows its members to achieve needs or wishes that they could not fulfill alone. Most suicidal people desperately want to live; they are just unable to see alternatives to their problems. The Buddhist emphasis is on sorrow as a part of life. However, people do not need to grapple with sorrow and pain alone, as shared pain has a therapeutic value. Suicide is preventable. The *koinonia* (fellowship) offered by the Christian church can act as a deterrent to sorrow leading to suicide.

GLOSSARY

amal .... distress, trouble or misfortune associated with wickedness

awwa .... desire springing from the depths of one's being

abidharma .... the higher teaching

akusala .... unskillful or unwholesome

anattā .... not a self

anicca .... impermanence

apunna, papa, bap .... ill fortune or demerit

arahant .... liberated person in their last birth

ariya .... one who is far removed from passions

asava .... mental intoxication

atta .... self

avidyā .... lack of light, the darkness of ignorance

avijja .... ignorance

bhava .... becoming

bhavana .... meditation

bhava-tanhā .... craving for existence or self-preservation which is the cause of rebirth

bhavatrisna .... embodiment

boon .... merit

Chenrezig .... Tibetan bodhisattva of compassion

citta .... the state of one's mind

cuti-citta .... death consciousness

dana .... alms-giving

dharma............................. *the true nature of things, the way things really are*

dhyana............................. *meditation*

Dukkha............................. *suffering due to birth, illness, decay, and death*

hamad.............................. *desire for something or someone visible to the eye*

jati................................... *birth*

kama-tanhā.................... *craving of happiness and sensual pleasure in the present life*

kamatrisna...................... *sensual pleasure*

Kannon........................... *Japanese bodhisattva of compassion*

karume .... *one's fate*

karuna............................. *compassion*

kilesa............................... *defilement*

kusal .... *wholesome acts*

Kwan Yin........................ *Chinese bodhisattva of compassion*

magga.............................. *the path to end suffering*

maitri bhavana.............. *loving kindness, mercy*

moha................................ *confusion*

nama-rupa .... *name and form*

nirodha........................... *the cessation of dukkha*

pancha sila .... *pillars of truth*

parilaaha........................ *fret*

pasko............................... *suffer or endure*

pathavi............................ *earth*

phassa .... *sense contact*

pii..................................... *spirit*

pirit .... *religious chanting prajna* .... *representing insight*

prasandi .... *the next rebirth*

pratitya-samutpada .... *chain of dependent arising*

puja .... *worship with offering*

punabbhava .... *rebirth*

rupa .... *matter*

salayatana .... *the six bases of sense impressions (eye, ear, nose, tongue, body, and mind)*

samadhi .... *concentration*

samkhara-dukkha .... *suffering as conditioned states*

samudaya .... *the truth of the cause of suffering*

sangha .... *Buddhist clergy (Theravada), Buddhist community (Mahayana)*

sankhāra-dukkhatā .... *the state of suffering due to mental formations*

samsara .... *cycles of reincarnation*

sanna .... *perception*

santana .... *process or stream of personality*

sarana .... *refuge*

sasana .... *religion*

sati .... *mindfulness*

shraddha .... *trust, faith*

sila .... *morality*

sunnatta .... *emptiness, devoid of self*

tanhā .... *craving or desire*

tanikama .... *loneliness*

ti-lakkhana .... *the three characteristics of all existence*

Tripitaka.......................... *Theravada Buddhist Pali canon*

trisna.............................. *thirst, craving, clinging, selfishness or blind demandingness*

upaayaasa .... *trouble*

upachhedika karma ...... *unexpected karma*

upadana .... *attachment*

upaghaata....................... *annoyance*

upaya-kausalya .... *skillful stratagems or liberative techniques adapted to each individual*

vedana .... *feeling*

vibhava-tanhā................ *craving for non-existence*

vibhavatrisna .... *deliverance through annihilation*

vijja .... *knowledge or truth*

vijnana............................ *departed consciousness*

vimukti .... *salvation, release*

vinyana .... *consciousness, spirit*

vipakakamma .... *result of karma*

viparinama-dukkha ...... *suffering caused by the fact that all things are temporary*

viparinama-dukkhatā ... *suffering inherent in change or concealed within the infidelity of happiness*

viragata........................... *non-attachment*

yathabhutam.................. *seeing things as they are*

REFERENCES

Chapter 1

Bodhi, Bhikkhu. 2003. *The Connected Discourses of the Buddha: A Translation of the Samyutta Nikaya*. Boston, MA: Wisdom Publications.

Buddhadasa. 1999a. *Christianity and Buddhism*. Sinclaire Thompson Memorial Lectures. Thailand Theological Seminary, Chiang Mai, 1967. Bangkok: Dhammasapha Publishing.

———. 1999b. *Tuagoo-khonggoo (I/Me–My/Mine)*. Bangkok: Dhammasapha Publishing.

———. 1999c. *Anattā of the Buddha*. Bangkok: Dhammasapha Publishing.

Chandrkaew, Chinda. 1982. *Nibbana: The Ultimate Truth of Buddhism*. Bangkok: Mahachula Buddhist University.

Crockett, William, ed. 1996. *Four Views on Hell*. Grand Rapids, MI: Zondervan.

Davis, John R. 1993. *Poles Apart: Contextualizing the Gospel in Asia*. Bangkok: Kanok Bannasan.

Harvey, Peter. 2002. *An Introduction to Buddhism: Teachings, History and Practices*. Cambridge: Cambridge University Press.

Küng, Hans. 1984. *Eternal Life?* Translated by Edward Quinn. London: Collins.

Lertjitlekha, Cherdchai. 1998. *Buddhist Panna: A Study of Theravada Buddhist Ethics in Dialogue with Christian Morality*. Bangkok: Saengtham College Press.

Lorgunpai, Seree. 1995. "World Lover World Leaver: The book of Ecclesiastes and Thai Buddhism." In *Voices From the Margin*, edited by R.S. Sugirtharajah. Maryknoll, NY: Orbis/SPCK.

Mejudhon, Nantachai. 1997. "Meekness: A New Approach to Christian Witness to the Thai People." DMiss diss., Asbury Theological Seminary.

Payutto, Prayuth A. 1988. *Kamma According to Buddhadhamma*. Bangkok: Buddhadhamma Foundation.

———. 1995. *Phutthatham*. New rev. ed. Bangkok: Chulalongkorn University.

———. 1999. *Dependent Origination*. Bangkok: Buddhadhamma Foundation.

Peck, M. Scott. 1999. *The Road Less Traveled and Beyond*. London: Ebury Press, Random House.

Phongphit, Seri. 1978. *The Problem of Religious Language: A Study of Buddha-dasa Bhikkhu and Ian Ramsay as Models for a Mutual Understanding of Buddhism and Christianity*. Ph.D. diss., University of Munich.

The Official Thai Dictionary. 1999. Bangkok: Nanmee Publishing.

Wright, N. T. 2006. *New Heavens, New Earth: The Biblical Picture of Christian Hope*. Cambridge: Grove Books.

Chapter 2

Anderson, Francis I. 1976. *Job: An Introduction and Commentary*. Vol. 13 of *Tyndale Old Testament Commentaries*, Edited by Donald J. Wiseman. Downers Grove, IL: InterVarsity Press.

Beker, Johan Christiaan. 1987. *Suffering and Hope: The Biblical Vision and the Human Predicament*. Philadelphia: Fortress Press.

Bodhi, Bhikkhu, and Bhikkhu Ñanamoli. 1995. *The Middle Length Discourses of the Buddha: A Translation of the Majjhima Nikaya (Teachings of the Buddha)*. Boston, MA: Wisdom Publications.

———. 2003. *The Connected Discourses of the Buddha: A Translation of the Samyutta Nikaya*. Boston, MA: Wisdom Publications.

———. 2005. *In the Buddha's Words: An Anthology of Discourses from the Pāli Canon*. Boston, MA: Wisdom Publications.

Boonyakiat, Satanun. 2009. "A Christian theology of suffering in the Context of Theravada Buddhism in Thailand." PhD diss., Fuller Theological Seminary.

Dhammapitaka. (P. A. Payutto). 2003. *Buddhadhamma*. Bangkok: Chulalong-korn University.

Dillard, Raymond B., and Tremper Longman. 1994. *An Introduction to the Old Testament*. Grand Rapids, MI: Zondervan.

Ford, David F. 2007. *Christian Wisdom: Desiring God and Learning in Love*. Cambridge: Cambridge University Press.

Hartley, John E. 1988. *The Book of Job*. Grand Rapids, MI: Eerdmans.

Humphreys, Christmas. 1990. *Buddhism*. 3rd ed. London: Penguin Books.

Kärkkäinen, Veli-Matti. 2002. "'Evil, Love and the Left Hand of God': The Contribution of Luther's Theology of the Cross to an Evangelical Theology of Evil." *Evangelical Quarterly* 74 (3): 215–34.

King, Winston L. 1962. *Buddhism and Christianity: Some Bridges of Understanding*. Philadelphia: Westminster Press.

Kitamori, Kazoh. 1965. *Theology of the Pain of God*. Richmond, VA: John Knox Press.

Koch, Klaus. 1983. "Is There a Doctrine of Retribution in the Old Testament?" In *Theodicy in the Old Testament*, edited by James L. Crenshaw. Philadelphia: Fortress Press.

Koyama, Kosuke. 1977. *No Handle on the Cross: An Asian Meditation on the Crucified Mind*. Maryknoll, NY: Orbis Books.

Luther, Martin. 1955. *Luther's Works*. Vol. 31. American ed. Edited by Jaroslav Jan Pelikan, Hilton C. Oswald, and Helmut T. Lehmann. St. Louis, MO: Concordia Publishing House.

McGrath, Alister E. 1994. *Luther's Theology of the Cross: Martin Luther's Theological Breakthrough*. Grand Rapids, MI: Baker Book House.

Michaelis, Wilhelm. 1967. "Πασχω." In *Theological Dictionary of the New Testament*, edited by Gerhard Kittel, Gerhard Friedrich, and Geoffrey William Bromiley, 904–24. Grand Rapids, MI: Eerdmans.

Moltmann, Jürgen. 1993. *The Crucified God: The Cross of Christ as the Foundation and Criticism of Christian Theology*. Translated by R. A. Wilson and John Bowden. Minneapolis, MN: Fortress Press.

Murphy, Roland E. 2002. *The Tree of Life: An Exploration of Biblical Wisdom Literature*. 3rd ed. Grand Rapids, MI: Eerdmans.

Nyanatiloka, ed. 1980. *Buddhist Dictionary: Manual of Buddhist Terms and Doctrines*. Kandy, Sri Lanka: Buddhist Publication Society.

Rahula, Walpola. 1996. *Gems of Buddhist Wisdom*. Kuala Lumpur, Malaysia: The Buddhist Missionary Society.

Thompson, David. 1997. "למע" In vol. 3 of *New International Dictionary of Old Testament Theology & Exegesis*, edited by Willem VanGemeren. Grand Rapids, MI: Zondervan.

Wood, James. 1966. *Job and the Human Situation*. London: Geoffrey Bles.

Chapter 3

Bercholz, Samuel, and Sherab Chödzin Kohn, eds. 2003. *The Buddha and His Teachings*. Boston, MA: Shambhala.

Bimal Krishna Matilal. 1980. "Ignorance or Misconception?—A Note on Avidyā in Buddhism." In *Buddhist Studies in Honour of Walpola Rahula*, edited by Somaratna Balasooriya, et al. London: Gordon Fraser Gallery.

Bodhi, Bhikkhu, and The Dalai Lama. 2005. *In the Buddha's Words: An Anthology of Discourses from the Pāli Canon.* Boston, MA: Wisdom Publications.

Bowers, Jr., Russell H. 2005. "Gentle Strength and *Upāya*: Christian and Buddhist Ministry Models." In *Sharing Jesus Effectively in the Buddhist World*, edited by David Lim, Steve Spaulding, and Paul De Neui, 109–46. Pasadena, CA: William Carey Library.

Burtt, E. A., ed. 1982. *The Teachings of the Compassionate Buddha: Early Discourses, the Dhammapada, and Later Basic Writings.* New York: Penguin.

Byron, Thomas. *The Dhammapada.* http://www.angelfire.com/ca/SHALOM/dhammapada.html.

Frauwallner, Erich. 1973. *History of Indian Philosophy.* Vol. 1 of *The Philosophy of the Veda and of the Epic.* Delhi: Motilal Banarsidass.

Gethin, Rupert. 1998. *The Foundations of Buddhism.* Oxford: Oxford University Press.

Jayatilleke, K. N. 1974. *The Message of the Buddha.* Edited by Ninian Smart. New York: Free Press.

Jones, Ian Charles. 1991. "The Continuity of Madhymaka and Yogācāra in Indian Mahāyāna Buddhism." Vol. 6 of *Brill's Indological Library.* Leiden: E. J. Brill.

Kempis, Thomas à. 1955. *Imitation of Christ.* Garden City, NY: Imagine Books.

Lacombe, Oliver. 1980. "Buddhist Pessimism?" In *Buddhist Studies in Honour of Walpola Rahula*, edited by Somaratna Balasooriya, et al. London: Gordon Fraser Gallery.

Larson, Gerald James. 1984. "The Relation between 'Action' and 'Suffering' in Asian Philosophy." *Philosophy East and West* 34 (4).

Nishitani, Keiji. 1982. *Religion and Nothingness.* Translated by Jan Van Bragt. Berkeley, CA: University of California.

Nyanaponika, Thera. 2003. "Seeing Things as They Are." In *The Buddha and His Teachings*, edited by Samuel Bercholz and Sherab Chödzin Kohn. Boston, MA: Shambhala.

Pye, Michael. 2003. *Skilful Means: A Concept in Mahayana Buddhism.* 2nd ed. London: Routledge.

Rice, Jonathan R. 2004. "The Tragic Failure of Britain's Evangelical Awakening." *International Journal of Frontier Missions* 21 (1): 23–25.

Smart, Ninian. 1984. "Action and Suffering in the Theravadin Tradition." *Philosophy East and West* 34 (4)

Thompson, Marianne Meye. 1989. "Eternal Life in the Gospel of John." *Ex Auditu* 5: 35–55.

Thurman, Robert A. F. 1978. "Buddhist Hermeneutics." *Journal of the American Academy of Religion* 46 (1).

Watson, Burton, trans. 1993. *The Lotus Sutra.* Colombia University Press.

Williams, Paul. 2002. *The Unexpected Way: On Converting from Buddhism to Catholicism.* Edinburgh and New York: T & T Clark.

Chapter 4

Chua, Chuang How. 2005. "Kitamori Kazoh and the Pain of God: An Expository Review of an Asian Theology." *Mission Round Table* 1 (1): 17–26.

———. 2006. "Divine Violence and Divine Grace: A Missiological Interpretation of Kitamori Kazoh." Unpublished paper presented at the Evangelical Missiological Society Annual Conference, Orlando, FL, September 28–30.

———. 2008. "A Missiological Appropriation of Kitamori's 'Pain of God' Theology." *Mission Round Table* 4 (2): 19–21.

Humphreys, Christmas. 1951. *Buddhism.* Middlesex, Great Britain: Penguin Books.

Jones, E. Stanley. 1933. *Christ and Human Suffering,* New York: Abingdon-Cokebury.

Kitamori, Kazoh. 1965. *Theology of the Pain of God.* Richmond, VA: John Knox Press.

Maguire, Jack. 2001. *Essential Buddhism: A Complete Guide to Beliefs and Practices.* New York: Pocket Books, Simon & Schuster.

Niles, D. T. 1967. *Buddhism and the Claims of Christ.* Richmond, VA: John Knox Press.

Rahula, Walpola Sri. 1974. *What the Buddha Taught.* New York: Grove Press.

Smith, Alex G. 2001. *Buddhism Through Christian Eyes.* Littleton, CO: OMF.

———. 2009. *A Christian Pocket Guide to Buddhism.* London: OMF UK.

Suzuki, Beatrice Lane. 1959. *Mahayana Buddhism: A Brief Outline.* New York: Macmillan.

Weerasingha, Tissa. 1989. *The Cross and the Bo Tree: Communicating the Gospel to Buddhists.* Taichung, Taiwan: Asia Theological Association.

Chapter 5

Appleton, George. 1961. *Christian Presence and Buddhism*. London: SCM Press.

Coward, Harold. 1985. *Pluralism: Challenge to World Religions*. Maryknoll, NY: Orbis.

Cracknell, Kenneth. 2006. *In Good and Generous Faith: Christian Responses to Religious Pluralism*. Cleveland, OH: Pilgrim Press.

Dalai Lama, and Tenzin Gyatso. 2001. *Compassion and Wisdom*. Singapore: Amitabha Buddhist Centre.

Davis, John R. 1993. *Poles Apart? Contextualizing the Gospel*. Bangkok: Kanok Bannasan.

———. 1997. *The Path to Enlightenment*. London: Hodder & Stoughton.

Dendo Kokai, Bukkyo. 1966. *The Teaching of Buddha*. Tokyo: Kosaido Printing.

Hiebert, Paul. 2008. *Transforming Worldviews: An Anthropological Understanding of How People Change*. Grand Rapids, MI: Baker Academic.

Humphries, Christmas. 1951. *Buddhism*. London: Penguin Books.

Johnson, Alan R. 2005. "A Contextualized Presentation of the Gospel in Thai Society." In *Sharing Jesus Holistically in the Buddhist World*, edited by David Lim and Steve Spaulding, 179–216. Pasadena, CA: William Carey Library.

Küng, Hans, et al. 1986. *Christianity and the World Religions*. Garden City, NY: Doubleday.

Lim, David. 1983. "Biblical Christianity in the Context of Buddhism." In *Sharing Jesus in the Two Thirds World*, edited by V. Samuel and C. Sugden, 175–203. Grand Rapids, MI: Eerdmans.

———. 2003. "Towards a Radical Contextualization Paradigm in Evangelizing Buddhists." In *Sharing Jesus in the Buddhist World*, edited by David Lim and Steve Spaulding, 71–94. Pasadena, CA: William Carey Library.

McDermott, Gerald R. 2000. *Can Evangelicals Learn from World Religions? Jesus, Revelation and Religious Traditions*. Downers Grove, IL: InterVarsity Press.

Paul VI. 1965. *Nostra Aetate: Declaration on the Relation of the Church to Non-Christian Religions*. Article 2. http://www.vatican.va/archive/hist_councils/ii_vatican_council/documents/vat-ii_decl_19651028_nostra-aetate_en.html.

Ramachandra, Vinoth. 1999. *Faiths in Conflict?* Leicester: InterVarsity Press.

Smith, Alex. 2001. *Buddhism Through Christian Eyes*. Littleton, CO: OMF.

Smith, Andy. 2009. "Many Starting Points Can Lead to Jesus." *Evangelical Missions Quarterly* 45 (2): 198–203.

Strauss, Robert, and Tom Steffen. 2009. "Change the Worldview ... Change the World." *Evangelical Missions Quarterly* 45 (4): 458–64.

Vasanthakumar, Michal Solomon. 2005. "An Exploration of the Book of Ecclesiastes in the Light of Buddha's Four Noble Truths." In *Sharing Jesus Holistically in the Buddhist World*, edited by David Lim and Steve Spaulding, 147–77. Pasadena, CA: William Carey Library.

Wagner, Paul. 2006. "Beyond Karma: A Model for Presenting Freedom in Christ in the Buddhist Context." In *Communicating Christ in the Buddhist World*, edited by David Lim and Paul De Neui, 210–32. Pasadena, CA: William Carey Library.

Yong, Amos. 2003. *Beyond the Impasse: Toward a Pneumatological Theology of Religions*. Grand Rapids, MI: Baker Academic.

Chapter 6

Bock, Carl A. 1884. *Temples and Elephants: Narrative of a Journey of Exploration Through Upper Siam and Lao*. London: Sampson Low, Marston, Searle and Rivington.

Coffman, Elesha. 2002. "The Cremation Question." *Christianity Today*. http://www.christianitytoday.com/history/newsletter/2002/feb22.html.

Cohen, Milton. 2002. "Death Ritual: Anthropological Perspectives." In *Perspectives on Death and Dying*, edited by Philip Pecorino. 5th ed. http://www.sunysuffolk.edu/pecorip/SCCCWEB/ETEXTS/DeathandDying_TEXT/table_of_contents.htm.

Cort, Mary L. 1886. *Siam: or the Heart of Farther India*. New York: Ansen D. F. Randolph.

Curtis, Lillian J. 1903. *The Lao of North Siam*. Philadelphia, PA: Westminster.

Davis, John. 1993. *Poles Apart*. Bangkok: Kanok Bannasan.

De Neui, Paul H. 2003. "Contextualizing with Thai Folk Buddhists." In *Sharing Jesus in the Buddhist World*, edited by David Lim and Steve Spaulding, 121–46. Pasadena CA: William Carey Library.

———. 2005. "Appropriate Typologies for Folk Buddhists." In *Appropriate Christianity*, edited by Charles Kraft, 415–36. Pasadena, CA: William Carey Library.

Dhammananda, K. Sri. 1998. *What Buddhists Believe*. Kuala Lumpa: Lasa Press.

George, Timothy. 2002. "Cremation confusion: is it unscriptural for a Christian to be cremated?" *Christianity Today* 46. http://www.christianitytoday.com/ct/2002/006/27.66.html.

Gustafson, James. 1970. "Syncretistic Rural Thai Buddhism." MA thesis, Fuller Seminary, Pasadena, CA.

Hauerwas, Stanley. 1990. *God, Medicine and Suffering*. Cambridge, MA: Eerdmans.

Hesselgrave, D., and E. Rommen. 1989. *Contextualization: Meanings, Methods and Models*. Leicester: Appollos.

Hughes, Philip. 1982. "Incarnation and communication of the Gospel in Thailand." In *To What Extent? Incarnation and the Thai Context*, edited by Herb Swanson, 24–33. Chiang Mai: Payap University Press.

James, Hugh, 2004. *A Fitting End*. Norwich: Canterbury Press.

Johnson, Alan. 2002. "*Wrapping the Good News for the Thai.*" http://www.agts.edu/syllabi/ce/summer2002/mthm639oleson_sum02_np_r3.pdf.

Kingshill, Konrad. 1991. *Ku Daeng—Thirty Years later: A Village Study in Northern Thailand 1954–1984*. DeKalb, IL: Center for Southeast Asian Studies, Northern Illinois University.

Kusawadee, Banjop. 2001. "Pastoral Care of the Dying and the Funeral Rite in The Evangelical Lutheran Church in Thailand." MA thesis, Luther Seminary, North Adelaide, S. Australia.

Le May, R. 1986. *An Asian Arcady: The Land and Peoples of Northern Siam*. Bangkok: White Lotus.

Ling, Trevor. 1970. *Buddhism*. Kettering, UK: Ward Lock Educational.

Mahidol University. 1996. "Religions in Thailand." July 23. http://www.mahidol.ac.th/thailand/relgions/buddhism.html.

Neely, A. 1995. *Christian Mission: A Case Study Approach*. Maryknoll, NY: Orbis.

Palmer, Marion. 1907. "Evangelistic Work for the New Missionary." *Laos News* April.

Perkin, W. H. 1923. "A Patriarch Passes On." *Siam Outlook*. January: 200–216.

Prometta, Tongpan. 2000. "Allowing Jesus to be Reborn at funerals." In *Proceedings of Isaan Congress II*, translated by Paul De Neui. Khon Kaen, Thailand. http://thaicov.org.

"*Religion in Thailand.*" http://www.mahidol.ac.th/thailand/religions/buddhism.html.

Segaller, Denis. 1995. *Thai Ways*. Bangkok: Post Books.

Smith, Richard. 2000. "A Good Death." *British Medical Journal* 320. http://www.bmj.bmjjournals.com/cgi/content/ full/320/7228/129.

Suvanno. 1996. *How a Theravadin Buddhist Chinese Funeral May be Conducted*. http://www.urbandharma.org/pdf/thera-chifuner.pdf.

Swanson, Herbert. 1984. *Kristchak Muang Nua*. Bangkok: Chuan Printing Press.

———. 2004. *Northern Thai Protestant Attitudes Towards Other Faiths: Analysis of a Questionnaire*. http://www.herbswanson.com/ProtestantAttitudes Towards/index.php.

———. 2004. *Protestant Attitudes to Other Faiths*. E-mail message to author, March 10.

Sze, Joanna. 2005. Sungei Way Subang Methodist Church, Malaysia. Unpublished text.

Tambiah, Stanley J. 1970. *Buddhism and the Spirit Cults of NE Thailand*. Cambridge: Cambridge University Press.

Walter, Tony. 2003. "Historical and cultural variants on the good death." *BMJ* 327: 218–20.

White, H. 1912. "Burial Customs Among the Laos of North Siam." *Laos News* July: 102–6.

Wright, N. Tom. 2008. *Surprised by Hope*. New York: HarperCollins.

Chapter 7

Bowker, John. 1970. *Problems of Suffering in Religions of the World*. Cambridge: Cambridge University Press.

Fernando, Ajith. 1995. *The Supremacy of Christ*. Reprint, Secunderabad: OM Books.

Jones, E. Stanley. 1968. *A Song of Ascents*. Nashville: Abingdon Press.

Kitamori, Kazoh. 1965. *The Theology of the Pain of God*. Richmond, VA: John Knox Press.

Lanka Library Forum. 2007. "Kirinda—Legend of Queen Viharamaha Devi." http://www.lankalibrary.com/phpBB/viewtopic.php?f=48&t=1795.

Narada, Maha Thera. 1980. *The Buddha and His Teachings*. Colombo: Vajirārāma.

Stott, John. 1986. *The Cross of Christ*. Leicester: InterVarsity Press.

Chapter 8

Jataka, Mahabodhi. 528:19.

Sze, Joanna Sze. 2005. Sungei Way Subang Methodist Church, Malaysia. Interview with Barnabas Mam.

Visuddhi-Magga, ch. XIX.

Chapter 9

Basham, Richard. 1989. "'False consciousness' and the problem of merit and power in Thailand." *Mankind* 19: 126–37.

Bhanthumnavin, Duangduen. 1997. *Religious Belief and Practice of Thai Buddhists: Socialization and Quality of Life*. Bangkok, Thailand.

Flemming, Dean. 2005. *Contextualization in the New Testament: Patterns for Theology and Mission*. Downers Grove, IL: InterVarsity Press.

Köstenberger, Andreas J., and Peter T. O'Brien. 2001. *Salvation to the Ends of the Earth: A Biblical Theology of Missions*. Downers Grove, IL: InterVarsity Press.

Mejudhon, Nantachai. 1997. *Meekness: A New Approach to Christian Witness to the Thai People*. DMiss diss., Asbury Theological Seminary.

Moreau, A. Scott, Gary R. Corwin, and Gary B. McGee. 2004. *Introducing World Missions: A Biblical, Historical, and Practical Survey*. Monrovia, CA: MARC.

Tambiah, Stanley Jeyaraja. 1985. *Culture, Thought and Social Action: An Anthropological Perspective*. Cambridge, MA: Harvard University Press.

Thailand Evangelism and Church Growth Committee. 2006. *Thailand: State of the Nation Research Data*. Overseas Missionary Fellowship. http://www.omf.org/omf/thailand/resources. Accessed 2 April 2010.

Chapter 10

Aronson, Harvey B. 2004. *Buddhist Practice on Western Ground: Reconciling Eastern Ideals and Western Psychology*. Boston, MA: Shambatha.

Beankston, William B., H. David Allen, and Daniel S. Cunningham. 1983. "Religion and Suicide: A Research Note on Sociology's 'One Law.'" *Social Forces* 62 (2): 521.

Bodhi, Bikkhu. 2000. *The Connected Discourses of the Buddha, A New Translation of the Samyutta Nikaaya.* Boston, MA: Wisdom Publications.

———. 2003. *The Connected Discourses of the Buddha: A Translation of the Samyutta Nikaya.* Boston, MA: Wisdom Publications.

Bowker, John. 2005. *The Concise Oxford Dictionary of World Religions.* Oxford University Press.

Bridges, Jerry. 1985. *True Fellowship: The Biblical Practice of Koinonia.* Colorado Springs: NavPress.

Canetto, Silvia Sara, and Morto M. Silverman. 1998. "Gender, Culture and Suicidal Behaviour." *Suicide and Life Threatening Behaviour* 28 (1): 69–81.

Dasayavanish, Chamlong, and Primpprao Dasayavanish. 2007. "A Buddhist Approach to Suicide Prevention." *Journal of Medical Association of Thailand* 90 (8): 1680–88.

De Silva, D., and S. Jayasinghe. 2003. "Suicide in Sri Lanka." In *Suicide Prevention: Meeting the Challenge Together,* edited by L. Vijayakumar. Chennai, India: Orient Longman.

De Silva, H. J., N. Kasturiarchachi, S. L. Seneviratne, A. Molagoda, and N. S. Fonseka. 2000. "Suicide in Sri Lanka: Points to Ponder." *Ceylon Medical Journal* 45: 17–24.

De Silva, Lily. 1986. *One Foot in the World: Buddhist Approaches to Present-day Problems.* Kandy, Sri Lanka: Wheel Publication No. 337/338; 1–35.

Dhammapada. 2001. *The Way of Truth.* Translated by Sangharakshita. Birmingham, UK: Windhorse Publications.

Dhirasekera, Jothiya. 1979. *Encyclopaedia of Buddhism.* Vol. 4, 5. Colombo: Department of Cultural Affairs.

Dissnayake, S. A. W., and P. de Silva. 1983. "Sri Lanka." In *Suicide in Asia and the Near East,* L.A. Headley ed. Berkeley, CA: University of California Press.

D'Oyly, John. 1919. *A Sketch of the Constitution of the Kandyan Kingdom.* Reprint, Dehiwela: Tisara, 1971.

Ferdinandis, T. G. H. C., and H. J. De Silva. 2008. "Illicit Alcohol Consumption and Neuropathy—A Preliminary Study in Sri Lanka." *Alcohol and Alcoholism* 43 (2): 171ff.

Ferguson, D. M., L. J. Horwood, and L. J. Woodward. 2001. "Risk Factors and Life Processes Associated with the Onset of Suicidal Behaviour During the Adolescence and Early Adulthood." *Psychological Magazine* 167: 747–53.

Gambrich , Richard, ed. 1991. *The World of Buddhism*. London: Thames and Hudson.

Giddens, Anthony. 1969. "The Social Meanings of Suicide." *Giddens Sociology* 3: 265–66

———. 1971. *Capitalism and Modern Social Theory: An Analysis of the Writings of Marx, Durkhaeim and Max Weber*. Cambridge: Cambridge University Press.

Guenther, H. V., trans. 1959. *The Jewel Ornament of Liberation*. Leiden: E. J. Brill.

Halverson, John. 1978. "Religion and Psychosocial Development in Sinhalese Buddhism." *Journal of Asian Studies* 37 (2): 221–32.

Hettiarachchi, J., and G. C. S. Kodituwakku. 1989. "Self-Poisoning in Sri Lanka: Motivational Aspects." *International Journal of Social Psychiatry* 35 (2): 204–8.

Jayatilleke, K. N. 1972. *Ethics in Buddhist Perspective*. Kandy, Sri Lanka: Wheel Publication No. 175.

Kasturiarachchi and V. P. Manawadu. 2002. "Deliberate Self-harm: Assessment of Patients Admitted to Hospitals." *Journal of the Ceylon College of Physicians* 35:1–12.

Kearney, Barbara N., and Barbara D. Miller. 1987. *Internal Migration in Sri Lanka and Its Social Consequences*. Littleton, CO: Westview Press.

Kearney R. N., and B. D. Miller.. 1985. "The Spiral of Suicide and Social Change in Sri Lanka." *The Journal of Asian Studies* 45 (1): 82–101.

———. 1988. "Suicide and Internal Migration in Sri Lanka." *Journal of Asian and African Studies* 23: 287–304.

Keown, Damien. 1986. "Buddhism and Suicide: The Case of Channa." *Journal of Buddhist Ethics* 3: 9–31.

Krug, Etienne G. 2002. *World Report on Violence and Health*. World Health Organization, 140–41.

Kuruppuarachchi, K. A. L. A., and C. A. Wijesinghe. 2009. "Suicidal Risk Assessment and Depression." *The Ceylon Medical Journal* 54 (1): 31–32.

Lamotte, E. 1987. "Religious Suicide in Early Buddhism." *Buddhist Studies Review* 4: 105–26.

Levinson, David. 2002. *Encyclopedia of Crime and Punishment*. Vol. 1. London: Sage Publications.

Malalasekere, G. P., Jothiya Dheerasekere, and W. G. Weeraratne. 1997-2009. *Encyclopedia of Buddhism*. 8 Vols. Colombo, Sri Lanka: Department of Buddhist Affairs.

Marecek, Jeanne, and Lakshmi Ratnayake. "Suicide in Rural Sri Lanka." In *Suicide Risk and Protective Factors in the New Millennium*, edited by Onja Grad. Ljubljana: Cankarjev Dom.

Marecek, Jeanne. 2006. "Young Women's Suicide in Sri Lanka: Cultural, Ecological and Psychological Factors." *Asian Journal of Counseling* 13 (1): 63–92.

Maris, Ronald W., Alan Lee Berman, Morton M. Silverman, and Bruce Michael Bongar. 2000. *Comprehensive Text Book of Suicidology*. New York: Guilford.

National Report on Violence and Health in Sri Lanka. 2008. World Health Organization. http://www.who.or.jp/CHP/2008/Report_on_violence_and_health_Sri_Lanka.pdf.

Obeyesekere, Gananatha. 1990. *Buddhism Transformed: Religious Change in Sri Lanka*. Delhi: Motilal Banarsidas.

O'Brien, John Anthony. 1974. *The Faith of Millions: The Credentials of the Catholic Religion*. Huntington, IN: Our Sunday Visitor.

Peiris-John, R. J., and A. R. Wickremasinghe. 2008. "Efficacy of Activated Charcoal in Yellow Oleander Poisoning." *The Ceylon Medical Journal* 53 (2): 33–35.

Phipps, William E. 1985. "Christian Perspectives on Suicide." *The Christian Century* October 30: 970–72.

Pickering, W. S. F., and Geoffrey Walford. 2000. *Durkheim's Suicide: A Century of Research and Debate*. New York: Routledge.

Premasiri, P. D. 2006. "A 'Righteous War' in Buddhism?" In *Buddhism, Conflict and Violence in Modern Sri Lanka*, edited by Mahinda Deegalle, 78–85. New York: Routledge.

Ratnayeke, Lakshmi. 1998. "Suicide in Sri Lanka." In *Suicide Prevention: The Global Context*, edited by Robert Kosky, et al., 139–42. New York: Plenum Press.

Ratnayake, Ruwan. 2008. "Building Capacity to Address Emerging Problems in Developing Countries: Intentional Self-Poisoning and Pesticide." *Open Medicine* 2 (2): 26–28.

Rhys Davids, C. A. F., and K. R. Norman, trans. 1989. *Therigatha*. Oxford, UK: Pali Text Society.

Ritzer, George. 1992. *Sociological Theory.* 3rd ed. New York: McGraw-Hill.

Samaraweera, Daya, and Atitayen Sanvardhanyag Pravesyak. 2006. *An Approach to Development through the Hidden Past of Monaragala.* Monaragala, Sri Lanka: Police Public Relations Unit.

Samaraweera, D. S. D. 2003. *A Community-based Study on Suicidal Behaviour in the Ratnapura District.* Thesis submitted to University of Colombo.

Sangharakshita. 1996. *A Guide to the Buddhist Path.* Birmingham, UK: Windhorse Publications.

Siyadav, Mahesi, trans. 1988. *Dammacakkapavattana Sutta.* Selangor, Malaysia: SukhiHotu Dhamma Publication.

Spiro, Melford E. 1970. *Buddhism and Society: A Great Tradition and Its Burmese Vicissitudes.* New York: Harper and Row.

Straus, Jaqueline, and Murray, A. Straus. 1953. "Suicide, Homicide, and Social Structure in Ceylon." *American Journal of Sociology* 58: 461–69.

Thanissaro, Bhikkhu, trans. 1993. *Dhammacakkappavattana Sutta: Setting the Wheel of Dhamma in Motion.* (SN 56.11). Accessed June 7, 2009. http://www.accesstoinsight.org/tipitaka/sn/sn56/sn56.011.than.html.

Vijayakumar, Lakshmi, Thilothammal N. 1993. "Suicide Pacts in India." *Crisis* 14: 43–46.

———. Jane Pirkis, Tran Thanh Huong, Paul Yip, Rohini De A. Seneviratne, and Herbert Hendin. 2008. "Socio-economic, Cultural and Religious Factors Affecting Suicide Prevention in Asia." In *Suicide Prevention in Asia,* edited by Herbert Henden, et al., 19–30. World Health Organization.

Vinaya Pitaka. Vol. 3.

Wexler, Lisa M. 2006. "Inupiat Youth Suicide and Colonization: Lessons Learned from Northwest Alaska." Community Health Education, Department of Public Health, University of Massachusetts Amherst. http://apha.confex.com/apha/134am/techprogram/paper_126026.htm.

WHO. 2005. *Mental Health Atlas.* Rev. ed. World Health Organization.

INDEX

SUFFERING